GOALS OF LINGUISTIC THEORY

GOALS OF LINGUISTIC THEORY

edited by
STANLEY PETERS
The University of Texas at Austin

Prentice-Hall, Inc., *Englewood Cliffs, New Jersey*

Library of Congress Cataloging in Publication Data
Main entry under title:

Goals of linguistic theory.

Papers presented at a conference held at the
University of Texas at Austin in October, 1969.
1. Linguistics–Congresses. I. Peters, Stanley,
1941- ed.
P23 1969.G6   415   72-159
ISBN 0-13-357095-9

©1972 by Prentice-Hall, Inc., Englewood Cliffs, N. J.

10 9 8 7 6 5 4 3 2 1

Printed in the United States of America.

Prentice-Hall International, Inc., *London*
Prentice-Hall of Australia, Pty. Ltd., *Sydney*
Prentice-Hall of Canada, Ltd., *Toronto*
Prentice-Hall of India Private Limited, *New Delhi*
Prentice-Hall of Japan, Inc., *Tokyo*

CONTENTS

PREFACE

In October 1969, a large number of generative grammarians gathered at The University of Texas at Austin for a conference on the goals of linguistic theory. This book comprises all but one of the papers given at that conference. Apparently divergent developments of transformational grammar had been perceptible for two or three years. Simply bringing together people who disagree is not guaranteed to produce agreement, as the reader will discover. But in this case it did at least promote in the conference participants a better understanding of all the positions involved and may, it is hoped, do the same for readers by the medium of this book.

In his contribution, Charles Fillmore considers how an ordinary working grammarian can use the linguistic data available to him to justify a generative grammar empirically. He argues that many of the things a generative grammar is supposed to do, while of great importance to a linguistic theorist, are little help to the linguist who is simply concerned to describe the structure of a given language as well as he can.

Joseph Emonds develops some consequences of the idea, proposed in his Ph.D. dissertation, that cyclic transformations apply only when they preserve structure. This highly original proposal leads to a nontraditional analysis of English sentential complements which may explain some of their idiosyncracies.

Noam Chomsky deals with objections raised by generative grammarians to his *Aspects of the Theory of Syntax* and certain subsequent proposals about the relations between syntax and semantics in grammar. He revises the *Aspects* theory and argues that extending interpretive semantic rules to operate on surface structure meets the criticisms of generative semanticists.

Paul Postal defends generative semantics (he suggests a different name), arguing its superiority over the revised *Aspects* theory. Generative semantics is the better motivated theory, he indicates, because it supplies a homogeneous apparatus to overcome the deficiencies of the *Aspect* theory.

My paper deals with evaluation measures and, more generally, the problem of explaining how a complete grammar is acquired on the basis of a small sample of a language. Recent results suggest that a different approach to this problem may work better than evaluation procedures.

Paul Kiparsky takes up the problem of irregularities in the application of phonological rules which are not explainable within current generative phonological theory. He shows that many such restrictions either minimize allomorphy or preserve a semantic contrast which would otherwise be phonetically neutralized in some environments, and indicates how these observations can explain the ‘irregularities’ when incorporated into linguistic theory.

Unfortunately, Sylvain Bromberger’s address to the conference cannot be included here. His perspective as a philosopher of science offers linguists valuable insights about linguistics. I hope that his paper will be published in the future.

Thanks are due to the Graduate School and the College of Arts and Sciences of The University of Texas at Austin for the financial support which made this conference possible. Mrs. Penny McAdoo took care of the many essential details involved in such an undertaking with tremendous skill. My colleagues here, students and faculty, provided much assistance and good advice.

Stanley Peters

GOALS OF LINGUISTIC THEORY

Chapter 1

ON GENERATIVITY

Charles J. Fillmore

1.

For some time I have been striving to understand just exactly what it takes for something to be a generative grammar. The nature of my concern with this question is not that of a metatheoretician within the discipline, nor that of a philosopher of science looking at our field from the outside; it is rather that of an easily confused "ordinary working grammarian" who is trying to be minimally clear about what it is that he is doing.

The ordinary working grammarian of whom I speak has fairly special and fairly limited ways of troubling himself with the problems I will be discussing, and he has special and limited reasons for being pleased or displeased with a theory. For example, when the ordinary working grammarian is told that a generative grammar of a language is a recursive device which demarcates exhaustively and exclusively the unlimitedly large set of sentences in the language, what that means to him is that he has a test for knowing whether what he has done, in describing a certain language, has been successful: if he discovers sentences in the language which his grammar fails to recognize, or if he notices sequences which his grammar allows but the language does not, then he knows that his efforts have fallen short of complete success.

If the ordinary working grammarian is told that he can capture generalizations that would otherwise escape him only by adopting a particular notation or a particular set of conventions regarding the form and interpretation of grammatical rules, what that means to him is that the grammatical descriptions he writes should be simpler if he uses these notations and conventions than if he does not, and that grammars written by people who adhere to the same conventions will be interpretable to him.

Similarly, when the ordinary working grammarian is told that the model of grammar with which he should work must contain in its notation or in an auxiliary set of conventions a body of assumptions about language universals, he is willing to accept this, not so much because he is pleased that in this way the theory abstracts properties of the basic human psychic apparatus for language out of the cultural diversity of individual languages, but because this decision makes it possible for him not to have to remember all the things he believes to be true about language in general: to the extent that his beliefs about language universals are embedded in the notations he uses, he will always know when to be surprised by new evidence which contradicts one or another of these beliefs. He knows that when he encounters linguistic facts which he cannot articulate with the notational and conceptual apparatus at his disposal, he has correctly detected a crisis in the theory and is now in a position to revise his beliefs about language.

Our grammarian, we have seen, is essentially lazy, and, indeed, almost "practical" in his views about what theories are for.

I am going to claim that the ordinary working grammarian is confused about what it takes for something to be a generative grammar. Before I go on to explain myself, I must report immediately that we do not find him guilty of the much-discussed confusion between "generate" as a stative verb used to relate a grammar and the sentences of the language it is a grammar of, and "generate" as an active verb used of a human being and the utterance he produces. The ordinary working grammarian knows and is careful about these distinctions. (It is not so easy to keep these notions distinct in one's unconscious, I must admit. I continually find that I am attracted to "generative semantics" or back again to "interpretive semantics" depending on whether I have recently been more impressed with my experiences of wanting to say things I do not know how to express, or with my experiences of having said things which I cannot understand. In the former mood I am convinced that the mechanism inside me for constructing well-formed messages is intact, and that what is malfunctioning is the component which maps messages into utterances; when I am in the latter state I feel that the mechanism for producing grammatical sentences is intact, and that what is defective is the apparatus for assigning meanings to them.)

I must explain also, before I go on, that the ordinary working grammarian I have in mind finds himself fairly solidly within the generativist camp. His doubts about generative grammar do not arise from any assumptions about the superiority of the research goals of the taxonomists or distributionists of a decade or two ago. To him, the data do not determine the conceptual base of the theory; they constitute, rather, the phenomena which the theory has to explain. And this was something he learned from the generativists.

For the sake of younger readers, let me interpret my allusions. I am old enough to remember the days when, as a typical classroom demonstration or analytic procedures in linguistics, the professor presented a pair of linguistic forms, showed on the basis of the distribution of their constituent elements that they are analogously constructed, and then continued by pointing out that their external distribution proves them to be distinct. I contribute the following examples to this discussion: the pair *maternity dress* and *paternity suit*. It is easy to believe that there are distributional parallels in English-language texts between *maternity* and *paternity*, and that the distributional properties of *dress* and *suit* are analogous. However, on examining the external distribution of the two-word expressions, we would discover that they are in fact quite distinct, in that they occur in vastly unlike total context sets. Some of my teachers took the trouble to say that when a linguist claims that two forms are grammatically distinct, what he means, precisely, is that their total context sets are distinct.

Today reasonable people are much more likely to say that there is something about what these expressions *are* which accounts for their different distributions, rather than the other way around; and such reasonable people might be said to be taking the generativist position. To the challenge that these two ways of talking about the facts amount to the same thing, I reply that in the development of a generative description, one would notice the internal similarity of *maternity dress* and *paternity suit* only by accident; in the development of a distributionist account, the comparison of these forms is a necessary step in the individual description.

2.

My topic, then, is the way in which a "generative" linguist conceives the relation between a grammar and the objects which the grammar is designed to identify and describe, i.e., the "grammatical" sentences of the language in question.

In the earliest discussions of generative grammars, a comparison was suggested between writing a grammar and specifying the set of well-formed formulas in a mathematical system. In Chomsky (1957, p. 13) we read;

> The fundamental aim in the linguistic analysis of a language L is to separate the "grammatical" sequences which are sentences of L from "ungrammatical"

sequences which are not sentences of L and to study the structure of the grammatical sequences. The grammar of L will thus be a device that generates all of the grammatical sequences of L and none of the ungrammatical ones.

A generative grammar recognizes certain strings of symbols as well-formed sentences in the language, but not others, much in the manner of the formation rules in a mathematical system.

This function of a grammar is interpretable as being identical to one of the unarticulated goals of the traditional grammarians, the difference being that a generative grammar is one in which the characterization of the totality of well-formed sentences is made explicit. To mention an aspect of such a suggestion which comes quickly to mind, it seems quite likely that some traditional grammarians, and many classroom grammarians, may indeed have been willing to think of a grammar as analogous to the system of formation rules in a mathematical system—that is, in the quite literal sense that in both cases the rules were devised by wise and rational creators, for the creators' own purposes, and that the admission or rejection of a presented formula or sentence was to depend on whether or not it was in conformity with these independently valued rules. A mathematical system and a system of grammatical rules upheld by proponents of the doctrine or correctness are both, after all, manmade.

Explicit generative grammars appeared on the scene, fortunately, at a time when the question of the membership of a sentence in a language was taken as an empirical issue. On the *de facto*, as opposed to the *de jure*, theory of grammaticality, the speaker is the source of the language, and a successful generative grammar is one which conforms in its predictions to certain kinds of judgments made by speakers of a language about the sentences in their language. A proposed grammar can be shown to be incorrect by a demonstration that the set of sentences in the language is not the same as the set of sentences recognized by the grammar.

That, at least, was the goal which grammarians learned to set for themselves. In the face of the first requirement, it is clear that what the ordinary working grammarian needs to *find* out is the identity of the set of *de facto* grammatical sentences, and what he needs to *figure* out is whether the grammar he constructs puts the good sentences in and rules the bad ones out. We shall soon see that this requirement is a difficult one.

In addition to this requirement that a grammar identify each of the grammatical sentences of language, the concept of generative grammar comprises the further condition that it associate with each of the sentences it generates a structural description—a display of all the grammatical information about the sentence which the speakers of the language can be said to possess. As these first two requirements are phrased in Katz (1966, p. 123),

the rules of a linguistic description must not only be capable of producing an infinite list of formal objects, but the formal objects on the list must be the sentences of the language under study and the list must exclude any string in the vocabulary of the language that is not a sentence in the language. Furthermore, these rules must somehow specify all the information about the sentences that a speaker utilizes to produce and understand them.

The second requirement does not commit us to anything new in the actual workings of a grammar. The very rules which play a part in the successful generation of the sentences of the language can be used, *via* a structure-assigning algorithm taken to be part of linguistic theory, to provide the correct structural descriptions. As stated in Thorne (1968, p. 302), "The set of rules involved in the generation of a sentence is equivalent to an analysis of it."

With the concept of generative grammars thus elaborated to contain the notion "correct structural description," the relation between a grammar and the set of linguistic objects it generates is subtler than was apparent at first. The native-speaker judgments to which the analyst needs to appeal for convincing himself that his work is adequate involve not only acceptance or rejection of sentences, but also assent to various kinds of assertions about the sentences that are accepted.

Our ordinary working grammarian looks at this new responsibility and sees two problems: first, whether he can determine what the correct structural descriptions of the sentences in the languages are; and second, whether the rules needed for generating the sentences in the first sense are indeed precisely those which will succeed in assigning correct structural descriptions. The ordinary working grammarian worries, in other words, about whether there really is a definitional relation between a description of everything speakers know about the sentences of their language and grammatical rules of the type he has learned.

From the beginning, but only with seriousness in work later than Chomsky (1957), the concept of generative grammar has been further enriched by the requirement that it be capable of ranking sentences along a dimension ranging from the fully grammatical to the totally unstructured. It was apparently believed by Chomsky that for this new role there need be no new requirements on the form and operation of the generative apparatus itself. In Chomsky and Miller (1963, p. 291) we read that a generative grammar, *defined as* a device which enumerates the grammatical sentences of a language and which assigns structural descriptions to each of these, may also be *regarded as* a device which assigns to any string presented to it a relative-grammaticality index. What is needed, apparently, is some system of conventions which governs the way in which the structure-assigning apparatus is to be consulted for determining, for any nonsentence, its degree of departure from full grammaticality.

The ordinary working grammarian, confronting this added responsibility, sees now three things to worry about. The first is whether he or anyone he trusts knows how to rank sentences according to their degree of deviation from full grammaticality; the second is whether there is a general way of determining, from the rules of grammar, a ranking of sentences which conforms to these judgments. His third problem is that he fails to understand why knowing what is wrong with each of two sentences should entail knowing whether one of them is worse off than the other.

One final enrichment of the concept of generative grammar is found in the view that a grammar which a grammarian constructs is a claim about something which speakers of the language have inside their skins and which makes them able to produce and comprehend the sentences, and many of the near-sentences, of their language (see Chomsky 1965, pp. 3-9). With this addition the study of grammar takes on a new interest and importance, naturally; but with this addition one finds it particularly difficult to imagine in advance the precise nature of criteria for success. I will argue, nevertheless, that the most intelligible view of grammatical research sees it as the attempt to discover the internal rules which account for the rule-guided aspect of human linguistic abilities.

3.

The most simply conceived goal of a generative grammar, to go back to the beginning, is that of determining, for any sequence of elements in the vocabulary of the language, whether it is grammatical or ungrammatical.

The details of the technical side of this task are of little real interest to the ordinary working grammarian. He knows that to the extent that any genuine generative grammar is an effective theory, it will always be possible to tell, *if* a sentence is generated by the grammar, *that* it is generated by the grammar: one tries out the rules, using whatever heuristic tools one has at hand, until one finds the sentence in question, and declares that it is in the language. There is, to be sure, another issue—that of knowing for certain that a presented string is *un*grammatical according to the grammar—but that question is related to subtle properties of grammars that are of little concern to the ordinary working grammarian. He is willing to assume that an interpreter of a generative grammar, given wit, luck, and patience, will be able to find out one way or another whether a given sentence is in or out.

What does concern him is the nontechnical problem of knowing whether the sentences that get in are the good ones and whether the sentences that get left out are the bad ones—whether, in other words, the grammar and the speakers make the same choices. He sees this as a problem because he knows that judgments about grammaticality are subject to all sorts of confusions between grammaticality and significance, acceptability, or intelligibility; he knows that even when speakers say they understand that they are to make judgments about grammaticality rather than these other things, they still disagree; he knows that sometimes people change their minds about whether a sentence is grammatical; and he finds the appeal to unending idiolectal variation somewhat unsatisfying.

There was a time when these uncertainties would not have bothered our grammarian: a decade or so ago there was little reason to doubt the "clear cases principle" proclaimed in Chomsky (1957, pp. 13-14). On this principle, native-speaker judgments are criteria of grammar-constructing success only with respect to the clear cases. The grammarian begins by considering sentences like *I like ice cream* that are clearly grammatical and sequences like *Ice cream me the* that are clearly ungrammatical, and he constructs the simplest grammar which generates all the incontrovertibly grammatical sentences and fails to generate all the incontrovertibly ungrammatical sentences. The grammar, then, and not the grammarian, makes the decision about the unclear cases.

Today's grammarian finds little comfort in this principle, because he knows, if he has read Ross's thesis (Ross 1967), that the kinds of arguments that seem to bear very crucially on the nature and operation of syntactic systems involve him in grammaticality decisions that are extremely difficult to make. If he has seen studies of speech variation by Elliott, Legum, and Thompson (1969), he knows that properties of grammars and sentence configurations figure importantly in the description of idiolectal and stylistic differences, but not at all in a way that gives any primacy to a simple distinction between being in the language or out, being generated or not generated by the grammar.

The simplest criterion of success, which was to consist of checking the identity of being "in the language" to being "generated by the grammar," does not do, in short, what our ordinary working grammarian had hoped it would do for him.

4.

But let us turn to another problem, that of designing a grammar capable of assigning degrees of grammaticality. Chomsky's theory of relative grammaticality (Chomsky 1965, pp. 148-54) takes roughly the following form. The grammar generates the set of fully grammatical sentences in a more or less straightforward way. For a string of words not found among the fully grammatical sentences, its degree of deviation from full grammaticality can be computed by comparing it with the grammatical sentences to which it is in some ways similar.

The procedure may be thought of as including something like the following steps. For each deviant string one identifies the set of sentences maximally similar to it. One identifies the properties which the deviant and grammatical sentences have in common, and in doing that one isolates just those properties which are "out of place." If an "out-of-place" element is a constituent of a major category not found in that position in the grammatical sentences, the deviation is particularly serious—we may say that the string loses three points. Where an out-of-place element is of an appropriate category but has grammatical properties not found in that position in any of the fully grammatical sentences, the deviation is of minimal seriousness—the string loses one point. Where an out-of-place element is of an appropriate major category according to part of its context but ordinarily requires a categorial environment of a type not found in the string in question, the offense is of medium seriousness—the string loses two points. The degree of deviance of the string as a whole might be registered, in the most simple-minded rendering of this procedure, as the sum of the values of these various offenses.

The deviance-computing procedure I have just sketched, as well as subtler variations on it, has to be based on the assumption that it is in principle possible to identify, for a deviant string, just those lexical items or features which are out of place, or just those orderings of elements which are appropriate. Even if we agree to allow multiple ways of recognizing the out-of-place elements—that is, even if we are willing to record certain strings as ambiguously deviant—we still must face the ill-defined problem of determining which portion of a deviant string provides the framework within which the rest can be described as out of place.

For any attempt to deal with this task, we have to distinguish between a deviant string of words taken in the abstract and a deviant or mistaken utterance. We shall find for the former that there is simply no possibility of determining in any absolute way its degree of departure from full grammaticality. In the latter case, an account of deviant utterances must take two cases into account: mistakes, as in the speech performance of children, drunkards, and foreigners (and the rest of us when we are off our guard), where what is of interest is a comparison between what was intended and what was said; and figurative speech, where what is of interest is the structural type which the speaker wants the hearer to perceive as a framework upon which the hearer's "construing" abilities can impose some sort of interpretation—hopefully the intended interpretation.

To see what is involved for strings of words considered *in vacuo*, we can take the most favorable case—that of strings which happen to be identical to sentences generated by a grammar which differs in minor ways from the grammar which provides the measure. Suppose, for example, that we wish to say something about the sentences produced by a speaker of a nonstandard dialect of English and suppose that we wish to determine whether it makes sense to talk about the degree of deviation of his sentences from those of the standard dialect.

Given sentence (1), what we need to know first of all is whether it is to be compared with (2) in the standard dialect or with (3).

(1)   I seen it.
(2)   I have seen it.
(3)   I saw it.

Depending on which of the latter two is taken to be the basis of comparison, sentence (1) is deviant either by virtue of an omission or by virtue of a substitution. If the index we need is something which grades strings of words along the grammaticality dimension, it must be a meaningful question to ask whether the string comes out as more ungrammatical under one of these interpretations than under the other, and it must likewise make sense to ask whether the intuitions of native speakers of the standard dialect can be called on to decide which interpretation is correct. Such inquiry, surely, does not lead to an understanding of where (1) fails with respect to the standard dialect.

Of course, in order to know which comparison is the "right" one, we need to know whether the rules of the dialect from which we have taken our sample allow the perfect auxiliary *have* to be contracted to zero (where the standard dialect requires retention of the final fricative), or whether these rules specify *seen* as the preterite form of *see*. In case the source dialect has nothing corresponding to the standard dialect contrast between (2) and (3), our problem is more serious still: are we to say that the dialect has only the perfect form, with the auxiliary deleted; that it has only the preterite form, realized phonologically as *seen*; or that, having the two constructions distinct at some level of analysis, the rules neutralize them in surface sentences? The answers to these questions involve detailed comparison of the grammatical rules of the separate dialects, but can in no meaningful way, as far as I can tell, be expressed as information about (1) as viewed from the standard dialect.

With (1) we have the simplest possible case, and yet there were these uncertainties. The situation with random word sequences is totally beyond hope. That becomes obvious as soon as we realize that the possibilities available for matching any one of these with a set of grammatical sentences include the operations of order change, insertion, deletion, or replacement of elements, and unrestricted combinations of these.

For utterances that are deviant by mistake, the relevant comparison is between the actual utterance and the intended utterance; but in this case, (*a*) it is not always possible to know what the intended utterance is, and (*b*) it does not matter whether the actual occurring utterance is, in the abstract, grammatical or not.

What is needed is some apparatus for pairing any string of words with any structural description, and providing some index of the degree of fit between the description and the string, the value of this index determined by an operation which relates the lexical information associated with the individual words of the string with the structural description. Such a device is what we find elaborated in Lakoff (1965). By Lakoff's procedure, any string will have an indefinitely large number of grammaticality values according to the infinite number of structural descriptions that can be brought into association with it. For a fully grammatical sentence there will be at least one structural description which it satisfies completely. An ambiguous grammatical sentence will show perfect fit with two or more structural descriptions — one for each of its possible interpretations. Working out the details requires giving different weight to distinct types of "poor fit." All such decisions will involve appeals to native-speaker judgments of some sort, but technically the thing seems feasible.

But notice what happens to our understanding of the working of a generative grammar when we adopt Lakoff's device. The syntactic component specifies the set of well-formed structural descriptions. The dictionary component associates with each lexical item a set of syntactic, semantic, and phonological properties, the syntactic properties understood as including information about insertability into deep-structure configurations and sensitivity to grammatical rules. The relative-grammaticality algorithm automatically assigns a grammaticality index to each ordered pair in which the first element is a sequence of lexical items and the second is a structural description.

Under Lakoff's proposal a generative grammar can do what I think Chomsky suggested a generative grammar ought to do, i.e., serve as a grammaticality-index assigning mechanism. But the whole thing depends crucially on having correct information about the lexical items of the language. How are we to discover, our ordinary working grammarian asks, what are the correct lexical properties of the words and morphemes of a language? Can it be, he frets, that the difficulties of knowing correctly the grammar and semantics of lexical items are of the same order of magnitude as those of determining the grammaticality of sentences?

These worries of his are, I think, justified. Presumably, we are to determine the grammatical properties of lexical items by comparing deviant with nondeviant uses of them. We know that *resemble* is unpassivizable, for example, because speakers of English tell us that while (4) is grammatical, (5) is not.

(4) John resembles a horse.
(5) A horse is resembled by John.

But, of course, there are in fact some speakers of English who tell us that the passive sentence is not ungrammatical. That means that when we observe a seemingly deviant use of a lexical item, we must ask whether this usage constitutes a departure from conventions provided by that speaker's language, whether the speaker's language differs in relevant ways from the language we have been considering, or whether his judgments on grammaticality are sometimes inaccurate. In other words, we must be able to ask whether the speaker regularly uses the word in ways of which the observed usage in an instance, or whether in this situation he made a mistake.

Two examples will demonstrate the difficulty in knowing what the facts are. The first is an elementary case of figurative speech. Although it is certainly possible to come up with clear cases, it is frequently in practice impossible to know, even in one's own speech, whether a word has been used figuratively, in the creative sense, or whether it is simply polysemous in the needed way. The use of the word *bitch* in referring to an unpleasant adult female human was clearly figurative in its first instance, but when we find people who hesitate to use the word when speaking of a female dog, it is apparent that for them the insulting sense of the word does not draw on their creative abilities. A description of this state of affairs in terms of the marking of deviance would run like this: somebody whose lexicon contains only the literal interpretation of the noun but who is observed to use it nevertheless when referring to human beings has made a creative extension of the scope of the word that is accounted for by reference to the knowledge that participants in our civilization use attributions to human beings of nonhuman animal properties for pejoration; somebody who does not use the word when referring to female dogs lacks the original sense and has a lexical entry for *bitch* with the pejorative sense built in rather than acquired by a construal principle.

Unfortunately, an empirically indistinguishable account is found in the claim that some speakers have two descriptions of the word, others only one. On this interpretation, the acquisition of the nonliteral sense is an event in the history of the language. I know of no reasonable proposals for evaluating these alternative accounts.

For a second example, I turn to the fact that some speakers of English do not use *convince* in the same ways they use *persuade*. They allow themselves to say (6) but not (7).

(6) We persuaded him to come.
(7) We convinced him to come.

Suppose, knowing that, we hear our informant say (7). We may say that his internal grammar makes the distinction just mentioned, but that he has generalized the infinitive complement construction to the verb *convince* this one time; or that he is in the process of acquiring the more generalized rule; or that he was imitating speakers of a lesser dialect; or that he mistakenly produced this utterance by choosing the word *convince* when he intended *persuade*; or, of course, we might simply say that in his lexicon *convince* and *persuade* are given, apart from their phonology, identical descriptions.

There are, then, uncertainties about the proper way of interpreting apparently different uses of lexical items and uncertainties about the accessibility of correct lexical information in general. Appeals to introspection, the compilation of questionnaire results, and claims about idiolectal variation seem not always to point to the truth. Grammatical theory needs instead to consider deviance marking as a precise formal problem, and this it can do by applying to lexical descriptions something akin to Lakoff's proposal for computing relative grammaticality. The lexicon is a device which characterizes well-formed lexical entries but fails to associate phonological material (i.e., "lexical items") with lexical descriptions. Grammatical theory can now be thought of as providing a way of registering the degree of grammaticality of word strings with respect to structural descriptions *if the lexical descriptions of the words are known.* This is accomplished by associating any sequence of clusters of lexical features—minus the phonological content—with any structural description. The grammar is able to assign indices of relative grammaticality, but only to ordered pairs of lexical description sequences and structural descriptions. The grammar says, in effect: if you can find strings of words that have such-and-such properties, then I can tell you exactly how well they fit any structural description.

If this is what a generative grammar is to do, it has managed to get as far as possible from its initial goal of specifying the well-formed sequences of words. The fact is, of course, that we have by this time completely lost the attention of our ordinary working grammarian. He wants to know just what these deviance markings are for, and he has serious doubts about whether the speaker's intuitive judgments on grammatically deviant sentences can be accounted for in general in terms of misordering errors and category substitutions of the sort he sees this device capable of detecting. Our grammarian knows first of all that the construal principles for a great many instances of metaphor involve understandings about objects and events rather than properties of the linguistic elements which give expression to these objects and events. More than that, he can think of many cases of what he insists on considering deviant uses of language but which cannot be described by any of the grammar-bound plans for characterizing deviance that have been proposed.

I have in mind a situation like the following. Journalists these days have been made conscious of the jeopardy to justice (or at least the danger of a libel suit) that results from public assignment of guilt to their fellow citizens. They have been instructed to heed certain rules of thumb that are supposed to keep them out of trouble, and among these, I assume, are the following: "Never say of a person who committed a crime that he did it, only that he *allegedly* did it." "Never call the person who committed the crime the culprit, or the murderer, or the burglar, until after the trial; call him instead the *suspect.*"

As a result of sincere obedience to these injunctions, journalists (perhaps most noticeably in Columbus, Ohio) have acquired odd uses of the adverb *allegedly* and the noun *suspect.* Recently I heard on the evening news in Columbus:

(8) Six members of the Students for a Democratic Society were charged with allegedly distributing inflammatory literature.

(I am assuming, incidentally, that they were charged with *actually* distributing inflammatory literature; if they were only charged with allegedly doing this, then they were surely guilty, and my point is lost.) In a report on the burglary of a milk store in my city, the local evening newspaper reported:

(9) The police have no clues as to the identity of the suspect.

There was of course no suspect: they had no clues on the identity of the burglar.

These are assuredly deviant uses of the words in question, and I believe they would be recognized as such by their authors if they had had time to edit what they had written. But it seems to me that a correct description of the nature of the deviance is not the sort of thing that can be provided by a generative grammar rigged to assign grammaticality indices. I may be wrong, but I find it difficult to imagine how such an algorithm could successfully mark the two sentences I came across as being more acceptable in journalese than such technically equally odd sentences as (10) and (11).

(10) He wanted the children to allegedly rob the flower girl.
(11) I hope no suspect burns our house down while we're on vacation.

The deviant uses I have been discussing simply do not involve category errors of familiar kinds.

Uncertainties about the ways in which lexical items figure in the operation of a deviance-marking apparatus brings one face to face with the question of analogy in speech behavior. Although I have agreed with and once contributed to the body of unkind words people have directed toward a little book called *State of the Art* (Hockett 1968), I find myself convinced that in the description of changes in the lexicon, the appeal to changes in the content of grammatical rules faces a number of serious difficulties. Consider the recent popularity of event nouns used in the context of social protest in which the first element is a verb and the second element is the preposition *in*, as in *sit-in*, *love-in*, etc. I believe I am correct in my understanding that *sit-in* was the first of these. The ordinary working grammarian in me wonders how we are to describe what happened when *sit-in* became a part of the English lexicon. Were there changes in the derivational rules of the language? Was it registered as an unanalyzed lexical item? Or what?

If *sit-in* entered the language as an unanalyzed lexical item, then it had no influence on the rules, since only generative rules assign structural descriptions. If the word did have an analysis, then there either must be some supplementary apparatus for assigning structure to lexical items, or it must be taken as being generated by a possibly newly created generative rule.

Suppose we take this last position, since it is the only one that is intelligible within the framework of generative grammar. What is the nature of this newly created rule? If the rule is stated as one which takes any verb, shall we say that *sit* was marked, for a while, as the only verb to which it could apply? Shall we say that the scope of the rule was perfectly general, and merely observe as a fact about the history of usage that nobody bothered to use it for anything but the verb *sit* for the first few months after the introduction of the rule? (If the answer to this second question is yes, then we must understand the occurrence of the later words in the way that we understand the constructibility of novel sentences.)

But if the original rule was an exceptional one, applying only to *sit*, then what are we to say about such later additions as *wade-in, pray-in,* and *strip-in*? Are we to say that at the later stage the rule became generalized so as to include any verb, or any of a certain type of verb, or are we to say that the grammar became more complicated by virtue of having the relevant exception features added to the verbs *wade, pray, love,* and the rest? If we accept that the rule was originally general enough to include any verb, in some strict sense of "verb," was it in fact general enough to include the later hippie creation, *be-in*? If not, with the extension to *be* are we to say that the rule was further generalized or that it was made more specific so as to include *be*?

These are all, quite obviously, senseless questions. It would never occur to anyone today to line up all these alternatives and to worry seriously about which is to be preferred, if only because we remember how silly certain older works seem in which we are taught five alternative analyses of the word *took*. We have here one of those cases where we might indeed agree to say, with Hockett, that somebody made up a word, the word caught on, other people apprehended a pattern and made up some new words on the same pattern. A reconstruction of this history in the form of a sequence of changes in systems of generative rules would strike the ordinary working grammarian as nothing more than allegiance to a ritual form. However we eventually manage to deal with descriptive problems of this sort, it is at least very clear that in none of this inquiry would it have been of any help to have available to us a metric of relative grammaticality.

5.

I have said that it is difficult to see how a generative grammar can be required to demarcate all and only the grammatical sentences of a language in view of some rather serious questions about the empirical determinability of that set; and I have said that it is impossible to imagine any way in which a generative grammar can assign grammaticality indices to deviant sentences. I turn now to a brief consideration of the ways in which a grammar assigns structural descriptions to the sentences which it generates.

The theory of transformational grammar makes available for structural descriptions of sentences (1) the categories of the base rules; (2) the domination relations that are defined initially by the rules of the base and are adjusted by the transformations; (3) the left-to-right sequence of elements; (4) information about permitted co-occurrences in particular structures; and (5) information found in the lexicon regarding (*a*) insertability into deep-structure configurations, (*b*) sensitivity to grammatical rules, and (*c*) the semantic structure of lexical items. A grammar is judged as adequate in one important respect if it describes sentences in ways which match certain sorts of intuitive judgments on the part of native speakers, if it captures certain aspects of their knowledge about the sentences.

One specific descriptive problem, ordinarily taken to be the easiest, is that of knowing whether a grammar gives the correct constituent-structure analysis to the surface sentence. Considering the variety of ways in which complex verbal expressions in English get parsed, I am ready to assume that native-speaker intuitions about constituent structure are among the least important criteria for judging the adequacy of proposed descriptions.

But it is also likely that there are a great many facts about the grammatical interpretation of sentences which the devices of categories and sequence and domination fail to capture altogether, yet which must be a part of the generative grammarian's added burden if the goal of achieving descriptive adequacy is to be seriously sought after. I have in mind a number of descriptive problems connected with the treatment of focus, topicalization, reference, deep-structure cases, presuppositions, and illocutionary-act potential. The brute-force method of incorporating all these matters into the theory is to let assertions about them find their place in proposed underlying structures for sentences. Consider sentence (12) in this connection.

(12) Did I give you the other book?

The people called generative semanticists have been accumulating arguments according to which the underlying linguistic structure of (12) will ultimately have to be something which, when rendered into English, would read like (13).

(13) There is a set of books that both you and I know about and the cardinality of that set is some number *n* and you and I have just had in mind a subset containing *n* - 1 of those books and I am now calling your attention to the remaining *n*th book. There was a time when I had that book in my possession and I am now asking you to tell me whether I did anything in the past which would count as causing that book to be in your possession

The speech-act function of the sentence is made explicit in the part about the speaker's requesting an answer from the hearer; the presuppositions are captured in the clauses preceding the operative clause; the category of definiteness is reconstructed as a set of assumptions about what the speaker believes the hearer to be "having in mind"; and so on.

When the ordinary working grammarian sees such demonstrations, he is properly overwhelmed, but he has trouble believing that the principles by which these maximally abstract representations are to be mapped into the sentences of his language are principles that today's grammarians are equipped to discover. He feels, in fact, that he finds himself in the age of what we might call the New Taxonomy, an era of a new and exuberant cataloguing of the enormous range of facts that linguists need eventually to find theories to deal with. The attempt to capture fully the native speaker's intuitions about the structure and content of his sentences has led to observations which make it extremely difficult to believe in the simple and comforting things we believed in, about grammatical theory, just a few years ago.

6.

I see in much recent work a shift of interest away from the properties of an apparatus needed solely for generating the proper set of sentences, toward the mechanisms which speakers of a language can be shown to have, on the basis of any evidence within reach, which account for their ability to do what they do when they communicate with each other using their language. This switch of emphasis to the system itself, and away from the in-or-out judgments associated with the strict notion of generative grammar, makes it possible to ask new kinds of questions. Let me give an example of what I mean.

When grammar construction is seen as a purely formal task, one of the desiderata of a grammar must be its completeness. In evaluating a grammar which is to generate all and only the sentences of a language, we cannot tolerate a situation in which symbols are introduced at one point and never interpreted or operated on by later rules. It is possible, I want to suggest, that a grammar which exhibits the workings of a natural language cannot meet such a requirement.

It may be that an earlier portion of a grammar allows the introduction of a structure even though the remaining rules of the grammar fail to assign it an acceptable surface form. For types of phenomena that have concerned Perlmutter (in Perlmutter 1968), such a failure is to be accounted for in terms of surface-structure constraints. Surface-structure constraints, however, make up a fairly clearly defined segment of the grammar itself, and their justification is based on their contribution to the task of isolating grammatical from ungrammatical strings. The issue I am about to bring up is different.

In general, tag questions in English are constructed by adding to any assertive sentence an interrogative piece which contains as subject a pronoun which matches the surface subject of the main sentence, and a pro-verb-phrase which corresponds to the predicate of the main sentence and which is negative in case the main sentence is affirmative, and vice versa. What we need to be able to say about English is that a tag question formative can be chosen with any assertive sentence but the rules for constructing tag questions out of such combinations fail to cover all cases.

People have trouble with tag questions after such sentences as (14), (15), (16), and (17).

(14) Somebody's out there.
(15) Somebody tried to get in.
(16) I'm competent to do that.
(17) *One* of us could go.

The rule for forming the tag question requires the selection of an appropriate pronoun. *Somebody* is human and singular and unmarked for gender. *It* is nonhuman, *he* and *she* are marked for gender, and *they* is plural. There is no pronoun which matches it. From the paraphrasability of (14) with (18), many people say (19), but others end up with (20) or (21) and still others give up.

(18) There's somebody out there.
(19) Somebody's out there, isn't there?
(20) Somebody's out there, isn't he?
(21) Somebody's out there, aren't they?

For a sentence like (15) some people say (22), and others give up; I have heard myself say (23).

(22) Somebody tried to get in, didn't they?
(23) Somebody tried to get in, didn't there?

For (16) some people accept (24), a great many allow themselves to say (25), but many others simply do not know what to say.

(24) I'm competent to do that, aren't I?
(25) I'm competent to do that, ain't I?

For (17) the best thing is to make a joke out of it:

(26) *One* of us could go, couldn't you?

Our grammar sometimes fails us.

Observations like these are certainly familiar, and for illustrating my point I could just as well have considered the rules for subject-verb agreement and their failure to yield grammatical sentences corresponding to (27) and (28).

> (27) Either he or I is always on duty.
> (28) Either he or I am always on duty.

The recognition of problems of this sort is the recognition of what people try to say, how their grammars fail them, and how eventually they invent a new form, they go ahead and say something they feel is ungrammatical, or they give up. To account for such situations we must allow grammars to be "incomplete" in just the right ways, that is, for just those situations in which the creative part of a grammar sets up something which the interpretive part cannot cope with.

It should be pointed out, incidentally, that the discovery of this sort of operative failure in a grammar offers no comfort to those persistent spokesmen for the inherent vagueness of grammars. Grammars may indeed have areas of unimprovable vagueness, but the facts about English that I have been discussing can be made totally explicit. What gives the native speaker the impression of vagueness is his uncertainty about knowing what to do when he wants to say something which his grammar—in ways unknown to him—fails to allow him to say.

7.

The ordinary working grammarian learns what he can about the grammatical processes which are available to the producers of sentences, and he uses what he knows of these processes for describing these sentences. He welcomes Chomsky's discussions of the nonaccessibility of correct grammaticality judgments, because without the "clear cases principle" to guide him, he knows of no way to bring to his task of writing a grammar the evidence of grammaticality judgments. He wants to know what sorts of things can go wrong in the production of an utterance, and what kinds of freedom creative users of language have for constructing sentences or near-sentences in their language. He does not want to be responsible for a relative grammaticality ranking of utterances or utterance-description pairs.

He will be glad if he can be reassured that his success as a grammarian will not be measured on the basis of his ability to demonstrate that his grammar does everything that generative grammars have been said to have to do. I believe he deserves such reassurance.

Knowing what he does not have to do will not give him reliable insights into what he does have to do, unfortunately, but that is because the ordinary working grammarian I have in mind is exactly as confused as I am about that. If he is a practitioner of the New Taxonomy, he is having a good time. It is possible to remain happy, for a while, without well-defined goals.

REFERENCES

Chomsky, N. 1957. *Syntactic structures.* The Hague: Mouton.

_____. 1965. *Aspects of the theory of syntax.* Cambridge: M.I.T. Press.

Chomsky, N., and Miller, G. A. 1963. Introduction to the formal analysis of natural languages. In *Handbook of mathematical psychology, vol. II,* ed. R. D. Luce et al., pp. 269-321. New York: Wiley.

Elliott, D., Legum S., and Thompson, S.A. 1969. Syntactic variation as linguistic data. In *Papers from the fifth regional meeting of the Chicago Linguistic Society,* ed. R. Binnick et al., pp. 52-59. Chicago: University of Chicago Linguistics Department.

Hockett, C. F. 1968. *The state of the art.* The Hague: Mouton.

Katz, J. J. 1966. *The philosophy of language.* New York: Harper & Row.

Lakoff, G. 1965. On the nature of syntactic irregularity. Ph.D. dissertation, Indiana University.

Perlmutter, D. 1968. Deep and surface structure constraints in syntax. Ph.D. dissertation, M.I.T.

Ross, J. R. 1967. Constraints on variables in syntax. Ph.D. dissertation, M.I.T.

Thorne, J. P. 1968. Grammars and machines. In *Language,* ed. R. C. Oldfield and J. C. Marshall, pp. 293-306. New York: Penguin.

Chapter 2

A REFORMULATION OF
CERTAIN SYNTACTIC TRANSFORMATIONS

Joseph Emonds

INTRODUCTION

In this paper, I will be principally concerned with reformulating the extraposition transformation of Rosenbaum (1967) in accordance with a general constraint on transformations proposed in my doctoral dissertation (Emonds 1970). It is therefore appropriate to begin by stating and explaining this "structure-preserving constraint."

The general theoretical and heuristic motivation for such a constraint is essentially the same as that found in Ross (1967). Like Ross, I start from the premise that certain restrictions on the applicability of various transformations are not *ad hoc* specifications forming part of individual rules, but are rather reflections of some deeper grammatical principles (constraints) which define the formal framework in which transformational rules operate.[1]

A principal direction of Ross's work was to define the structural conditions under which movement transformations operate. That is, Ross's constraints (for example, the coordinate structure constraint or the complex NP constraint, but the others as well) essentially specify that constituents *cannot be moved out of certain structural configurations*, even though these configurations otherwise satisfy the structural description of a transformation which would move these constituents.

The direction of my dissertation (Emonds 1969) is to try to define the conditions when the structural changes of transformations are actually applicable (more correctly, "satisfied"). That is, my constraint (the structure-preserving constraint) essentially specifies that constituents *cannot be moved into certain structural configurations.*

From a study of English transformations, I arrive in my dissertation at the following tentative hypothesis, subject of course to testing and refinement and perhaps rejection on the basis of other languages.[2] Constituents are to be divided into "phrase nodes" (NP, S, VP, PP, AP) and "nonphrase nodes." Various ways in which the class of phrase nodes may be formally characterizable are suggested, but in any case they can be listed as a set of substantive universals in linguistic theory. The structure-preserving constraint then requires that a phrase node X in a tree T can be moved, copied, or inserted into a new position in T, according to the structural change of a transformation whose structural description T satisfies, only if at least one of two conditions is satisfied: (*a*) In its new position in T, X is immediately dominated by the highest S. (A transformation having such an effect is a "root transformation.") (*b*) The new position of X is a position in which a phrase-structure rule, motivated independently of the transformation in question, can generate the category X. (A transformation having such an effect is a "structure-preserving transformation.")

Nonphrase nodes may also be moved, copied, or inserted by either a root or a structure-preserving transformation, but they may also be moved by a third type of transformation: a single, specified nonphrase node may be moved over a single, specified *adjacent* node (but not over more than one such node or over a variable). Such a rule is a "minor movement rule." (Further restrictions can be placed on this type of rule, but they are not of interest here as I will be concerned here only with rules which move phrase nodes.)

In defending the structure-preserving constraint in my dissertation, I show that a number of phrase node movement or insertion rules which apply freely in embedded sentences can be formulated as structure-preserving by making at most small modifications (which, on reflection, can be independently justified) in the usual statements of these rules. The rules which relate the second sentences in the pairs of (1) to the first ones (by moving or inserting the italicized constituents) are examples of this type of rule.

(1) John wrote the letter.
  The letter was written by *John*. (passive rules)

  It seems to John that Mary prefers fish.
  Mary seems to John to prefer fish. (subject raising)

  It wouldn't be easy to clean this house.
  This house wouldn't be easy to clean. (object raising)

  The girls behaved as well as the boys.
  The girls behaved *themselves* as well as the boys (identical or reflexive object)

  There couldn't be any truth in that report.
  That report couldn't have any truth in it. (*there*-replacement)

  A man who hasn't got a family won't work as hard.
  A man won't work as hard *who hasn't got a family*. (extraposition from NP)

For other such rules, more justification is required to show that they are structure-preserving.[3] For example, limiting ourselves to NP movement rules for the moment, three rules which have rarely if ever been formulated as structure-preserving by transformationalists are *wh*-fronting, *there*-insertion, and dative movement. (The formal mechanism for expressing a structure-preserving rule adopted in my dissertation is that the node of category X which is moved, copied, or inserted replaces another node of category X, already present in the tree, which dominates either nothing or some recoverable form such as *it, do, there,* etc.) The arguments that *wh*-fronting and *there*-insertion are structure-preserving are too long to reproduce here, but it might be helpful to see what kind of formulation of dative movement is required by the structure-preserving constraint.[4]

The dative movement rule encompasses two formal operations, the deletion of the preposition *to* or *for,* and the reversal of the order of the direct and the indirect object NP's. Thus, the dative movement rule derives (3) from (2).

(2) John read a long paper to the students.
(3) John read the students a long paper.

If we exclude extending the phrase structure rules of English in an *ad hoc* way, there is no way to state dative movement as a structure-preserving rule which moves a single constituent. However, if we make crucial use of the fact that dative movement reverses the order of two constituents *of the same category*, we can state the rule as structure-preserving. That is, a formulation of dative movement in which both the direct and the indirect object NP's move, as in (4), is structure-preserving, since both NP's are replacing other (recoverable) NP's already present in the tree.

(4)

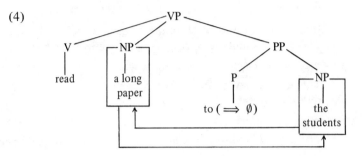

In most cases, the preposition which is deleted by the dative movement rule is not replaced in surface structure by another preposition. However, after some verbs, *with* is inserted in this position (in the structure-preserving fashion):

(5) John supplied typing paper to the students.
John supplied the students *with* typing paper.

The coach credited the victory to the lineman.
The coach credited the lineman *with* the victory.

Thus, the structure-preserving formulation of dative movement is as in (6).

(6) $[_{VP}$ X + V – NP – $\left\{\begin{smallmatrix}\text{to}\\\text{for}\end{smallmatrix}\right\}$ – NP – Y] $\Longrightarrow 1$ - 4 - $\emptyset$ - 2 - 5

$\quad\quad\quad$ 1 $\quad$ 2 $\quad\quad$ 3 $\quad\quad$ 4 $\;$ 5

(There are other conditions on dative movement not taken up here; only certain verbs govern the rule, there are many inanimate indirect object NP's which cannot undergo the rule, after some verbs like *read, pay,* and *teach* the preposition drops even if no direct object is present, etc.)

Dative movement, as formulated here, is an instance of a rule in which more than one constituent is moved by a single transformation. Since it is desirable to limit possible complex transformational rules of this type, it might be concluded that the fact that the structure-preserving constraint gives rise to formulating dative movement in this way is a theoretical consideration which lessens the value of this constraint. Upon reflection, however, we can see that in fact the structure-preserving constraint automatically limits such rules in very strong ways. For example, the structure-preserving constraint requires that the only movement rules which can interchange constituents in embedded sentences must interchange constituents of the same category. (It implies that a rule which interchanges a verb and an indirect object is impossible.)

Now it turns out that there is strong independent evidence that dative movement *must* be formulated as structure-preserving. This evidence is based on the placement of post-verbal particles (*in, out, up, down,* etc.) in sentences with indirect objects, and is presented in Emonds (1972). Thus, the structure-preserving constraint makes exactly the right prediction in the case of dative movement, and may well serve as a useful guide in research for correctly reformulating (and for discovering) other syntactic transformations.

1. THE STATUS OF SENTENCE AND INFINITIVE COMPLEMENTS

The principal subject of this paper is a more far-reaching reformulation of a grammatical transformation in view of the structure-preserving constraint: a reformulation of the extraposition rule of Rosenbaum (1967). However, I will begin not by considering the extraposition rule directly, but by justifying a claim which basically explains certain conditions on that rule. The claim is that embedded sentences are *not* instances of the constituent NP[5] if they either have a finite verb and are introduced (optionally) by *that* or have an infinitive (with or without expressed subject). Examples of such constituents are indicated in (7).

> (7) John believed *(that) Mary was a foreign agent.*
> John will see to it *that you have a reservation.*
> Bill would prefer *for Mary to stay awhile.*
> Barbara decided *to buy a car.*
> *That Bill knows German thoroughly* is obvious to all.
> *To read so many magazines* is a waste of time.
> *For the house to be painted* would irritate him.

The arguments in this section will differentiate such constituents not only from NP's with head nouns but also from the gerund constructions italicized in (8).[6]

> (8) John regretted *stealing Mary's book.*
> John will see to *your getting a ticket in time.*
> Bill would prefer *buying fewer foreign books.*
> *Your being able to find a new job* would be surprising.
> *Reading so many magazines* seems a waste of time.
> *Mary's having so many books* surprised him.

I claim that the last examples of (7) and (8) should be represented in surface structure as (9) and (10) respectively.

(9)

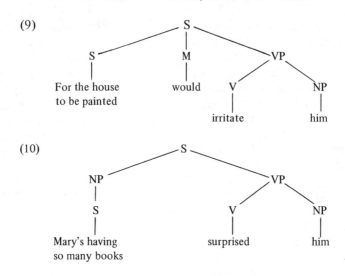

(10)

The deep structure I propose for (9) will be given in the course of the arguments to be presented.

The analysis of sentence and infinitive subject and object complements to be given here is at variance with that given in Rosenbaum (1967). Nonetheless, many of the grammatical facts elucidated in that work are important for establishing certain aspects of my analysis. What I believe to be flaws in Rosenbaum's arguments will be discussed in this section. In section 2, I show how an alternative analysis, which makes crucial use of the structure-preserving constraint, accounts both for the facts accounted for by Rosenbaum and for certain *ad hoc* conditions which must be placed on his extraposition rule.[7]

1.1 Two Exceptional Classes of Gerunds

Although I will argue that only gerunds (and not sentences and infinitives) are instances of NP's, I agree with Rosenbaum (1967) that there are two classes of gerunds (i.e., VP's whose heads have *-ing* affixes and which are not participles) which are not NP's. One such class contains the complements to "verbs of temporal aspect," which includes *begin, start, finish, continue, commence, stop, keep, keep on, go on, resume, cease,* etc.:

(11)

John $\begin{Bmatrix} \text{began} \\ \text{kept} \\ \text{continued} \\ \text{resumed} \\ \text{stopped} \end{Bmatrix}$ eating that steak.

We are concerned here only with the sense in which *John* is understood as subject of *eat*. Two reasons for not considering *eating that steak* in (11) as an NP are that this constituent cannot be the subject of a passive sentence (this argument due to Rosenbaum), nor can it be the focus constituent in a cleft construction, as can other NP's:

(12)

$$\text{*Eating that steak was} \left\{\begin{array}{l} \text{begun} \\ \text{kept} \\ \text{continued} \\ \text{resumed} \\ \text{stopped} \end{array}\right\} \text{by John.}$$

$$\text{*It was eating that steak that John} \left\{\begin{array}{l} \text{began} \\ \text{kept} \\ \text{continued.} \\ \text{resumed} \\ \text{stopped} \end{array}\right\}$$

Another class of gerunds which are not NP's are the VP complements to many transitive verbs of perception (*see, watch, observe, notice, smell, hear, listen, feel*) and to a few other verbs like *find, catch,* etc.:

(13) I saw John *cleaning the table.*
     *It was cleaning the table that I saw John.

     They noticed some smoke *coming out of the window.*
     *It was coming out of the window that they noticed some smoke.

     John found her *studying algebra.*
     *It was studying algebra that John found her.

Gerunds of this second class are reduced progressive forms of infinitives, as I will show. First, note that infinitives generally occur after transitive verbs of perception (but lack a characteristic *to*);

(14) I saw John clean the table.
     They noticed some smoke come out of the window.

But infinitives in progressive form are superficially excluded after such verbs:

(15) *I saw John be cleaning the table.
     *They noticed some smoke be coming out of the window.

We can account for this gap in the paradigm by deriving the sentences of

(13) from the underlying strings of (15) by a *be*-deletion rule. The underlying progressive nature of the forms in (13) is confirmed by observations like the following:

> (16) *The prisoners died* implies *The prisoners are dead.*
> *The prisoners were dying* does not.
> *We saw the prisoners die* implies *The prisoners are dead.*
> *We saw the prisoners dying* does not.
> *We found the prisoners dying* does not.

> (17) Question: *Where are the children?*
> Appropriate answers: *They are running across the street.*
> *I can see them running across the street.*
> Inappropriate answers: *They run across the street.*
> *I can see them run across the street.*

These reduced progressive infinitives will be treated like other infinitives in the rest of this paper. Similarly, from here on, when I use the term "gerund," I mean to exclude these reduced progressive infinitives and also the complements to verbs of temporal aspect.

1.2. The Deep Structure of Sentence and Infinitive Complements.

I agree with Rosenbaum that an S is generable at the end of VP's, AP's, and NP's by phrase structure rules like (18), (19), and (20).[8]

> (18) VP → ... + (S)
> (19) AP → ... + (S)
> (20) NP → ... + (S)

The S in (18) is the source of at least the sentence and infinitive complements to Rosenbaum's verb classes containing, as typical members, *tend* and *persuade*. (I return to the arguments favoring Rosenbaum's analysis of these verbs below.) The S's in (19) and (20) are the source of sentence and infinitive complements to nouns like *tendency, belief, preference,* etc. and to adjectives like *eager, happy, ready,* etc.

The crucial difference between my analysis and Rosenbaum's is that I take the S in (18) also to be the deep-structure source for the sentential and infinitival subject and object complements italicized in (7) above (where the verbs are *believe, prefer, irritate, seem,* etc.). That is, the arguments to be presented below show that sentence and infinitive complements are not generable by the rule NP → S and hence cannot have any other source but (18), (19), and (20).

Such a claim immediately raises numerous questions, perhaps the most obvious being how I can account for the interpretations of the complements in (7) as objects and especially subjects, if I claim that these complements have the same postverbal deep-structure positions. I think this question can be adequately answered in a fairly simple way, and I return to it in section 2 after I have established my analysis on syntactic grounds. The question is essentially concerned with the semantic component, since it is in this component and not in syntax or phonology that grammatical relations are used.

An alternate way to state my position is to say that the phrase structure rule NP → S or alternatively NP → NP + VP always gives rise to gerunds and never to sentences and infinitives.

An initial advantage of my analysis is that the rule that differentiates between *to* and *-ing* can be related to structural difference between clauses which are NP's and those which are not, rather than in terms of an *ad hoc* syntactic feature, as in Rosenbaum (1967).[9]

I now turn to an examination of the various syntactic positions of the category NP and attempt to show that, in each such position, sentences and infinitives either do not occur or are not present in the given position in deep structure.

1.3 The Position of Object Complements.

It might at first be thought that the italicized clausal complements in (21) are NP's, whereas these same complements are extraposed to the end of the VP and are no longer NP's in the corresponding paraphrases of (22).

(21) John already said *that he will pay up* yesterday.
They proved *that John had taken bribes* in District Court.
Mary promised *to be quiet* reluctantly.
I like *it that they played those records* very much.

(22) John already said yesterday *that he will pay up.*
They proved in District Court *that John had taken bribes.*
Mary promised reluctantly *to be quiet.*
I like it very much *that they played those records.*

However, the adverbs which can precede or follow object clauses as in (21) and (22) are those adverbs which are not closely linked to the main verb: locative adverbs of space and time, manner adverbials, etc. These same classes of adverbs can in fact precede or follow *extraposed* subject clauses, as in (23).

(23) It seems *that victory is unattainable* today.
It seems today *that victory is unattainable.*

It means nothing *to speak of simultaneity* in Einstein's framework.
It means nothing in Einstein's framework *to speak of simultaneity*.

It isn't required *that the players be tall* in this school.
It isn't required in this school *that the players be tall*.

It pleased me *that they played those records* very much.
It pleased me very much *that they played those records*.

It doesn't frighten me *to watch horror movies* anymore.
It doesn't frighten me anymore *to watch horror movies*.

It isn't necessary *to be smart* on this campus.
It isn't necessary on this campus *to be smart*.

In my dissertation (Emonds 1969, sec. 4.3) I propose an adverb movement rule by which adverbs originally outside a VP may move inside it (so as to precede an extraposed S), in order to account for the alternations in (23). If we assume that the italicized complements in (21) and (22) have the same (extraposed) status as those in (23), this rule automatically accounts for (21) and (22), making an explanation of the latter alternation in terms of the extraposition rule redundant.

In other words, extraposition of S is not needed to explain (22). We can assume that extraposition is always *obligatory* from object position, and the rule which accounts for the variants in (23), whether it be an S movement or an adverb movement, automatically accounts for (21) and (22). Thus, (21) and (22) are irrelevant for deciding whether object clauses are ever found in the object NP position or whether they are always generated in extraposed position. The real test for deciding this question is the order of object clauses with respect to phrases which are subcategorized by the head verb, such as those italicized in (24).

(24) They told a fairy tale *to the children*.
      They told *the children* a fairy tale.
      *They told how to build a kite *to the children*.
      They told *the children* how to build a kite.

      *She won't tell she is sick *to the doctor*.
      She won't tell *the doctor* she is sick.

      You promised a new hat *to Mary*.
      You promised *Mary* a new hat.
      *You promised to be quiet *to Mary*.
      You promised *Mary* to be quiet.
      *You promised you would do the wash *to Mary*.
      You promised *Mary* you would do the wash.

The man taught the importance of books *to his sons.*
The man taught *his sons* the importance of books.
*The man taught that books were important *to his sons.*
The man taught *his sons* that books were important.

I take this responsibility *upon myself.*
*I take to fix the lamp *upon myself.*
I take it *upon myself* to fix the lamp.

They expect some cooperation *of (from) you.*
*They expect that you cooperate *of you.*
They expect it *of you* that you cooperate.

John said something nasty *to Mary.*
*John said to leave him alone *to Mary.*
John said *to Mary* to leave him alone.

Bill got a free meal.
Bill got to eat out.
Bill got a free meal *for Joe.*
Bill got *Joe* a free meal.
*Bill got to eat out *for Joe.*[10]
Bill got Joe to eat out.

I make no attempt to explain in a principled fashion why an *it* sometimes appears in object position in (24) and sometimes does not. The italicized PP's in (24) are deep-structure sisters to V, and in every case an infinitive or sentence object complement must follow them. Thus, there is no distributional evidence that such complements occur in object NP position in deep structure.[11]

1.4. Sentences and Infinitives after Exclusion of Prepositions.

A clearcut indication that infinitives and sentences are not in the same category as gerunds and noun phrases with head nouns is that the latter two but not the former two appear after the traditional class of prepositions (*from, at, into, toward, by, with, on account of, because of, despite,* etc.):

(25) John just came back from his job.
John just came back from driving a cab.
*John just came back from to drive a cab.
*John just came back from that he drove a cab.

He blamed it on Bill's strictness.
He blamed it on Bill's being too strict.
*He blamed it on for Bill to be too strict.

*He blamed it on that Bill was too strict.

Because of John's age, Mary gets a pension.
Because of John's being so old, Mary gets a pension.

*Because of for John to be so old, Mary gets a pension.
*Because of that John is so old, Mary gets a pension.

*Because John's age, Mary gets a pension.
*Because John's being so old, Mary gets a pension.
Because John is so old, Mary gets a pension.

It might be thought that the future participle, *"about* + infinitive," is an exception to the prohibition on infinitives after prepositions, but this *about* has no semantic or syntactic connection with the preposition *about;* for example, the future participle is not a PP:

(26) It is about New York that they are talking.
*It is about to leave that John seems.

Prepositions do appear in pseudo-cleft constructions which have sentences and infinitives in focus position, as in (27). This is sometimes taken as certain evidence that the traditional class of prepositions does appear before infinitives and sentences in underlying syntactic structure.

(27) What we are aware of is that she is poor.
What he insisted on was that we not pay for the food.

Whether (27) is evidence for this contention or not depends, however, on one's analysis of the pseudo-cleft construction of the form (28).

(28) $(_S (\begin{Bmatrix} \text{what} \\ \text{where} \\ \text{when} \end{Bmatrix}) \text{ - X - Y }_S) \text{ - be - } (_C \text{ Focus constituent }_C)$

Can (28) be derived by a deletion of the second X and Y in an assumed underlying structure of the form (29)?

(29) $(_S \text{ X - (wh-some } \begin{Bmatrix} \text{thing} \\ \text{place} \\ \text{time} \end{Bmatrix}) \text{ - Y }_S) \text{ - be - } (_S \text{ X - C - Y }_S)$

Suppose the answer is yes, and consider (30). In the first example, X = *John should be doing,* Y = ∅, and C = *working the bar.* [12]

(30) What John should be doing is working the bar.
What John was doing to Bill was kicking him in the shins.

In these sentences, X dominates *-ing;* but C dominates *-ing* also, implying two -*ing's* in the underlying right-hand S in (29), hardly a satisfying result. The problem is the assumption that (29) represents the underlying structure of a pseudo-cleft of the form (28).

The undesired consequence of this assumption can be avoided if we replace *wh-something* in (29) with W, where W dominates *wh-something* and is subject to other conditions. But then W can be constitutents like *doing wh-something* or *of wh-something*, and it no longer is necessarily so that prepositions must precede sentences and infinitives (i.e., be the last element in X in [29]) in deep structure.

Thus, any analysis of the pseudo-cleft construction which assumes that the focus constituent is the remnant of a deep-structure sentence on the right-hand side of the copula does not require that I abandon the claim that infinitives and sentences do not appear as NP's after prepositions. There are other possible approaches to pseudo-cleft constructions, but I think that arguments to the same effect as the one I have given here could be constructed for any precise alternative analysis of pseudo-cleft sentences.

Infinitives and sentences do not appear before *'s* in gerunds and noun phrases with head nouns, but this alone proves nothing, since gerunds and certain other "complex" noun phrases, from which we are trying to differentiate them, do not either. However, there is a discernible difference in ungrammaticality between gerunds before *'s* and infinitives before *'s*, the latter being less acceptable. Compare:

(31) *Does he know about smoking pot's being illegal?
    *(Worse) Does he know about to smoke pot's being illegal?

This intuition can be strengthened by noting that, in most American speech, *'s* can be omitted in many cases after the subject of a gerund. When this optional rule is applied to the sentences in (31), the result is that the first, but not the second, sounds completely acceptable:

(32) Does he know about smoking pot being illegal?
    *Does he know about to smoke pot being illegal?
    Cf. Does he know about it being illegal to smoke pot?

    We agree about shoveling snow being ridiculous.
    *We agree about to shovel snow being ridiculous.
    Cf. We agree about it being ridiculous to shovel snow.

Actually, the same kind of change in acceptability between (31) and (32) appears when NP's with N heads, as well as gerunds, lose their *'s:*

(33) *I didn't know about the purchase of a car's putting them into bankruptcy.
    I didn't know about the purchase of a car putting them into bankruptcy.

This further demonstrates the similarity between gerunds and other NP's, as well as the dissimilarity between gerunds and infinitives.

A few examples with NP's in appositive position to other NP's are perhaps in order. Very little is known about the special properties of this construction. However, in connection with our concern here, we can note that infinitives, although interpretable in this position, are not as natural as gerunds. Compare, for example, the infinitives and gerunds used as appositives in (34).

(34) All this constant activity, buying food twice a day and going out every night, is wearing me out.
*All this constant activity, to buy food twice a day and to go out every night, is wearing me out.

We have finished the most irksome part, filling out the long registration form.
*We have finished the most irksome part, to fill out the long registration form.

This concludes my examination of nonsubject NP positions, in which we have seen that infinitives and sentences do not occur.

1.5 Sentences and Infinitives in Subject Position.

Sentences and infinitives occur in surface structure in subject position, as in the examples of (7), repeated here for convenience:

(35) *That Bill knows German thoroughly* is obvious to all.
To read so many magazines is a waste of time.
For the house to be painted would irritate him.

According to the analysis I am pursuing, these sentences must be derived from the corresponding sentences in (36), since the only source for sentence and infinitive complements is the "extraposed" S (and perhaps VP) generated by (18).

(36) It is obvious to all that Bill knows German thoroughly.
It is a waste of time to read so many magazines.
It would irritate him for the house to be painted.

A straightforward rule to accomplish this derivation would be one which replaces a subject NP dominating *it* (or, perhaps, dominating nothing at the point when the rule applies) with the complement S, as in (37). I will call this rule "subject replacement." (Care will have to be taken to insure that the only S's which undergo subject replacement are those which are in fact interpreted as deep-structure subjects. I take up this question in section 2.)

$$(37) \quad (_S (_{NP} \text{ it}) (_M \text{ would}) (_{VP} (_V \text{ irritate}) (_{NP} \text{ him}) (_S \underbrace{\text{for the house}}_{\text{to be painted}})))$$

The result of applying subject replacement to (37) was given earlier as (9).

According to this formulation, subject replacement is not a structure-preserving rule. But the structure-preserving constraint then requires that it be a root transformation. That is, it must *not* apply in nonroot S's. This is in fact the case; gerunds, but not infinitives or sentences with finite verbs, are acceptable subjects in nonroot S's.[13]

(38) *That for Bill to smoke bothers the teacher is quite possible.
That it bothers the teacher for Bill to smoke is quite possible.
That Bill's smoking cigarettes bothers the teacher is quite possible.
?It is quite possible that for Bill to smoke bothers the teacher.

*For that you pay that tax to be necessary would be an inconvenience.
For it to be necessary that you pay that tax would be an inconvenience.
*It would be an inconvenience for that you pay that tax to be necessary.

*He protested the decision that for the bill to be marked paid meant nothing.
He protested the decision that it meant nothing for the bill to be marked paid.
He protested the decision that the bill's being marked paid meant nothing.

*John was happy that to own a car didn't disqualify you.
John was happy that it didn't disqualify you to own a car.
John was happy that owning a car didn't disqualify you.

*I don't believe for you to study history hurts you.
*I don't believe that you study history hurts you.
I don't believe your studying history hurts you.

*He didn't want that he was Indian to be known at his club.
He didn't want it to be known at his club that he was Indian.
*He didn't want his being Indian to be known at his club.
*His being Indian wasn't known at his club.

*A day at the beach is more fun than to play golf is.
A day at the beach is more fun than playing golf is.

*To go by car doesn't seem as rewarding as to ride a horse used to seem.
Going by car doesn't seem as rewarding as riding a horse used to seem.

*He exercises so rarely that to lift those bricks is bad for his heart.
He exercises so rarely that lifting those bricks is bad for his heart.

*Although that the house is empty may depress you, it pleases me.
*Although for the house to be empty may depress you, it pleases me.
Although the house's being empty may depress you, it pleases me.

*The children for whom to diagram sentences is easy often become mathematicians.
The children for whom it is easy to diagram sentences often become mathematicians.
The children for whom diagramming sentences is easy often become mathematicians.

*She forgets how expensive to go to the dentist is.
She forgets how expensive going to the dentist is.

*The reason why that you have insurance doesn't protect you is that you're a foreigner.
*The reason why for you to have insurance doesn't protect you is that you're a foreigner.
The reason why your having insurance doesn't protect you is that you're a foreigner.

*Situations in which to write out a check is necessary should be avoided.
Situations in which writing out a check is necessary should be avoided.

*The salesman who that I bought a car seemed most important to was a Southerner.
*The salesman who for me to buy a car seemed most important to was a Southerner.
The salesman who my buying a car seemed most important to was a Southerner.

*She likes the kind of man that to see a few movies a year will
satisfy.

She likes the kind of man that it will satisfy to see a few movies
a year.

She likes the kind of man that seeing a few movies a year will
satisfy.

The contrasts in grammaticality in (38) are a *necessary* consequence of the
structure-preserving constraint if we assume that sentence and infinitive
complements are generated at the end of the VP by (18), since a
non-structure-preserving rule like subject replacement *cannot* apply in
embedded sentences.

On the other hand, these contrasts must be accounted for in an *ad
hoc* fashion in Rosenbaum's framework. That is, the extraposition rule must
carry a condition that it is obligatory for a sentence or infinitive subject of a
nonroot S.

A previous attempt to attribute this condition to a more general
principle was made by Ross (1967). He proposed that it is due to a general
prohibition on the configuration $(_{NP} S)$ in the "sentence interior" position.
As Ross himself pointed out, however, the fact that gerunds, which may be
S's dominated by NP's, occur in sentence interior position casts doubt on the
generality of this constraint. A clearer counterexample is provided by
"headless" relative clauses, which occur quite freely in sentence interior
position:

(39) She won't tell $\begin{Bmatrix} \text{what she heard} \\ \text{*she is sick} \end{Bmatrix}$ to the doctor.

The man taught
$\begin{Bmatrix} \text{what he had learned from the missionaries} \\ \text{*that the missionaries were evil} \end{Bmatrix}$ to his sons.

He takes $\begin{Bmatrix} \text{whatever is necessary to prove his point} \\ \text{*that his assumptions are unchallengeable} \end{Bmatrix}$ for
granted.

John was happy (that) $\begin{Bmatrix} \text{what he had done} \\ \text{*to own a car} \end{Bmatrix}$ hadn't disqualified
him.

I never assumed $\begin{Bmatrix} \text{what I heard on the news} \\ \text{*that we were in danger} \end{Bmatrix}$ was true.

He drives so fast that $\begin{Bmatrix} \text{what we save on fares is spent on fines.} \\ \text{*for me to watch for signs is difficult.} \end{Bmatrix}$

Although $\begin{Bmatrix} \text{what I have learned} \\ \text{*that I own a yacht} \end{Bmatrix}$ doesn't impress you, it did her.

The children for whom $\begin{Bmatrix} \text{whatever the teacher says} \\ \text{*that the teacher is always right} \end{Bmatrix}$ is
gospel aren't very interesting.

He protested the decision that
{ however much had not been paid would be added to his taxes.
{ *for the bill to be marked paid meant nothing.

For { what that company makes
{ *that they make saddles } to be well-known would surprise me.

I conclude that the condition that infinitives and sentences *must* be extraposed in nonroot S's is an *ad hoc* condition in Rosenbaum's framework, and not the consequence of a universal principle.

The subject replacement rule (i.e., my counterpart to extraposition) has further similarities to root transformations. As Ross noted in formulating the constraint just discussed, a sentence or infinitive complement cannot appear in subject position if *anything* (at least, anything which is not separated from the subject by a comma) precedes this position:

(40) Why did { *that Mary liked old records
{ Mary's liking old records } irritate him?

Is { *that this stock will be sold
{ ?this stock's being sold } certain?

Cf. ? This stock's being sold is certain.

When was { *to arrive an hour early
{ arriving an hour early } a requirement?

*Never will for us to be comfortable be possible in this climate.
Never will it be possible for us to be comfortable in this climate.

A disease like that { *to take a lot of pills
{ ?taking a lot of pills
{ ?frequent exercise } won't cure.

This is automatically accounted for in the analysis I am pursuing, once we note that this is a general condition on all the fronting root transformations of English: only one of them can apply in a given S. To see that this is so, I first list the preposing root transformations studied in chapter 1 of my dissertation, along with sentences in which the italicized constituents have been fronted by each of the rules in question;

(41)   (a)   Directional adverb preposing:
Away ran John.
Into that house ran the boys.

(b)   Negated constituent preposing:
Never will she buy a car.
Only a few students did he meet in the East.

(c)   Direct quotation preposing:
"Bill likes corn," John said, "but I don't."

(d)   Nonfactive complement preposing:
All the people in the crowd, he assumed, were carrying flags.

(e)   Topicalization:
These steps I never swept with a broom.
Her John likes.

(f)   VP preposing:
She never has bought a car, and *buy one* she never will.
He said I would like her, and *like her* I do.

(g)   Left dislocation:
John, he ran away.
My brother, he met only a few students.

(h)   Comparative substitution:
Easier for us to solve would be a problem from number theory.
Equally as welcome would be a theorem from geometry.

(i)   Participle preposing:
Speaking to the president now is our top reporter.

(j)   PP substitution:
Among the guests was standing John.

Also subject to this condition on fronting transformations, for reasons unknown to me, is the nonroot transformation of *wh*-fronting:

(41)   (k)   *Wh*-fronting:
Which plays of his have we read?
What would be easier to solve?

Note, first, that the ungrammatical examples of (40) are forbidden combinations of the preposing root transformations of subject replacement with rules (41b), (41e), and (41k). Furthermore, combinations of rules (41a) through (41k) with each other, all of which produce ungrammaticality, are given in (42). The notation (x-y) after the examples in (42) means that first rule (41x) and then rule (41y) applies to yield the example in question.

(42)   *John, away he ran. (a-g)
*Away, John, he ran. (g-a)

*That house into ran the boys. (a-e)

*She never has bought a car, and buy one never will she. (b-f)

*She never has bought a car, and never $\begin{Bmatrix} \text{will buy one she} \\ \text{buy one she will} \end{Bmatrix}$ (f-b)

*These steps never did I sweep with a broom. (b-e)
*Never did these steps I sweep with a broom. (e-b)
*Never these steps did I sweep with a broom. (e-b)

*Which plays of his $\begin{Bmatrix} \text{never have} \\ \text{have never} \end{Bmatrix}$ we read? (b-k)
*Never $\begin{Bmatrix} \text{which plays of his have} \\ \text{have which plays of his} \end{Bmatrix}$ we read? (k-b)

*Who into the house dashed? (a-k)
*Into the house who dashed? (k-a)

*What $\begin{Bmatrix} \text{these steps did} \\ \text{did these steps} \end{Bmatrix}$ you use to sweep with? (e-k)

*These steps $\begin{Bmatrix} \text{what did} \\ \text{did what} \end{Bmatrix}$ you use to sweep with? (k-e)

What did he assume all the people in the crowd were carrying?
All the people in the crowd, he assumed, were carrying flags.
*All the people in the crowd, what did he assume, were carrying? (k-d)

*My brother, only a few students did he meet in the East. (b-g)
*Only a few students, my brother, did he meet in the East. (g-b)

*"Bill likes corn," John, he said, "but I don't." (g-c)
*John, "Bill likes corn," he said, "but I don't." (c-g)

*He said I would like her, and her like I do. (f-e)
*John said she would help him willingly, and help willingly him she does. (e-f)

*John, her he likes. (e-g)
*Her, John, he likes. (g-e)

*The president speaking to now is our top reporter. (i-e)
*Speaking to now the president is our top reporter. (e-i)

*Was among the guests standing John? (j-k)
*Among the guests was John standing? (k-j)

*What would easier to solve be? (h-k)
*Easier to solve what would be? (k-j)

Thus, all the preposing root transformations (and *wh*-movement) can apply only if no other transformation of the same type applies in the same root S. (I do not pretend to have captured this restriction in a formal way; I use it only to show that subject replacement is like other root transformations.) This restriction predicts, as a special case, the ungrammaticality of subject replacement in the root sentences of (40), since, in these examples, a constituent precedes the subject NP position as a result of a preposing root transformation (or *wh*-fronting).[14]

A study of the sentence and infinitive complements which occur in subject position thus favors the view that they originate at the end of the VP in deep structure. For it is this assumption, coupled with the structure-preserving constraint, which automatically predicts the ungrammaticality of the sentence and infinitive subjects in (38) and (40). In Rosenbaum's framework, on the other hand, these facts can be accounted for only by an *ad hoc* condition making extraposition of a sentence or infinitive complement not immediately dominated by a root S obligatory rather than optional.

1.6. Other Arguments Confirming the non-NP Status of Infinitives and Sentences.

(i) In noun phrases with noun heads, at some point in the transformational derivation a rule must insert *'s* in the context: $[_{NP}[_{NP}X\_] Y]$. This is not a deep-structure condition, because it is not an NP in this position in deep structure which receives the *'s* in phrases like *John's expulsion by the principal*. But according to this rule, gerunds should be noun phrases and sentences and infinitives should not be, since the initial (subject) NP in gerunds but not in infinitives and sentences can be followed by an *'s* suffix.

(ii) If sentences and infinitives are not NP's, they should not conjoin freely with NP's. It was pointed out by Gleitman (1965) that this is the case. On the other hand, gerunds and NP's with head nouns can be conjoined.

(43)   She used to like watching television and physical exercise both.
*She used to like watching television and to play volleyball both.
*She used to like to watch television and physical exercise both. (where *physical exercise* is object of *like)*
*She used to like physical exercise and to watch television both.

Outdoor bathrooms and pitching a tent every day would bother me.
*To pitch a tent every day and outdoor bathrooms would bother me.

*Eating canned foods and to pitch a tent every day would bother me.

He proposed a 20% reduction for the elderly and discontinuing the translation service.
*He proposed a 20% reduction for the elderly and that the office be moved to the suburbs.
*He proposed discontinuing the translation service and that the office be moved to the suburbs.

(iii) Rosenbaum noted that the extraposition does not apply to gerunds:[15]

(44)   *It was understandable John's owning two cars.
          *It is irritating everybody in the back seat John's driving fast.
          *It never scared him when he was young sleeping in the dark.

Some speakers of English find the starred sentences of (44) acceptable, but even these demand that a commalike pause precede the extraposed gerunds, so that what is probably involved is the right dislocation rule (a root transformation) discussed in Ross (1967) and in chapter 1 of my dissertation.

(45)   It was understandable, John's purchase of a gun.
          It irritates everybody in the back seat, John's big cigar.
          It never scared him when he was young, the skeleton in the closet.

Since gerunds do not appear "in extraposition" from the subject, the extraposition rule in Rosenbaum's framework must be made to depend on an *ad hoc* difference between gerunds and infinitives. But the counterpart of the extraposition rule in the framework of this study, the subject replacement rule, does not depend (is not formulated in terms of) such an *ad hoc* feature. This is because gerunds and infinitives have different rather than the same underlying sources. This formal advantage is the result of generating both subject and object sentence and infinitive complements at the end of the VP.

(iv) I will try to show in section 2 that certain (though not all) of Rosenbaum's conclusions about clausal complements from the way such complements behave in the pseudo-cleft construction are in error, and that this construction is not a diagnostic context for the category NP.

On the other hand, we can replace Rosenbaum's pseudo-cleft test for NP status (which I will show to be unsatisfactory) with a more appropriate one, the cleft test. Examples of the cleft construction, with the focus constituent italicized, are given in (46).

(46)   It's *the custard pie* that I disliked.
        It was *a tax break* that I counted on.
        Was it *John* that broke the window?
        It was *to John* that she spoke.
        It's *because of the flood* that they are leaving.
        It is *with great pleasure* that I present our speaker.
        It was *buying a new hat* that I enjoyed.
        It was *John's knowing the location of the mailbox* that surprised her.
        It was *because it was raining* that they left.

        *It's *very unhappy* that Bill is.
        *It was *useless* that the meeting seemed.
        *It was *explicitly* that he rejected our assumptions.
        *It was *too carefully* that she spoke.
        *It is *blow up some buildings* that you should do.
        *It is *playing for time* that they are doing.
        Cf. What you should do is blow up some buildings.
        Cf. What they are doing is playing for time.
        *It was *throwing away some letters* that John noticed Bill.
        *It was *ask John for money* that I heard you.
        *It was *stealing my money* that she caught him.
        *It was *drinking beer from the bottle* that she kept.
        *It was *to report on time* that we failed.
        *It was *that he passed out* that John drank so much.

The cleft construction appears to be a near-perfect diagnostic for the categories NP and PP.[16] In particular, the gerund can appear in focus position, as in two of the examples of (46). By this test, however, sentences and infinitives are not noun phrases:

(47)   *It was *to buy a new hat* that I wanted.
        *It's *for John to drive carelessly* that upsets me.
        *It is *to always be on time* that you should decide.
        *It was *that you explain your motives* that was important.
        *It's *that John has come too late* that Bill realizes.
        *Was it *that Mary had cashed the check* that Bill regretted?
        Cf. It's *John's driving carelessly* that upsets me.
        It was *explaining your motives* that was important.
        Was it *Mary's having cashed the check* that Bill regretted?

The ungrammaticality of the examples of (47) is automatically explained when we generate sentence and infinitive complements at the end of the VP (and not as NP's) and design the grammar so that just NP's and PP's appear in focus position in cleft sentences. (In chapter 4 of my dissertation, I show that this latter condition is in fact another automatic consequence of the structure-preserving constraint and not a special condition on rules that form the cleft sentence construction.)

(v) According to Rosenbaum's analysis, the italicized subject clauses in (48) are NP's.

(48)   *For John to arrive* would cause embarrassment.
        That the children are always late shows the necessity of discipline.
        That you spoke out of turn didn't help the situation.
        To suggest devaluation would anger the bankers.
        That the boys were dancing together was amusing John.

However, the agent-postposing (passive) rule does not apply to these supposed NP's. Rosenbaum apparently was under the impression that agent postposing and a subsequent rule deleting *by* would produce grammatical sentences, but this is not the case either:

(49)   *Embarrassment would be caused (by) for John to arrive.
        *The necessity of discipline is shown (by) that the children are always late.
        *The situation wasn't helped (by) that you spoke out of turn.
        *The bankers would be angered (by) to suggest devaluation.
        *John was being amused (by) that the boys were dancing together.

Rosenbaum was probably led to this conclusion by the existence of sentences like those in (50).

(50)   John was disturbed (*by) that the neighbors were so noisy.
        Mary was pleased (*by) that she had found a job.

But such sentences are due to the fact that *disturbed* and *pleased* are "passive adjectives," similar to *sorry* and *glad* in (51), as well as passive verb forms:

(51)   John was sorry (*by) that the neighbors were so noisy.
        Mary was glad (*by) that she had found a job.

We know the passive forms that appear in sentences like (50) are adjectives because they can be modified by characteristically adjectival modifiers like *very*.

(52)   John was very disturbed that the neighbors were so noisy.
Mary was very pleased that she had found a job.
John was very sorry that the neighbors were so noisy.
Mary was very glad that she had found a job.

*Embarrassment would be very caused by his arrival.
*The necessity of discipline is very shown by their tardiness.
*The situation wasn't very helped by your comments.
*John was being very amused by their antics.

(*Angered* and *amused* are also passive adjectives and can be used alone with *very*; the ungrammaticality of the last two examples in [49] is due to the fact that these adjectives cannot be used with infinitive complements or with the progressive.)

Another proof that the passive forms in (50) are adjectives is their ability to appear after *seem*:

(53)   John seemed $\begin{Bmatrix} \text{disturbed} \\ \text{sorry} \end{Bmatrix}$ that the neighbors were so noisy.

Mary seemed $\begin{Bmatrix} \text{pleased} \\ \text{glad} \end{Bmatrix}$ that she had found a job.

*Embarrassment seemed caused by his arrival.
*The necessity of discipline seemed shown by their tardiness.
*The situation didn't seem helped by your comments.

Finally, we know the passive forms in (50) are not verbs because they could occur with the progressive if they were:

(54)   That the neighbors were so noisy was disturbing John.
That John is looking for a job is pleasing Mary.
That John didn't have a job was depressing Mary.

*John was being disturbed that the neighbors were so noisy.
*Mary is being pleased that John is looking for a job.
*Mary was being depressed that John didn't have a job.

These three arguments show that agent postposing does not move sentences and infinitives. This means that the extraposition rule requires an *ad hoc* condition in Rosenbaum's framework. This condition simply states that sentences and infinitives do not act like NP's as far as the agent postposing rule is concerned, thus reflecting directly my contention that these constructions are never NP's.

In the framework I am proposing, the italicized subject clauses in

(48) are generated at the end of the VP, and moved to subject position by the subject replacement rule. By ordering subject replacement after the passive rules, the generation of examples (49) is avoided. We know on independent grounds that this ordering is correct because sentence and infinitive clauses can also replace deep-structure object instances of *it* which are moved to the subject position by the NP-preposing rule:

> (55) That John is brilliant is known by few people.
>
> For John to be arrested would be condemned by the newspapers.
>
> That we have permits will be proven by our willingness to show our luggage.
>
> That Mary stay the night was insisted on by Susan.
>
> To remain silent was preferred by everyone.
>
> That the house was old was denied by John.

I conclude that the fact that agent postposing does not apply to sentence and infinitive subjects in Rosenbaum's framework is a fault that can be eliminated if we assume that sentence and infinitive complements are always generated at the end of the VP.[17]

In this section, I have given several supporting arguments that sentences and infinitives are not instances of the configuration $(_{NP}S)$. I now turn to the task of showing how certain grammatical phenomena which are accounted for adequately in Rosebaum's grammar can equally well be described in the revised grammar I am proposing, though in somewhat different ways.

2. AN ALTERNATIVE TO ROSENBAUM'S EXPLANATIONS

2.1 Rosenbaum's Noun Phrase Complements.

Sentences such as those in (56) are often taken as evidence that the italicized antecedents of *it* must be NP's:

> (56) John tends *to eat too much*, although Mary disapproves of it.
>
> John guessed *that Mary would be coming*, although I had said nothing about it.
>
> If *this house had fewer windows,* it would bother me.
>
> It would have been pointed out by John if *there had been any danger.*

However, it seems to me that the sentences of (56) only show *either* that the underlined antecedents of *it* are NP's *or* that *it* may have antecedents which are S's.[18] In the absence of other pertinent arguments, these sentences could not decide for us which conclusion it would be correct to draw.

In the previous section, I gave several independent arguments that the italicized constituents in (56) are *not* NP's. Hence I conclude that *it* may also have S antecedents. Assuming that a pronoun and its antecendent are marked with coreferential indices, the fact that S's do not appear in NP positions in deep structure (as shown previously) suggests a theory of coreference in which some (perhaps all) anaphoric pronouns are generated in the base and in which structural conditions for coreferentiality of constituents are stated for various grammatical levels.

This is, of course, the "interpretive theory" of pronominalization, argued for extensively recently by Jackendoff (1969), Dougherty (1969), Bresnan (1971), and others. (Such theories can differ, it shoudl be kept in mind, from author to author). One obvious condition which must ordinarily be fulfilled in order for two constituents to be co-referential, however, is that one of them be a pronoun (or an epithet).

Given such a theory, a natural way to explain how a sentence or infinitive complement "in extraposition" (at the end of the VP) in deep structure is interpreted as a subject or object of a given verb is to assume that such a complement is coreferential with an *it* in the appropriate subject or object NP position. Thus, the embedded S in (57) is interpreted as the subject of the verb, and the embedded S in (58) is interpreted as the object of the verb.

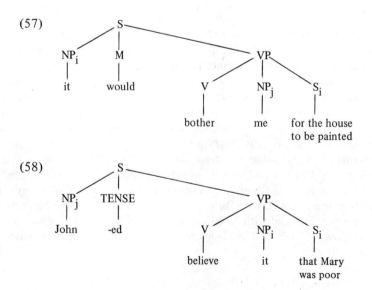

The embedded S's in (59), and hence the larger trees of which they form a part, are uninterpretable because the meanings of the main verbs in these trees do not admit of "oblique" S complements,[19] but only of subjects and objects. That is, no special subcategorization conditions are needed to exclude the trees of (59); the projection rule for forming the meaning of an S from the lexical meaning of the main verb of S cannot operate on trees with superfluous constituents not specified in the meaning of that verb.

(59)

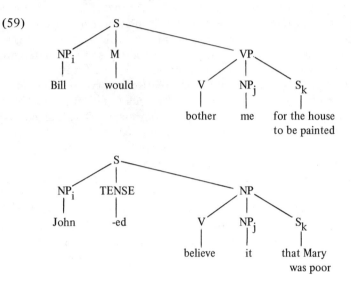

The theory of verb complementation I am proposing agrees with that of Rosenbaum's in that the distribution of the deep-structure *it*'s whose antecedents are sentence and infinitive (but not gerund) complements is essentially the same in both theories. In Rosenbaum's analysis, NP complement clauses are generated by the phrase structure rule: NP → IT + S, where a surface-structure IT dominates the terminal symbol *it*. In each case (excepting the complements to a very few verbs like *seem*, which I discuss in the next section) in which Rosenbaum postulates a deep-structure configuration $[_{NP}$ IT S] for a sentence or infinitive complement, I postulate a deep structure $[_{NP_i}$ it], where S_i appears simultaneously at the end of VP "in extraposition." The difference between the two analyses is that Rosenbaum considered IT to always be a deep-structure sister to its S antecedent, while I consider the corresponding *it* to be a coreferential with its antecedent S, which is in extraposition.

Rosenbaum's rule of IT-deletion, ordered after his extraposition rule, is essentially (60).

(60) $[_{NP}$ IT - S] $\emptyset$ - 2

Certain discrepancies, as in (61), must be accounted for in Rosenbaum's framework by special conditions either on (60) or on the extraposition rule itself.

(61)   John believed (it) that Mary was coming.
        John thought (*it) that Mary was coming.
        John liked it that Mary was coming.
        *John liked that Mary was coming.

In the framework I am proposing, the corresponding special conditions which determine the examples of (61) aside, *it*-deletion can be restated as (62), since NP_i can only dominate *it* if a coreferential S_i appears in the same tree.

(62) $NP_i - S_i \Rightarrow \emptyset - 2$

Similarly, the subject replacement rule must be stated in terms of coreferential indices, as in (63).

(63) $NP_i - X - S_i - Y \Rightarrow 3 - 2 - \emptyset - 4$, where no NP, PP or S dominates
        3 but not 1.

The condition on (63) prevents S's which are "too far down" in the tree from replacing the subject. An example of such an S is the one italicized in (64).

(64) It would have been pointed out by John if *there had been any danger.*

The formulation of subject replacement in terms of coreferential indices prevents subject replacement from applying to the italicized S's in (65).

(65) The government's action wasn't surprising, but it persuaded John *that the president wasn't lying.*
     That observation is interesting, but it doesn't prove *that we should abandon our efforts.*

A third rule in the grammar of English besides *it*-deletion and subject replacement (as they are formulated here) which is stated in terms of coreferential indices is the equi-NP deletion rule, also discussed in Rosenbaum (1967).

There is a further condition on subject replacement which it is appropriate to discuss here. The rule is obligatory when a verb has both a subject complement *and* an object or oblique complement, as in (66).

(66) That John has blood on his hands proves that Mary is innocent.
     *It proves that Mary is innocent that John has blood on his hands.

To see that movie is to relive the past.

*It is to relive the past to see that movie.

That John was late persuaded me that the train was delayed.
*It persuaded me that the train was delayed that John was late.

In fact, when such a verb is in a nonroot S (which means subject replacement is impossible), there is no way to obtain grammaticality without resorting to paraphrase:

(67) *The decision that (that) John has blood on his hands proves that Mary is innocent is ridiculous.
*The decision that it proves that Mary is innocent that John has blood on his hands is ridiculous.
Cf. The decision that John's having blood on his hands proves that Mary is innocent is ridiculous.

I will now show how the ungrammatical examples in (66) are a natural consequence of other factors in the grammar, and not of a special condition on subject replacement. In the discussion of passive noun phrases in section 2.6 of my dissertation, I introduced the concept of a "doubly filled node" in deep structure, whereby two constituents of the same category can occupy one phrase-structure position, as in (68), provided that only one such constituent is present at the level of surface structure.

(68)

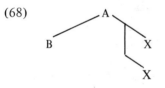

For verbs like *prove, mean, imply, be, persuade, convince, show*, etc. as exemplified in (66) my analysis requires that I assume a deep structure (69), which is a special case of (68).[20]

(69)

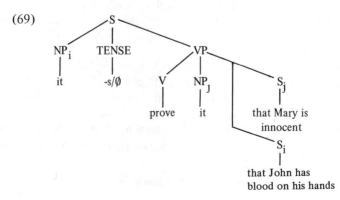

That fact that subject replacement, (63), is formulated in terms of coreferential indices means that S_i in (69) *may* move to the position of NP_i in a root S. The fact that a doubly filled node is never permitted in surface structure means that S_i *must* so move. This explains the ungrammaticality of the starred examples in (66) and (67).

2.2 Rosenbaum's Verb Phrase Complements.

Rosenbaum noted that some verbs which take object clause complements appear in the passive, as in (70), and that some do not, as in (71).

(70) That the house was old was denied by John.
      It was denied by John that the house was old.

      To remain silent was preferred by John.
      It was preferred by John to remain silent.

(71)

*To buy the *Times* would be my friends.
$\begin{cases} \text{tended} \\ \text{started} \\ \text{continued} \\ \text{condescended} \\ \text{hesitated} \\ \text{hastened} \\ \text{failed} \end{cases}$ by many of

*It would be the *Times*.
$\begin{cases} \text{tended} \\ \text{started} \\ \text{continued} \\ \text{condescended} \\ \text{hesitated} \\ \text{hastened} \\ \text{failed} \end{cases}$ by many of my friends to buy

*That he could pass without trying was $\begin{cases} \text{guessed} \\ \text{quipped} \end{cases}$ by John.

*It was $\begin{cases} \text{guessed} \\ \text{quipped} \end{cases}$ by John that he could pass without trying.

*Sobbing mournfully was $\begin{cases} \text{begun} \\ \text{started} \\ \text{kept on} \\ \text{resumed} \\ \text{continued} \\ \text{ceased} \\ \text{stopped} \end{cases}$ by John.

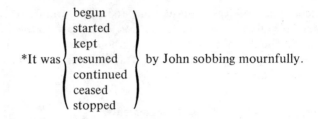

Rosenbaum attributed this difference to the difference between the underlying structures (72) and (73).[21]

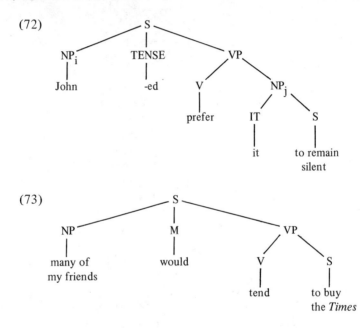

In my analysis of complementation, (72) is replaced by (74), as discussed in the preceding section. However, I retain Rosenbaum's structure (73) for the complements of the verbs in (71) without modification. Thus, I attribute the difference between (70) and (71) to the difference between the underlying structures (74) and (73).

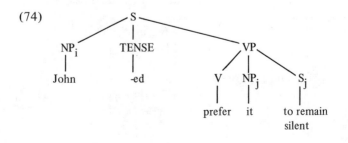

In either my analysis or Rosenbaum's, NP preposing cannot apply to (73) because there is no NP following the main verb. This accounts for the examples in (71).

Similarly, *wh*-fronting cannot apply to the nonexistent object NP in (73).[22]

(75)

$$\text{*Whatever he} \left\{ \begin{array}{l} \text{tended} \\ \text{hesitated} \\ \text{condescended} \\ \text{hastened} \\ \text{quipped} \\ \text{kept on} \\ \text{resumed} \\ \text{ceased} \end{array} \right\} \text{was usually a failure.}$$

$$\text{*John wonders what she} \left\{ \begin{array}{l} \text{tended} \\ \text{hesitated} \\ \text{hastened} \\ \text{condescended} \\ \text{quipped} \\ \text{kept on} \\ \text{resumed} \\ \text{ceased} \end{array} \right\} \quad .$$

In connection with the impossibility of applying *wh*-fronting to a (nonexistent) object NP in structures like (73), it is appropriate to comment on Rosenbaum's conclusions about the nonappearance of the verbs in (71) in the left-hand-side sentences of the pseudo-cleft construction:

(76)

$$\text{*Under pressure, what I} \left\{ \begin{array}{l} \text{tend} \\ \text{start} \\ \text{continue} \\ \text{condescend} \\ \text{hesitate} \\ \text{hasten} \\ \text{fail} \end{array} \right\} \text{(to) is to visit my psychiatrist.}$$

$$\text{*What John} \left\{ \begin{array}{l} \text{guessed} \\ \text{quipped} \end{array} \right\} \text{was that he could pass without trying.}$$

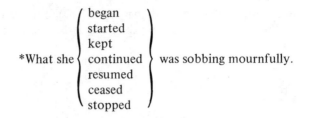

*What she { began / started / kept / continued / resumed / ceased / stopped } was sobbing mournfully.

It seems to me that Rosenbaum applied a faulty argument to data like (76) and yet came to the right conclusion. Rosenbaum assumed that the ungrammaticality of the examples in (76) was due to the fact that only NP's could appear to the right of the main copula in the pseudo-cleft construction (i.e., in "focus" position). But this assumption obliterates the well-motivated distinctions among the phrase nodes NP, AP, PP, VP, and S. In particular, the fact that just NP's and PP's appear in focus position in the *cleft* construction (discussed in section 1) could not be stated if this assumption were accepted.

The examples of (77) show that the opposite of Rosenbaum's assumption holds: any of the five major phrase nodes can appear in focus position in the pseudo-cleft construction:

(77) What I dislike is custard pie. (NP)
      What we counted on was getting a tax break. (NP)
      What John is is very brave. (AP)
      What Bill seems is quite dishonest. (AP)
      What upsets me is for her to be late. (S)
      What you don't realize is that John is cheating. (S)
      What you should do is blow up some buildings. (VP)
      What John is doing is kicking me in the shins. (VP)
      Where he rolled was down the hill. (PP)

The limitations on what can appear in focus position in the pseudo-cleft constructions are due to limitations on what *wh*-words can occur in the "headless relative" S on the left side of the copula. In the most restricted dialect, only *what* can so appear (meaning that the last example in (77) is ungrammatical). In my dialect, *what, where*, and *when* can so appear; in still another, I understand that any *wh*-word can so appear, as in (78).

(78) ?How I came was by boat.
      ?Why John left was because he had a cold.
      ?Who Mary likes is John.

In spite of this misleading assumption about the nature of the focus constituent in pseudo-cleft construction, the structure assigned by Rosenbaum to the verbs appearing in (76) can account for the ungrammaticality in (76) adequately. According to him, a typical verb in (76) appears in the following basic structure:

(79) $(_S$ NP $(_{VP}$ V S))

Now suppose the pseudo-cleft construction is formed by deleting the second X−Y (under identity with the first X−Y) in (80), where C stands for the focus constituent.

(80) $[_S$ X - W - Y] - TENSE - be - $[_S$ X - C - Y]

It is clear that W must be able to dominate *wh* if a pseudo-cleft is to be formed from (80). But suppose that the sentence X-C-Y is *I condescended to visit my psychiatrist,* and the pseudo-cleft sentence to be formed has as focus constituent the VP *to visit my psychiatrist.* (I differ from Rosenbaum in that it is perfectly permissible in my analysis for a VP to be the focus constituent in a pseudo-cleft construction.) This means that in (80), X = *I condescended* and Y = ∅. But W cannot be an NP dominating only *what,* since *condescend* only appears in the configuration (79); thus, **What I condescended was to visit my psychiatrist* is impossible. On the other hand, W may be the VP "to do *wh*-something," so as to yield *What I condescended to do was to visit my psychiatrist.*

A similar argument can be constructed if one assumes the pseudo-cleft is formed by moving a constituent out of a "headless relative" S subject into focus position, leaving behind a *wh* in an appropriate position. Whatever the analysis of the pseudo-cleft one adopts, the basic point about verbs whose S complements are not antecedents to a subject or object *it* (i.e., the verbs under consideration in this section) is that the lack of an object NP makes it impossible for *wh*-fronting to apply to produce the pseudo-cleft sentences of (76). These sentences are *not* excluded because of any limitation on the type of phrase nodes that may appear in focus position in the pseudo-cleft construction.

There remains one further improvement I believe can be made on Rosenbaum's analysis of complementation in terms of the concepts developed in this paper. Suppose we call the sentence and infinitive complements which are antecedents to a deep-structure *it* "antecedent complements" (these correspond to Rosenbaum's "noun phrase complements") and those which are not, "oblique complements" (these correspond to Rosenbaum's verb phrase complements"). An interesting question is whether the S complements italicized in (81) are antecedent complements or oblique complements.

(81) It seems to John *that we ought to leave.*
It happens *that I am out of money.*
It appeared to him *that the train had left.*

If these complements are antecedent to the subject *it,* as seems apparent on first glance, then we would expect that subject replacement could operate, as in (82), but it cannot.

(82)   *That we ought to leave seems to me.
          *That I am out of money happens.
          *That the train had left appeared to him.

We can account for this by assuming that in fact the verbs *seem, appear,* and *happen* (in one of its senses) do not take subjects, i.e. that the subject NP's of these verbs is empty in deep structure and that their S complements are oblique complements. (By contrast, the subject NP of predicates like *show, irritate, be necessary, be a lie,* etc. is a deep-structure *it* if they have a subject complement clause.) Since the subject replacement rule is formulated in terms of coreferential indices, it will not operate if a subject NP is empty.

The source of the *it* surface subject for *seem, appear,* and *happen* in (81) is then the same rule that provides the dummy subject to verbs like *rain, snow,* etc., in the cleft construction, and in *it's me, it's the Beatles,* etc.

Confirmation of the claim that the subject of *seem, appear,* and *happen* is empty in deep structure is given by the fact that, for the senses of these verbs in question, this subject cannot be questioned as shown in (83). This is behavior which is typical of nonreferring (dummy) subjects.

(83)   *What seems to John?
          *What happens?
          *What appeared to him?

          *What is raining?
          *What is John that he is talking to?
          *What was to the boy that I was speaking?
          *What's you?
          *What is the Beatles?
          Cf. Is it the Beatles?
             Who is it?

          *What seemed to John was that the food was stale.
          *What happens is that I don't have any money.
          *What appeared to him was that the train had left.

The predicates *seem* and *appear* should not be confused with the predicates *seem*-AP and *appear*-AP. The latter construction is derived from the former by means of the subject raising rule discussed in Rosenbaum (1967) and in section 2.4 of my dissertation, according to the following sequence of steps (Tense omitted):

(84) Deep-structure string: empty NP - seem - that it$_i$ be A that S$_i$:

Subject raising: it$_i$ - seem - be A that S$_i$
be-deletion: it$_i$ - seem - A that S$_i$.

According to this analysis, the derived predicates *seem-(to be)*-AP and *appear-(to be)*-AP have antecedent, not oblique, complements. That is, the complement S's at the end of the VP are coreferential in the derived predicates with the subject *it*. This is confirmed by the fact that such subjects can be questioned and removed by subject replacement:

(85) What seems to you to be strange?
What appeared interesting?
What seems strange is that John has left.
What appears to be obvious is that Mary is guilty.

That John has already left seems strange.
That we buy these books appears to be necessary.
For us to understand this would seem to me to be important.
To finish the assignment appeared useless at the time.

In summary, my antecedent complements correspond exactly to Rosenbaum's sentence and infinitive (not gerund) noun phrase complements. The only exception to this is that I analyze the sentence complements to *seem, appear,* and *happen* (in one of its senses) as oblique (i.e., "verb phrase") complements.

CONCLUSION

The main result of this paper is the conclusion that sentences introduced by *that* and infinitives are never noun phrases, but are always S (and perhaps VP) complements generated by the phrase structure rules at the end of VP's, AP's, and NP's. A phrase-structure rule NP - VP gives rise to gerunds, and not to *that* or *for-to* complements. The most important factor in the arguments for this position has been the realization that the inverse of Rosenbaum's extraposition rule has all the properties of a root transformation. Replacing extraposition with its inverse, "subject replacement," eliminates several irregularities and deficiencies in Rosenbaum's analysis of complementation. A secondary result of the paper is therefore the addition of subject replacement to the list of fronting root transformations compiled in chapter 1 of my dissertation, and given here again in section 1.5.

NOTES

Research on material in this paper was made possible by a fellowship at the Center for Advanced Study at the University of Illinois. I am indebted to Noam Chomsky, Morris Halle, and Michael Brame for careful readings, criticisms, and discussions of preliminary versions of this material.

[1] See also the discussion of the "A over A principle" in Chomsky (1968).

[2] The universal principle involved may be more general, but it reduces down to the constraint proposed here for English as a special case.

[3] See chapters 2 and 4 of my dissertation (Emonds 1969).

[4] The arguments concerning *there*-insertion are straightforward; the claim is made and supported that this rule moves a deep-structure subject to the predicate nominative position. This in turn provides an argument that, say, the italicized construction in "There may be some children *playing in the garden.*" is a constituent, a claim often advanced on other grounds.

[5] This does not mean that they cannot be part of an NP, as in *the fact that John came, the decision to leave town,* etc. I am not treating here embedded sentences introduced by *wh*-constituents rather than *that* (in particular, indirect questions). They are discussed in section 4.4 of my dissertation (Emonds 1969), where I point out that they share certain distributional characteristics of NP's that *that* clauses do not exhibit.

[6] Gerunds should be distinguished from participles, which will not be discussed here. Gerunds substitute for an NP, whereas participles modify NP's. Another difference is that participles never have an expressed subject apart from the NP they modify, whereas gerunds sometimes do have an expressed subject.

[7] Rosenbaum's extraposition rule, as he formulated it, need not be a counterexample to the structure-preserving constraint. If we assume his analysis of sentence and infinitive complements is correct, it is easy to see how the extraposition rule is structure-preserving.

Extraposition derives, for example, the second sentence of the following pair from the first:

For the house to be painted would irritate him.
It would irritate him for the house to be painted.

Since Rosenbaum's VP expansion rule generates an optional S in final position, extraposition (from subject position, in this case) has the following structure-preserving effect:

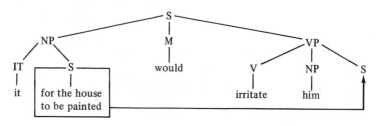

In fact, given the assumption that Rosenbaum's analysis is correct, confirmation that extraposition *must* be structure-preserving is given by the fact that if the S under VP is nonempty, a subject S may not be extraposed:

That John has blood on his hands proves (that) Mary is innocent.
*It proves (that) Mary is innocent that John has blood on his hands.

To see this movie is to relive the past.
*It is to relive the past to see this movie.

That John is late persuades me that the train is delayed.
*It persuades me that the train was delayed that John is late.

Thus, Rosenbaum's analysis *supports* the structure-preserving constraint. On the other hand, the structure-preserving constraint leads to a reformulation of Rosenbaum's work which, as will be seen in the text, also accounts for the above sentences.

It should be remarked that I am assuming an S expansion rule $S \rightarrow$ Comp + NP + TENSE + (M) + VP, where Comp is *that, than, as* or *for* and where Tense is -s (Present) or-*ed* (Past).

[8]If infinitives are ever generated directly in the base, instead of being derived from sentences, it may be that S in (18) and (19) should be replaced by $\left\{ \begin{matrix} VP \\ S \end{matrix} \right\}$. I take no stand on this question here.

[9]The complements to verbs of temporal aspect *(begin, finish, continue, resume,* etc.) introduced by V-*ing* which were discussed above are irregular exactly in that they are exceptions to the correspondence between clauses which are NP's and clauses whose first verb is marked with an -*ing* suffix. One possible way to explain this irregularity would be to assume the analysis, often advanced on other grounds (cf. Newmeyer, forthcoming), that the VP complements to verbs of temporal aspect originate in the subject NP, and are postposed by a (structure-preserving) rule in the following way:

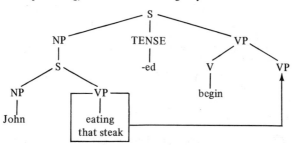

We could account for the presence of -*ing* rather than *to* in (11) by inserting -*ing* in gerunds before this postposing applies. However, this would mean either that *John began eating that steak* and *John began to eat that steak* have different deep structures or that *ing*-insertion is optionally ordered (with some verbs) before or after this postposing.

[10]This sentence is grammatical but cannot receive the interpretation required here, i.e., *Joe* understood as the subject of *eat out.*

[11]That is, in Rosenbaum's framework extraposition from object position is always obligatory. Also, for a thorough justification of treating post-verbal particles as (intransitive) PP's see Emonds (1972).

[12]In the second example of (30), X = *John was doing,* Y = *to Bill,* and C = *kicking him in the shins.*

[13]When gerunds are not acceptable subjects in nonroot S's, they are not acceptable as subjects of root S's either: *John's going downtown was false, etc.

[14]Michael Brame has pointed out to me the possibility that the condition that no two preposing root transformations may apply in the same S may be a principle of universal grammar, and hence not a formal problem in the grammar of English.

[15]The few exceptions to this, such as it's fun talking to foreigners, belong with the non-NP ing-complements to verbs of temporal aspect discussed earlier.

[16]I am treating adverbs like before, inside, now, here, etc. as intransitive prepositions, and subordinating conjunctions like because, before, now that, and while as prepositions with S rather than NP complements. This topic is discussed in detail in section 4.3 of my dissertation (Emonds 1969).

[17]One further point merits discussion here. As should be clear, I assume the deep-structure strings for the sentences of (48) to be the following:

> It would cause embarrassment for John to arrive.
> It shows the necessity of discipline that the children are always late.
> It didn't help the situation that you spoke out of turn.
> It would anger the bankers to suggest devaluation.
> It was amusing John that the boys were dancing together.

Suppose now we form the passive construction *without* applying subject replacement:

> *Embarrassment would be caused by it for John to arrive.
> *The necessity of discipline is shown by it that the children are always late.
> *The situation wasn't helped by it that you spoke out of turn.
> *The bankers would be angered by it to suggest devaluation.
> *John was being amused by it that the boys were dancing together

I must be able to explain this unexpected ungrammaticality in order to preserve the integrity of my analysis.

In section 2.1 of my dissertation (Emonds 1969), I argue that the passive by-phrase is present in deep structure, being distinguished from other deep-structure PP's only by the fact that its object NP is empty. If such a PP is not so present, agent postposing cannot apply, since this rule is structure-preserving.

Now there is a general prohibition against a great many (but not all) combinations of PP's and complement S's. I attribute the ungrammaticality of the above examples to the same prohibition.

> *I agree with it that John walked out.
> *We talked about it that the weather was warm.
> *John spoke against it for Bill to receive the prize.
> *We took a vote on it that John had a right to speak.
> Cf. John saw to it that we had reservations.

If one objects that the above underlying strings are permitted, but are simply changed into gerunds transformationally (see examples following), the same reasoning can be applied to the combination by + NP + S. In either case, the by-phrase has the same status as a number of other PP's.

I agree with John's walking out.
John spoke against Bill's receiving the prize.
We talked about the weather's being warm.
We took a vote on John's having the right to speak.

Embarrassment would be caused by John's arriving.
The necessity of discipline is shown by the children's always being late.
The situation wasn't helped by your speaking out of turn.
The bankers would be angered by suggesting devaluation.
John was being amused by the boys' dancing together.

[18] Assuming, as I will throughout this section, that infinitives are reduced S's.

[19] An oblique S complement is one which is not coreferential with a subject or object *it*; such complements will be discussed in the next section. They correspond roughly to Rosenbaum's "verb phrase complements."

I am assuming that each verb V has a lexical semantic meaning M(V) which contains some combination of the symbols X ("subject position"), Y ("object position"), and Z ("oblique position"). Thus, M(V) ... X ... Y ... Z ... for a verb with three complements. The definitions of grammatical relations in terms of deep-structure trees specify the constituents whose meanings are to be placed in the X, Y, and Z positions of M(V) so as to obtain (at least part of) the meaning M(S) of the sentence of which V is the main verb.

[20] The "positions" of the two embedded S's in (69) are assigned arbitrarily.

[21] In this section, I omit writing out deep-structure NP's deleted by equi-NP deletion.

[22] There are, however, some verbs which appear in the structure (73) which alternatively take object NP's, such as *start*. These do of course appear in sentences with *wh*-fronted object NP's.

REFERENCES

Bresnan, Joan. "An Argument against Pronominalization." *Linguistic Inquiry* I, 122-123, 1970.

_____. "A Note on the Notion "Identity of Sense Anaphora." *Linguistic Inquiry* II, 589-597, 1971.

Chomsky, Noam. *Aspects of the Theory of Syntax.* Cambridge, Mass.: M.I.T. Press, 1965.

_____. *Language and Mind.* New York: Harcourt Brace and World, 1968.

Dougherty, Ray. "An Interpretive Theory of Pronominal Reference." *Foundations of Language,* 5, 488-519. 1969.

Emonds, Joseph. "Evidence that Indirect Object Movement Is a Structure-Preserving Rule." *Foundations of Language,* 8, 1972.

_____. *Root and Structure-Preserving Transformations.* Cambridge, Mass.: Unpublished M.I.T. doctoral dissertation, 1970.

Fraser, Bruce. *The Verb-Particle Construction of English.* Cambridge, Mass.: M.I.T. Press, 1968.

Gleitman, Lila. "Co-ordinating Conjunctions in English." *Language* 41: 1965, 260-293. 1965.

Jackendoff, Ray. *Some Rules of Semantic Interpretation for English.* Cambridge, Mass.: Unpublished M.I.T. doctoral dissertation, 1969.

Newmeyer, Frederick. "On the Alleged Boundary between Syntax and Semantics." *Foundations of Language,* 6, 176-186, 1970.

Rosenbaum P. 1967. *The grammar of English predicate complement constructions.* Cambridge: M.I.T. Press.

Ross, J. R. 1967. Constraints on variables in syntax. Ph.D. dissertation, M.I.T.

Chapter 3

SOME EMPIRICAL ISSUES IN THE
THEORY OF TRANSFORMATIONAL GRAMMAR

Noam Chomsky

1.0

The most recent attempt to give a general synthetic view of the
theory of transformational grammar was in the mid-sixties, in such books as
Katz and Postal (1964) and Chomsky (1965), which summarized and
extended much work of the early sixties. Since then, there has been a great
proliferation of papers and dissertations, and a flood of underground
literature that has kept the mimeograph machines humming. In this work,
many new and original ideas have been developed and a great variety of
phenomena have been studied, often with quite penetrating analyses. There
is an appearance of a considerable diversity of points of view—and to some
extent, the appearance is correct. However, I think that the dust is beginning
to settle, and that it is now perhaps possible to identify a number of real,
empirically significant theoretical questions that have been raised, if not
settled, in this work. I also think much of the apparent controversy is
notational and terminological—including many issues that appear to be

fundamental and have been the subject of heated, even acrimonious dispute. This is unfortunate, because it sidetracks serious work, and because occasionally certain questions of some interest are embedded, sometimes buried in these terminological debates.

1.1

As an example, consider the matter of grammaticalness, certainly a fundamental issue; What does a grammar generate? An answer that has been widely accepted and used is: a grammar generates sentences with structural descriptions. Recently, George Lakoff has made what appears to be a radically new proposal (Lakoff 1969a). He suggests that a grammar should not generate sentences in isolation, but rather "pairs, (P, S), consisting of a sentence, S, which is grammatical only relative to the presuppositions of P." He raises the question whether it makes sense to speak of the well-formedness of sentences in isolation, removed from all assumptions about the nature of the world, and argues that competence includes the study of the relationship between a sentence and what it presupposes about the world by way of systematic rules. Knowledge of language must include knowledge of these rules.

For example, consider the sentence (1):

(1) John called Mary a Republican and then *she* insulted *him*.

(where the italicized words are more heavily stressed). Lakoff observes that the speaker's judgments as to well-formedness will depend on his beliefs, and he says: "I find [this sentence] perfectly well-formed, though those with other beliefs may disagree." Actually, the situation is still more complicated. Thus the decision as to whether (1) is "well-formed," in this sense, depends also on John's and Mary's beliefs. I can insult someone by attributing to him a property that I think admirable but that he regards as insulting. Similarly, even someone sharing Lakoff's beliefs couldn't insult Barry Goldwater by calling him a Republican.

With this qualification, Lakoff's observation is correct. What follows from it? I think very little. "Well-formedness" is a theoretical term. We are free to define it so that it takes its place within a sensible theory. One terminological proposal—the one I would advocate as the most natural—would be this:

(I) define "well-formed" so that sentence (1) is well-formed independently of the beliefs of John, Mary, or the speaker;

(II) assign to the semantic component of the grammar the task of stipulating that (1) expresses the presupposition that for John to call Mary a Republican is for him to insult her.

The relation between (1) and the presupposition of course holds independently of anyone's factual beliefs; it is part of the knowledge of the speaker of English, quite apart from his beliefs, or John's, or Mary's. In general, according to this terminology, the grammar generates sentences and expresses the fact that these sentences carry certain presuppositions. It makes no reference to specific beliefs.

Lakoff's proposal is different: it is to define "well-formed" as a relative concept, and to have the grammar generate pairs (S, P) such that S is well-formed relative to P.

For sentences with presuppositions in this sense, nothing hinges on this terminological decision. All the problems remain exactly where they were—in particular, the problem of characterizing the relation between a sentence and its presupposition. The latter is an interesting question. For the moment, I see nothing more that can be said about this particular case, which is typical of those that Lakoff cites, beyond the unilluminating comment I have just made. What may appear at first sight to be a profound issue dissolves into nothing on analysis, though important questions are nevertheless involved.

1.2

Consider a second example, from the same volume. There Ross (1969a) presents "ten arguments that indicate that auxiliaries and verbs are really both members of the same lexical category, *verb*...[and] two arguments which indicate that they must be main verbs."[1] Ross's argument is that the analysis presented in, say, Chomsky (1957) should be replaced by an analysis with the two features [V] and [Aux], where words such as *read, eat,* etc. are specified as [-Aux] as distinct from *be, have,* and the modals which are [+Aux], and [+V] is subcategorized into [±Aux]. Consider, in contrast, the analysis he rejects. There, the symbol V was used for such words as *read, eat,* etc. and the feature v was proposed[2] characterizing V's as well as *be, have,* and the modals. Thus Ross's proposal is to replace v by [+V] and V by [+V, -Aux]. So far, at least, nothing is at stake except the use of the term "verb": shall we use it to refer to V or to v, i.e., in the new notation, to [+V, -Aux] or to [+V]?[3] Again, there is an interesting question involved in what appears here largely as a notational issue. Perhaps there are arguments for deriving auxiliaries, or some auxiliaries, by the rules that generate "true verbs" with their various complements. But it is important to distinguish such arguments, if they exist, from merely notational points.

These examples I have given merely for purposes of illustration. I will turn, in a moment, to more difficult cases.

2.0

I will sketch a framework for discussion that would, I believe, be fairly generally accepted (apart from questions of terminology) by many people working on transformational grammar, and then go on to identify some points of controversy that go beyond terminology, that appear to involve empirical issues. I will also indicate my own views on these issues, at present, and sketch briefly what leads me to them.

2.1

To begin, I will repeat some material from my paper (Chomsky 1971), which was an attempt to do something rather similar. Let us assume given the notion "phrase-marker" and the notion "grammatical transformation" as a mapping of phrase-markers into phrase-markers. We may say, then, that a grammar G generates a class K of derivations Σ, where Σ is a sequence of phrase-markers:

$$(2) \quad G \rightarrow K = \left\{ \Sigma : \Sigma = (P_1, \ldots, P_n) \right\}$$

where Σ is maximal, in the obvious sense, $P_i = T(P_{i-1})$, by some transformation T of G.

The grammar G specifies a set of transformations and various conditions on them—for example, ordering conditions. We may assume that P_n, which we shall call the "surface structure," determines the phonetic form of the sentence generated by phonological rules.[4]

Apart from the rules and conditions established in a particular grammar there are general principles that belong to universal grammar: for example, the condition of cyclic ordering; the conditions on application of transformations discussed in various forms in Chomsky (1964a, b, c; 1968) and Ross (1967); and the various conditions on cyclic and noncyclic transformations suggested by Emonds (1969). Among these are, for example, conditions that preclude extraction of noun phrases from the italicized positions of "John saw Bill and *Tom*," "The fact that *Bill* was here surprised me," "John believed the claim that Tom read *the book*," "John saw that picture of *Tom*," "John wondered whether Bill had seen *Tom*," etc.; conditions relating deep-structure representation to the possibility of deletion;[5] and conditions that prevent too wide a variation between deep and surface structures.[6] Such universal restrictions are of critical importance.

The gravest defect of the theory of transformational grammar is its enormous latitude and descriptive power. Virtually anything can be expressed as a phrase-marker, i.e., a properly parenthesized expression with parenthesized segments assigned to categories. Virtually any imaginable rule can be described in transformational terms. Therefore, a critical problem in making transformational grammar a substantive theory with explanatory force is to restrict the category of admissible phrase-markers, admissible transformations, and admissible derivations, for example, in the ways just mentioned and perhaps others to which I will return.

2.2

The general point may be worth a slight digression. The fundamental problem of linguistic theory, as I see it at least, is to account for the choice of a particular grammar, given the data available to the language learner.[7] To account for this inductive leap, linguistic theory must try to characterize a fairly narrow class of grammars that are available to the language learner; it must, in other words, specify the notion "human language" in a narrow and restrictive fashion. A "better theory," then, is one that specifies the class of possible grammars so narrowly that some procedure of choice or evaluation can select a descriptively adequate grammar for each language from this class, within reasonable conditions of time and access to data. Given alternative linguistic theories that meet this condition, we might compare them in terms of general "simplicity" or other metatheoretic notions, but it is unlikely that such considerations will have any more significance within linguistics than they do in any other field. For the moment, the problem is to construct a general theory of language that is so richly structured and so restrictive in the conditions it imposes that, while meeting the condition of descriptive adequacy, it can sufficiently narrow the class of possible grammars so that the problem of choice of grammar (and explanation, in some serious sense) can be approached.

Notice that it is often a step forward, then, when linguistic theory becomes more complex, more articulated and refined—a point that has been noted repeatedly (see, for example, Chomsky 1965, p. 46). For example, it is a step forward when we complicate linguistic theory by distinguishing among all imaginable rules the two categories of "transformational rules" and "phonological rules," with their specific properties, and formulate conditions on their application and interrelation. Similarly, conditions of the sort cited a moment ago complicate linguistic theory and constitute a step forward in that they restrict the class of possible sets of derivations (hence languages) that can be generated by theoretically admissible grammars; i.e., they restrict the choice of K in (2). It can be expected that further progress will come with the discovery of additional formal and substantive universals:

a more explicit and detailed articulation of the properties of various parts of grammars, their interrelation, the kinds of rules that can appear in them, and so on.

Given the framework already outlined, it is correct to say that the "most conservative" theory is one that has no more theoretical apparatus than what was described: phrase-markers and transformations. The descriptive power of such a system is enormous. Hence this is a rather uninteresting theory. It can be made still more uninteresting by permitting still further latitude, for example, by allowing rules other than transformations that can be used to constrain derivations. This further weakening of the notion "grammar" would permit more grammars and more sets of derivations. Improvements from the worst possible case will come by placing more restrictive conditions on the choice of grammars, limiting the kinds of rules that can appear in them and the ways in which these rules can operate. Permitting a broader class of "derivational constraints" within particular grammars is a step toward a worse theory;[8] but general conditions on the choice of rules and the way they may apply, no matter how complex and detailed these conditions may be, could be a step toward empirical adequacy—specifically, toward that aspect of empirical adequacy that I have called "explanatory adequacy" (Chomsky 1964, 1965).

Thus it is misleading to say that a better theory is one with a more limited conceptual structure, and that we prefer the minimal conceptual elaboration, the least theoretical apparatus. Insofar as this notion is comprehensible, it is not in general correct. If enrichment of theoretical apparatus and elaboration of conceptual structure will restrict the class of possible grammars and the class of sets of derivations generated by admissible grammars, then it will be a step forward (assuming it to be consistent with the requirement of descriptive adequacy). It is quite true that the burden of proof is on the person who makes some specific proposal to enrich and complicate the theoretical apparatus. One who takes the more "conservative" stance, maintaining only that a grammar is a set of conditions on derivations, has no burden of proof to bear because he is saying virtually nothing.

Consider, for example, the issue of "autonomous phonemics." Suppose that we have a theory that defines "phonological rule" and "derivation" in the sense of Chomsky and Halle (1968). Suppose further that someone were to propose, as a general condition, that there is a level of representation meeting the conditions of "autonomous phonemics" (i.e., linearity, invariance, and so on, in the sense of Chomsky 1964, Postal 1968), and that in every derivation, one step must be a representation in terms of the level of autonomous phonemics. This might be a theoretical advance, in that it limits the class of grammars and the possible sets of derivations, *if* it could be shown that no linguistically significant generalizations are lost by placing this additional condition on grammar. (If it could be shown, further, that this additional condition leads to explanation of certain phenomena, then of course it would be additionally confirmed.) It is for this reason that Halle's argument against autonomous phonemics (Halle 1959) is of such importance: it demonstrates that significant generalizations are indeed lost if we impose this condition on derivations. In the absence of such a demonstration,[9] the advocate of autonomous phonemics would have something of a case, simply because he was offering a way to restrict the class of possible grammars with no loss of descriptive adequacy. Thus in a weak sense, he meets the "burden of proof" simply by imposing a restrictive general condition that does not lose descriptive adequacy. His argument would, in fact, be considerably strengthened if there were some reason to believe that the task of choosing a grammar—that is, taking the inductive leap—is facilitated by this new general condition.[10]

Perfectly analogous general considerations hold in syntax. Suppose, for example, that we discover two categories of transformation, L (lexical) and non-L (nonlexical), with rather different formal properties. Consider the following hypothesis: no linguistically significant generalizations are lost if all transformations of L are applied before any transformation of non-L, in forming derivations. Suppose we complicate linguistic theory by imposing on grammars the condition that all transformations of L apply before any transformation of non-L. This proposal constitutes a potential step forward in that it restricts the class of grammars. It expresses the claim that the hypothesis just cited is an essential, not an accidental property of language. We must ask questions analogous to those appropriate in the case of autonomous phonemics. Is the hypothesis correct in the case of particular grammars? Is the class of grammars restricted in a way that facilitates the choice of grammars? Are there further conditions on derivations that can be expressed in terms of the level of representation ("deep structure") defined as the set of phrase-markers that appear in derivations after all transformations of L have applied? Is there any further explanatory value to this concept? And so on.

I will try to show that the status of deep structure, though conceptually somewhat on a par with that of autonomous phonemics (as has been observed, correctly, by McCawley, Postal, and others), differs in a fundamental way in that, in the case of deep structure, the questions just asked receive positive answers, whereas in the case of autonomous phonemics, they do not. My point at the moment is that the question, in both cases, is an empirical one. There is almost nothing to say of any significance on a "methodological" level. One can point out, *a priori*, that further elaboration of linguistic theory, in both cases, complicates the theory. Although one wants the "simplest" linguistic theory,[11] in some sense that cannot be specified in a useful way, elaborations and complications of linguistic theory are all to the good insofar as they narrow the choice of grammars and the range of admissible languages (i.e., sets of derivations). Thus the hypothesis of general linguistic theory that deep structures exist, in the sense just explained, is on a par, methodologically, with other conditions on the form of grammar (e.g., those of sec. 2.1). In all of these cases, similar considerations apply.

2.3

Let me now return to the problem of outlining a linguistic theory that has the latitude to meet requirements of descriptive adequacy, but is sufficiently complex, highly articulated, and specific in its constraints so that the problem of explanatory adequacy can at least be placed on the agenda. Suppose that a grammar is of a form outlined in (2) of section 2.1. I have cited a number of restrictive conditions on transformations. The transformations that meet these conditions I will call "nonlexical transformations." In addition, grammars contain "lexical transformations" with very different properties:

> (3) A lexical transformation T replaces a subphrase-marker Q by a lexical item I.

3.0

The minimal framework outlined so far is common to all those varieties of linguistic theory that I want to discuss here. A number of specific questions now arise, in particular, the following:

> (4) (a) What is the relation of the lexical to the nonlexical transformations? What is the nature of the lexical items and the lexical transformations?
>
> (b) How is Σ of (2) related to a representation of the meaning of the sentence in question, and what is the character of semantic representation and the rules that relate it to Σ (if any)?
>
> (c) Are there any further conditions on K of (2) in addition to those cited? Specifically: Are there "input conditions" on the class of phrase-markers that appear as P_1 in some $\Sigma \in K$ (given a grammar G)? Are there output conditions on the surface structures P_n? Are there conditions on intermediate stages of derivations?

3.1

In the paper cited earlier (Chomsky 1971) I cited three variants of the general framework for linguistic theory outlined so far. The first of these

I called the "standard theory." It is the theory developed (in several variants, in fact) in Katz and Postal (1964) and Chomsky (1965), the most recent attempt at a general synthesis. Let us consider how questions (a), (b), (c) of (4) are answered in the standard theory.

Consider first the questions (a). It is assumed in the standard theory that all lexical transformations precede all nonlexical transformations. Furthermore, the subphrase-marker Q of (3) is always a designated dummy symbol $\triangle$. Lexical transformations are unordered. Each lexical item is a system of phonological, semantic, and syntactic features. The syntactic features specify the lexical transformation uniquely. The concept "deep structure" is well defined: the deep structure of a derivation $\Sigma = (P_1, \ldots, P_n)$ is the phrase-marker P_i such that for $j < i$, P_j is formed from P_{j-1} by a lexical transformation, and for $j > i$, P_j is formed by a nonlexical transformation. Since lexical transformations are constrained as just outlined, the deep structure P_i differs from P_1 only in that occurrences of $\triangle$ in P_1 are replaced by lexical items. The general form of P_1 is otherwise preserved in the deep structure.

Consider next the questions (b). According to the standard theory, the deep structure, defined as above, completely determines the semantic representation of the sentence. Thus there is a mapping that assigns to the deep structure a "reading" (or a set of readings, in the case of ambiguity) that contains a specification of all of its semantic properties in some universal notation. Various proposals have been made regarding notations for representation of conceptual structures: complex systems of features, case systems, networks of "thematic" relations, notations modeled on familiar logical systems, and so on (see, for example, Katz 1966, 1967, Gruber 1965, Weinreich 1966, McCawley 1968a, Jackendoff 1968, and many others).

Turning next to the questions of (c), the standard theory assumes both "input conditions" and "output conditions" on K. That is, there are independent conditions on deep structures and surface structures. The conditions on deep structures are determined by base rules: a context-free grammar that generates the initial structures P_1 of (2), and a lexicon which assigns to each lexical item contextual features that permit the item in question to be inserted into P_1, replacing some occurrence of $\triangle$. It is assumed that these base conditions may vary to some extent from language to language, but within certain general limits (for example, it is suggested in Chomsky 1965 that there exists a fixed set of grammatical functions that the rules of the categorial component may determine, and that lexical transformations are restricted to strictly local transformations or to rules that refer to heads of related phrases; in Chomsky 1970 still narrower conditions are suggested).

Furthermore, surface structures must meet certain output conditions. Specifically, it is assumed that there is a designated symbol # which cannot appear internally to a well-formed surface structure. [12] Obligatory transformations can be defined, in some cases at least, in terms of this notation, as discussed in Chomsky (1965).

It is also possible to extend the same notation to the description of certain types of deviance. For example, # may be introduced when some rule is violated in a derivation, indicating that the sentence is not well-formed, though perhaps still interpretable. To mention one example of some interest, consider the matter of violations of constraints on application of transformations. Thus such structures as *what did John believe the claim that John read* (from *John believed the claim that John read something*, or *who did John see the picture of* are formed only by violation of these conditions on application, though *what did John believe that John read* or *who did John see a picture of* are well-formed (see the references of sec. 2.1. for discussion). Suppose that # is assigned to the category X when a transformation is applied in violation of a constraint on the phrase dominated by X. Then the sentence will be interpretable, as it in fact is, though designated as not well-formed.

That this may be more than a mere notational point is suggested by an interesting observation by Ross (1969*b*). He argues plausibly that (5) is derived by applying a *wh*-inversion transformation (followed by deletion of *Bill saw*) within the second conjunct (6) of the structure underlying (5):

(5) He believes that Bill saw someone, but I don't know whom.
(6) I don't know [Bill saw whom].

He observes, however, that such sentences as (7) are well-formed,[13] although the structure (8), which presumably underlies the second conjunct, is not well-formed:

(7) He believes their claims about some products, but I don't know which (ones).
(8) I don't know which products he believes their claims about.

These observations would be accounted for by the notational device just proposed. Thus when the *wh*-inversion transformation is applied to form (8), the NP *their claims about* is assigned #, since a general constraint on application of transformations is violated. Accordingly, (8) is interpreted as deviant. But if we go on to form (7) along the lines Ross suggests, the NP is deleted. Thus the derivation is not "filtered out" as deviant by the output condition that # cannot appear internally in a surface structure. Thus (7) is well-formed. The same is true in many other cases, e.g., *he has plans to send some of his children to college, but I don't know which (ones)*, but *I don't know which children he has plans to send to college;* etc.

The point is of some interest because Ross is led, by these observations, to suggest that some general notion of "derivational constraint" might be needed to account for the facts. Everyone would agree that unless further elaborated, the suggestion that grammars contain "derivational constraints" is vacuous. Any imaginable rule can be described as a "constraint on derivations." The question is, what kinds of rules ("derivational constraints") are needed, if any, beyond those permitted by the standard theory? It is therefore of interest to see that in this case (which is, to my knowledge, the only plausible one that has been discovered in recent work—see below) a very simple and specific device, not unnatural on other grounds, suffices to account for the observed phenomena, so that a trivial modification of the standard theory suffices. The point is important for the reasons already given: the great weakness of the theory of transformational grammar is its enormous descriptive power, and this deficiency becomes more marked to the extent that we permit other rules beyond transformations (i.e., other sorts of "derivational constraints").

3.2

The work of the past few years has revealed quite a few inadequacies in the standard theory, as just outlined, and much of the theoretical debate now in progress has to do with attempts to overcome some of these problems. Two are discussed in Chomsky (1971). The first accepts the standard theory approximately as given, and proposes a few revisions and extensions; I will refer to this as the "extended standard theory" (henceforth, EST). Referring to questions (a), (b), and (c) of (4), EST retains the assumptions of the standard theory with regard to (a) and (c), but modifies the answers proposed for (b), as follows: semantic interpretation is held to be determined by the pair (deep structure, surface structure) of Σ, rather than by the deep structure alone; further, it is proposed that insofar as grammatical relations play a role in determining meaning, it is the grammatical relations of the deep structure that are relevant (as before), but that such matters as scope of "logical elements" and quantifiers, coreference, focus and certain kinds of presupposition, and certain other properties are determined by rules that take surface structure (more precisely, phonetically interpreted surface structure) into account. A number of examples were given there. For much more extensive discussion, along somewhat similar lines, see Jackendoff (1969).

3.3

An alternative to EST that has been developed quite extensively in the past few years has come to be known as "generative semantics," and this is the third theory discussed in Chomsky (1971). At that time, there was no clear formulation to which one could refer, but this difficulty has been remedied by the appearance of Lakoff (1969b, c). Comparison of the alternatives is facilitated by the fact that these papers adopt, with only a few changes, the general framework and terminology of Chomsky (1971), so that differences between EST and generative semantics, as so conceived, can be identified with relative ease. Let us consider, then, how generative semantics deals with the questions (a), (b), and (c) of (4).

With regard to questions (a), this approach interprets the notion of lexical transformation as follows: Q in (3) is a subphrase-marker which expresses the meaning of the item I,[14] and I now contains no semantic features, but only phonological and syntactic features. Furthermore, Lakoff insists that Q contain no lexical items; thus the lexical transformation is a one-step mapping from a notation involving no lexical items into another notation, with a lexical item replacing Q. Furthermore, the requirement that nonlexical transformations precede lexical ones is relaxed; now they may be interspersed freely. Thus in general, the notion "deep structure" is not defined, as it is in the standard and extended standard theory.

Turning now to the questions (b), there are two different versions of generative semantics that have been proposed. Postal (1969) appears to take the position that the initial phrase-marker P_1 of Σ [cf. (2)] can be taken as the semantic representation, as was suggested also by McCawley (1968a). Lakoff, however, takes a rather different position. For him, the semantic representation is a sequence such as (9):

(9) Semantic representation = $(P_1, PR, Top, F, \ldots)$, where PR is a conjunction of presuppositions, Top is an indication of the "topic" of the sentence, F is the indication of the focus, and . . . indicates other elements of semantic representation that might be needed (Lakoff 1969b).

Accordingly, a semantic representation is not a phrase-marker at all, and hence is not part of a derivation. Rather, it is a formal object that contains the initial phrase-marker P_1 of the derivation Σ, along with much else.[15]

As regards questions (c), generative semantics permits a wide range of conditions on derivations beyond the input and output constraints of the standard and extended theory. I return to this matter directly.

4.0

Summarizing so far, we have specified a general framework and three specific variants: the standard theory, the extended standard theory, and generative semantics. In my opinion, the standard theory is inadequate and must be modified. The evidence now available seems to me to indicate that it must be modified to the extended standard theory (EST). Furthermore, when some vagueness and faulty formulations are eliminated, I think we can show that generative semantics converges with EST in most respects. There are a few differences, which I will try to identify and discuss, but in most cases I think that the differences are either terminological, or lie in an area where both theories are comparably inexplicit, so that no empirical issue can, at the moment, be formulated. The clearest and probably most important difference between EST and generative semantics has to do with the ordering of lexical and nonlexical transformations. This, in fact, seems to me perhaps the only fairly clear issue with empirical import that distinguishes these theories. My feeling is that present evidence supports the narrower and more restrictive assumption of the (extended) standard theory that nonlexical transformations follow all lexical transformations, so that "deep structure" is a well-defined notion, and that the conditions on deep structure given by base rules narrowly constrain K (the class of derivations Σ). This, however, is an empirical issue, as distinct from a number of others that seem to me to be terminological, or in an area of indeterminacy and vagueness.

5.0

Before turning to this empirical issue, let me comment briefly on several issues that seem to me not to be so.

5.1

Lakoff maintains that perhaps the most fundamental innovation of generative semantics is the claim that semantic representations and syntactic phrase-markers are formal objects of the same kind, and that there exist no projection rules (rules of interpretation) but only grammatical trans- formations (see Lakoff 1969b, p. 37). Notice, however, that in his own formulation, a semantic representation is not a phrase-marker, but rather a sequence containing a phrase-marker as its first term [see (9), above]. However, this is a small point, since as noted (note 15), the semantic representation can no doubt be reformulated as a phrase-marker, to the extent that its properties are made clear. More generally, virtually any proposal that has been made concerning semantic representation can, in equally uninteresting ways, be reformulated so as to use phrase-markers for semantic representation. In particular, this is surely true of Katz's semantic representations. It is difficult to imagine any coherent characterization of semantic content that cannot be translated into some "canonical notation" modeled on familiar logics, which can in turn be represented with properly bracketed expressions where the brackets are labeled (phrase-markers). The whole question is a pseudo-issue. The real question is whether phrase- markers provide the most "natural" or the most "illuminating" way to represent semantic content. I cannot really believe that anyone would be willing to take a stand on this issue with any conviction, given the present state of descriptive semantics. In fact, it is quite unclear just what would be the content of such a claim. Thus this innovation, far from being fundamental, seems to me nothing more than a terminological proposal of an extremely unclear sort.

5.2

A second pseudo-issue was discussed briefly in Chomsky (1971), but perhaps an additional word of clarification is in order. It was pointed out earlier that EST differs from the standard theory only with respect to questions (4b), specifically, in its assumption that surface structures determine certain aspects of semantic interpretation. There is, of course, a trivial way to modify the standard theory so that it will be compatible with virtually anything that might be discovered about the relation between surface structure and semantic interpretation, yet still retaining the condition that deep structures determine semantic interpretation fully. Suppose, for example, that focus and presupposition[16] are determined by rules applying to surface structure; call them the rules R. Let us now modify the standard theory so that alongside of the rules of the categorial component (with S as the initial symbol) a grammar may have in addition the rules (10), where f_i and p_j are chosen freely from the categories of formal objects that serve as focus and presupposition, respectively:

(10) $S' \rightarrow S\ f_i\ p_j$

Thus the initial phrase-marker P_1' generated by the categorial component of the base will be of the form (11), instead of P_1, as before:

(11)

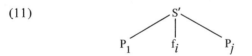

Transformations now apply as before, paying no attention to f_i, p_j. Thus instead of $\Sigma = (P_1, \ldots, P_n)$, we have (12):

(12) $\Sigma' = (P_1\ f_i\ p_j, P_2\ f_i\ p_j, \ldots, P_n\ f_i\ p_j)$,

where each term $P_k\ f_i\ p_j$ is a phrase-marker. Finally, we add an output condition C that accepts Σ' as well-formed just in case P_n, f_i, and p_j are related by the rule R. This revision of the standard theory (call it "version II" of EST) preserves the condition of the standard theory that deep structures alone determine semantic interpretation. Version II differs from the standard theory precisely in that it permits new kinds of output conditions, a greater latitude with respect to question (4c). Of course, the two versions of EST are empirically indistinguishable (in the respect cited).

As noted in Chomsky (1971), if certain aspects of semantic interpretation are determined from surface structure, then the standard theory must be modified (in either of the two ways just outlined) and, *a fortiori*, generative semantics is untenable in the forms in which it had been so far discussed, with P_1 of Σ serving as the semantic representation. Of course, generative semantics could be modified along the lines of version II of EST. This modification is precisely what Lakoff (1969*b, c*) presents as his formulation of the revised theory of generative semantics. Thus he permits new output conditions (which he calls "derivational constraints") relating semantic representation and surface structure.[17] The only difference is that, in the specific case of focus and presupposition, he chooses the notation (9) instead of (10), taking semantic representation to be a sequence of formal elements rather than a phrase-marker.[18]

There is only one apparent difference between the revised "generative semantics" as based on (9) and the second version of EST formulated in Chomsky (1971) and just restated; namely (apart from focus, presupposition, etc.), Lakoff assumes that P_1 "is" the semantic representation whereas EST assumes that P_1 "determines" the semantic representation. This apparent difference also seems to fade away under analysis (as we shall see below), leaving only the issue of ordering of various kinds of transformations and perhaps wealth of descriptive devices.

5.3

Putting aside for the moment the apparent difference in how P_1 is viewed, we note that Lakoff's revised generative semantics is simply a notational variant of EST. What leads him, then, to assert that it is an entirely different system? In part, this may result from a misstatement in his presentation of the empirical content of EST (either version). The proposal of EST is that semantic interpretation applies to the pair (deep structure, surface structure), with the qualifications noted above concerning surface structure. In particular, grammatical relations are determined by deep structure, focus and presupposition (in the sense discussed) by surface structure, and certain other aspects of semantic interpretation, such as coreference, by both deep and surface structure. Lakoff asserts that to say that specific aspects of semantic representation (say, focus and presupposition) are determined by principles operating on surface structure is equivalent to "the more neutral locution 'semantic representation and surface structure are related by a system of rules," (1969*c*). EST, however, makes a stronger claim: that the relation between surface structure and these specific aspects of semantic representation is independent of other terms in the derivation. This may be right or wrong, but it is quite different from the more neutral locution that Lakoff offers as a paraphrase.

The belief that Lakoff's revised generative semantics (except in the respect that we have put off until later) is a substantive alternative to the formulation of EST that Lakoff paraphrases in his exposition may also be fostered, in part, by some variation in the use of the term "derivational constraint." For Postal (1969, p. 235) a derivational constraint is a restriction on the sequence of trees which can occur in a well-formed sentential derivation: it is, then, a condition of Σ of (2). This is a natural terminology, given that Σ is called a "derivation." Lakoff does not define "derivation," but he uses the term "derivational constraint" not only for constraints on terms of Σ, but also for any condition relating Σ, or some term of Σ, to some aspect of the semantic representation. For example, he writes that "semantic representation and surface structure are related by a system. . .of derivational constraints" (1969b, p. 120). Thus a "derivational constraint" can relate the formal object (9), which is not a phrase-marker, to surface structure, which is a term of a derivation. If Lakoff were to accept the terminological proposal of version II of EST [i.e., with (10), (11), and (12)], his term "derivational constraint" would be synonymous with "constraint on derivation," as presumably intended. In this case, however, it is evident that this version of generative semantics (except for the status of P_1 and the matter of ordering) is compatible with anything that might be discovered about the relation of syntax and semantics. Postal's concept of derivational constraint, though it enormously increases the descriptive power of transformational grammar, at least may leave some empirical content to the theory. But in Lakoff's sense, where a "derivational constraint" is any conceivable principle relating some term of a derivation to another or to some aspect of semantic representation, it is difficult to see what is excluded by the theory which proposes that grammars include "derivational constraints." As this theory is presented, it is not even required that derivational constraints be pairwise constraints; they are merely conditions that limit the choice of derivations and semantic representations.

To simplify terminology, I suggest that we replace the term "derivational constraint" by its equivalent, "rule of grammar." Then the standard theory asserts that the rules include transformations, the base rules, and the output condition noted, along with the rules that map deep structures onto semantic representations. EST identifies certain aspects of semantic representation that are determined by deep structure, others that are determined by surface structure, but otherwise permits no new sorts of rules (or in version II, it allows a new type of output condition in place of rules relating surface structure and semantic interpretation). Generative semantics in Postal's sense claims that rules of interpretation of deep structures can be eliminated in favor of transformations, and permits other rules of an unspecified sort restricting derivations. Lakoff goes further, permitting any rule imaginable, so far as I can see.

Of course, all would agree that the fundamental problem of linguistic theory is to determine what kinds of rules (derivational constraints) exist. EST and Lakoff's generative semantics agree that there are transformations and rules relating surface (or shallow) structure to certain aspects of semantic representation, and they agree that there are general conditions on transformations.[19] They differ with respect to the rules introducing lexical items. Further, Lakoff suggests that many other kinds of rules are necessary. Of course, to say this is not to provide an alternative theory. Rather, any indication that this may be so simply poses a problem, for which a theoretical account is awaited. I return to this matter below.

6.0

Let us consider next the matter of the lexical-insertion transformations. Here there appears to be a substantive difference between EST and generative semantics.

6.1

Generative semantics holds that a lexical transformation replaces a subphrase-marker Q by an item I, where I is a set of phonological and syntactic features. Furthermore, it has been proposed (see McCawley 1968*b*, Morgan 1969) that Q must be a constituent of the phrase-marker. This is almost never the case, it would appear. For example, we must presumably insert *uncle* in place of the subphrase-marker "brother of (mother or father)," but the latter is no constituent. Rather, underlying the phrase *uncle of Bill*, we would presumably have "(*brother of [(mother or father) of Bill]*)," where the italicized item is what is replaced by *uncle*. Of course, the italicized item could be made a constituent by a new and otherwise un-motivated rule of "collapsing." This is the approach taken by McCawley in the case of words such as *kill* 'cause to die'. In the proposed underlying structure, *John caused Bill to die* (or *John caused Bill to become not alive*), the unit that is replaced by *kill* is not a constituent, but it becomes one by the otherwise quite unnecessary rule of predicate raising. Such a device will always be available, so that the hypothesis that Q is a constituent has little empirical content.[20]

If we insist that there be a "natural" or a "motivated" rule to make Q a constituent, then the claim that Q is a constituent in a lexical-insertion operation seems untenable. Consider, for example, the word *assassinate*, which, in terms of this approach, should replace everything but X in *kill X by unlawful means and with malice aforethought, where X is human, reasonably important, etc.* There is no way, without extreme artificiality, to make all of this, except for *X*, a constituent. Yet it is just this that would be required by the assumption that a lexical transformation inserts an item with only phonological and syntactic features for a subphrase-marker Q that is a constituent.

What is true of *assassinate* is true of most words. Consider, for example, the tone of sinister intent that is associated with *cohort* or *henchman* as compared with *colleague*; or consider the many examples analyzed in an illuminating way by Fillmore (1969) in terms of assertion and presupposition. Or compare, say, the word *dissuade* with *persuade not*, where the former, but not the latter presupposes some sort of intention on the part of the person dissuaded—thus you would not speak of dissuading John from standing on the corner or from being optimistic, unless he was doing so with some particular intent and exercise of will, though you might speak of persuading him not to, in such cases. (See also note 20.) The point is general, and indicates that condition (3) of section 2.3 can be met by generative semantics only if lexical transformations are operations of a markedly different sort from nonlexical ones. This is not to deny that certain (perhaps all) aspects of meaning can be paraphrased in a canonical notation using phrase-markers, which are then mapped onto phrase-markers with lexical items by "transformations." Given the enormous descriptive power of the concepts "phrase-marker" and "transformation," this thesis can hardly be doubted.

6.2

One might try to retain some substance for the view that lexical items are inserted by transformation in a different way. Suppose that we restrict principle (3) of section 2.3 as follows. Let us distinguish between assertion and presupposition in the case of lexical items, along the lines of Fillmore (1969), and say that the lexical-insertion transformation applies in a derivation, replacing a subphrase-marker Q by a lexical item I, where Q represents what is "asserted" by I, but only under the condition that what is presupposed by I is indicated in the semantic representation. This proposal is given by Lakoff (1969c,p. 31). Thus, instead of inventing some exotic transformation to insert *assassinate* for its paraphrase, we insert *assassinate* for Q = "killed" (approximately), but only when the presupposition is expressed that the person killed is reasonably important, etc. Recall that the semantic representation, in Lakoff's terms, is a sequence $(P_1, PR, \ldots)$, where PR is a conjunction of presuppositions. Presumably, what is intended is that the presupposition of *assassinate* is one term of this conjunction. Now the lexical-insertion transformations can be more restricted, and perhaps one can even preserve the principle that Q is a constituent.

As it stands, this proposal too is untenable. Thus to insert the word *assassinate, criticize, dissuade, accuse,* etc., it is not enough that the presuppositions associated with these words appear as conjuncts of PR, which is one term of the semantic representation. It is necessary, furthermore, to relate the presupposition in question to the position in the phrase-marker which is to be filled by the verb with this presupposition. It is difficult to see how this can be done unless the term PR of the semantic representation virtually duplicates the structure of the phrase-markers that constitute the derivations. For example, if lexical insertion is to take place in an embedded constituent, the presupposition associated with this insertion must be restricted in some way to this position of embedding. Even this elaboration, which is bad enough, would be insufficient if, indeed, lexical insertion can take place at arbitrary stages of derivation, so that there is no way to duplicate in PR the structure of the phrase-markers in which insertion takes place (except by arbitrary coding devices).

Furthermore, it is not at all clear what would now be "meant" by PR. Thus PR is intended to express the presuppositions of the utterance, and it is defined as a conjunction of presuppositions. But it is obvious that the presupposition associated with a lexical item in an embedded sentence need not be a presupposition of the entire sentence.[21] Or, to illustrate some of the difficulties with an oversimplified example, suppose that *accuse* NP *of* V*ing* means *state that* NP V*'s* where it is presupposed that it is wrong for NP to V. Then, given the proposal under consideration, the sentence *For John to accuse Bill of lying is worse than for John to state that Bill lied*, derives from *For John to state that Bill lied is worse than for John to state that Bill lied,* with the presupposition that John regards it as wrong for Bill to lie, where *accuse* replaces the first occurrence of *state.* Not only is this an unacceptable conclusion in itself, but we must also conclude that the same source underlies the sentence *For John to state that Bill lied is worse than for John to accuse Bill of lying.* There are many similar problems. Somehow, the presupposition must be linked in the underlying "semantic representation" to the specific point in the phrase-marker to which it is relevant.

I do not see any way to make sense of this proposal except by having PR, in some way, reflect the internal structure of the phrase-markers of Σ that are subject to lexical insertion. If, in fact, lexical insertion can take place at any point in Σ, the problem seems utterly hopeless. If lexical insertion were restricted to a particular term of Σ, as in the standard theory, the proposal would be intelligible, but rather pointless. It would amount to duplicating this term of Σ in PR. But quite apart from this, it is merely a play on words to use the term "transformation" for an operation that inserts an item I for a subphrase-marker Q of term P_i of a derivation $\Sigma = (P_1, \ldots, P_n)$, *on the condition that PR* [a term of $(P_1$ PR, . . .), which is the semantic resentation of Σ *contains a certain conjunct.* Such an operation is radically different in its properties from any nonlexical transformation, even though of course it could be described as a mapping of phrase-markers onto phrase-markers, if we modify Lakoff's theory along the lines of version II of EST (see note 15).

6.3

Once again, it seems that there is no substance to the proposal that lexical insertion is an operation inserting a lexical item for a phrase-marker representing its meaning, since no empirical issue is raised by this proposal. There seems no way of avoiding the usual assumption that a lexical entry contains a complex account of conceptual structure, nuance, presuppositions, and so on, and that this account involves grammatically related elements in the sentence. One can no doubt use the notation of phrase-markers and transformations to present this information, but this, if true, merely testifies to the enormous descriptive power of these devices. In any event, these "lexical-insertion" transformations bear little resemblance to nonlexical transformations, and no insight is gained by this approach, which seems to raise only terminological issues.

Generative semantics has attempted to incorporate the following two assumptions regarding lexical-insertion operations: (1) each such operation introduces an item I with no intrinsic semantic content; (2) this item I replaces a subphrase-marker. In Lakoff's version, assumption (2) is partially abandoned, only to raise still further problems. It is quite unclear what the content of a workable proposal might be, incorporating some version of the assumptions (1) and (2). In particular, it is difficult to see how such a proposal might differ from the standard theory, with regard to lexical insertion, unless it can be shown that independently motivated transformations precede lexical insertion. The latter question thus appears to be the only relatively clear empirical issue differentiating generative semantics and EST, so far as lexical items are concerned.

6.4.0

Let us consider, then, the question whether all nonlexical transformations follow all lexical transformations, as asserted in the standard (and extended standard) theory, or whether there are reasons for abandoning this hypothesis, and with it, the hypothesis that deep structures exist as a well-defined level of linguistic structure determined by base rules. I know of four lines of argument that have been explored in an attempt to refute this assumption. The first was McCawley's discussion of *respective-respectively* (McCawley 1968a). He attempted to construct an argument patterned on Halle's refutation of taxonomic (autonomous) phonemics, that is, to discover a generalization that is unformulable if deep structure is assumed to exist as a level of representation in a generative grammar. I am frankly unable to piece together his argument with any certainty, but I think there is no doubt that he did not succeed in constructing such a generalization. And his own positive suggestions seem to reduce merely to a variant of the standard theory.[22]

A second argument was presented by Lakoff in his interesting discussion of instrumentals (Lakoff 1968). However, this argument collapses when a wider variety of facts are considered.

These two cases are discussed in Chomsky (1971), and I will say no more about them here.

6.4.1

A third argument appears in Lakoff (1969*b,c*). It has to do with the words *persuade, dissuade*. The entire argument, when analyzed in detail, turns on the following factual claim, and only this. Consider the sentences (13), (14), and (15):

> (13) I persuaded John to date many girls.
> (14) I persuaded John not to date many girls.
> (15) I dissuaded John from dating many girls.

As Lakoff interprets the facts, sentence (13) can mean *There are many girls that I persuaded John to date*; sentence (14) cannot mean *There are many girls that I persuaded John not to date*; sentence (15) cannot mean *There are many girls that I dissuaded John from dating*. Putting the same point differently, we can say (16) but not (17):

> (16) I persuaded John to date many girls, in particular, Mary, Jane, ...
> (17) I dissuaded John from dating many girls, in particular, Mary, Jane, ...

Similarly, he regards (17) as not well-formed when *dissuade* is replaced by *keep, prevent, deter*, etc. Judgments about these cases can hardly be very firm, but I see no reason to accept these factual claims. The word *dissuade* does indeed seem to be rather like *prevent, deter, keep,* and other verbs that take *from*-complements, with respect to the interpretation of a following quantifier. In all cases, the interpretation in question seems to me as acceptable as in the case of verbs such as *persuade*, though I stress again the indecisiveness of the factual judgments. In no case do I see any motivation for assuming that part of the "meaning" is an abstract positive verb (underlying *prevent, keep,* etc.) accompanied by a negative particle. Since these are the only relevant empirical observations cited, I will not pursue the argument based on them.[23]

6.4.2

There is a fourth argument due to Jerry Morgan (1969). He observes that the sentence (18) has two senses when *almost* takes *kill* as scope (and a third, which we can disregard, when it takes *kill John* as scope):

(18) I almost killed John.

The two senses in question are as in (19) and (20), respectively:

(19) I shot at John and missed him by a hair—I almost killed him.
(20) I wounded John almost mortally—I almost killed him.

Morgan argues that we can explain this fact by supposing that underlying *kill* is the phrase-marker *cause to die*,[24] and that one reading of *almost kill* "involves the scope of *almost* being internal to *kill*; i.e., the reading paraphrased by 'I caused John to become almost dead' " [i.e., (20)]. He claims further that these two readings of *kill John* are differentiated more explicitly in (21), (22):

(21) What I did was almost kill John.
(22) What I did to John was almost kill him.

His point, I believe, is that (22) has the interpretation of (20), whereas (21) has the interpretation of (19). To me it seems, rather, that (21) is ambiguous as between (19) and (20), and that (22), as he holds, has the reading of (20). But this, if true, would hardly support his theory, since on his assumptions it should follow that (22) is also ambiguous.

Quite apart from this, there are further difficulties. The range of meaning he perceives seems to be characteristic of many—perhaps all—verbs that specify a process that can reach a terminal point; e.g., *I almost solved the problem, I almost persuaded Bill to leave, The planes almost destroyed the city*, etc. The latter, for example, might be interpreted along the lines of (19) or (20). Furthermore, *What the planes did was almost destroy the city* parallels (21) in interpretation, while *What the planes did to the city was almost destroy it* has, as its natural interpretation, the analog to (20). Yet in this case, there is little sense to the idea of an internal analysis, and surely no causative analysis. Again, the factual judgments seem to me insecure, but so far as they are clear at all, it seems that the whole matter simply has to do with verbs of process with a terminal point. One might, further, speculate that this is a universal characteristic of such verbs, and hence not to be described in a particular grammar. In any event, I see no argument here for the assumption that such verbs as *kill* must be introduced by transformations replacing phrase-markers such as *cause-to-die*.

Other difficulties in such an approach have already been discussed (see p. 79). Fodor (1970) presents several arguments in support of a much stronger assertion, namely, that the causative analysis is not only unmotivated but in fact unacceptable. His conclusion is approximately what Jackendoff (1969) formulates as the "extended lexical hypothesis," namely, that "the only changes transformations can make to lexical items is to add inflectional affixes such as number, gender, case, person, and tense." Another line of argument leading to the same conclusion has been explored by Joan Bresnan (1971). She suggests that the rules of the phonological cycle apply not to surface structures, as supposed heretofore, but in the course of the transformational cycle. It would follow that either the extended lexical hypothesis is accepted, or else fairly radical modifications have to be introduced in the principles of the phonological cycle. I will not go into these questions here. My own guess is that the extended lexical hypothesis is probably correct, in essence.

6.4.3

There have been a number of other attempts, some quite detailed, to show that certain lexical items must be introduced after certain transformations. To be at all convincing, such an argument against the standard (or extended standard) theory must show that some *syntactically motivated* transformation precedes the operation of lexical insertion—that is, some transformation motivated independently of the expression of the meanings of lexical items. As already noted, it will in general be quite difficult to distinguish between rules of semantic interpretation for lexical items and transformations that introduce such items in place of certain phrase-markers in a distinct "semantic" notation. Lakoff (1969c) discusses quite a number of such attempts. I will not try to review them all in detail, but will discuss only the case which he appears to regard as the strongest of the group.

Consider the word *remind*, as in the sentence (23):[25]

(23) John reminds me of a gorilla.

The proposal is that the underlying structure is, approximately, (24):

(24) I [perceive]$_V$ [John is similar a gorilla]$_S$.

Subject-raising and a permutation rule ("Psych-movement") give (25):

(25) John [perceive]$_V$ me [similar a gorilla]$_S$.

Predicate raising produces the phrase [*perceive similar*]$_V$ which is replaced by *remind*, by a lexical-insertion transformation.

The first question to be asked is whether these transformations are syntactically motivated. Predicate-raising surely is not; it is simply a device to convert phrases that are to be replaced by a lexical item into a single constituent. Though the matter is not relevant here, I might mention that the permutation rule that gives (25) as well as subject-raising into object position seem to me to be at best dubious rules. However, I will not pursue the issue here, because even if these rules are assumed, the case for lexical insertion after they apply seems to me extremely weak.

Lakoff asks (1969*c*) correctly, whether there is any syntactic evidence for the transformational derivation of (23) from (24). He offers the following evidence. Consider the sentences (26):

(26) To shave oneself is to torture oneself (is like torturing oneself).

The rule that forms such sentences applies freely if the subject is the impersonal, but is restricted in other cases. Thus we cannot have (27) or (28), although (29) is grammatical:

(27) To shave himself is to torture himself (is like torturing himself).
(28) Mary says that Bill thinks that shaving herself is torturing herself.
(29) Bill says that to shave himself is to torture himself.

The generalization he suggests is that the rule can apply "when the clause where the deletion takes place is a complement of a verb of saying or thinking and when the NP's to be deleted are coreferential to the subject of that verb of saying or thinking." This principle would permit (29), while excluding (27) and (28).

Suppose, now, that (24) underlies (23), and that the rule in question applies to the underlying form (24). Then from (30) we shall derive (31), which becomes ultimately (32):

(30) John perceive [shaving him similar torturing him].
(31) John perceive [shaving himself similar torturing himself].
(32) Shaving himself reminds John of torturing himself.

However, the principle just formulated will exclude (33):

(33) Mary says that shaving herself reminds John of torturing herself.

These conclusions are correct: (32) is grammatical but not (33). Therefore,

Lakoff concludes, there is independent syntactic evidence for the proposed derivation of *remind*, because the transformational rule that gives (31) must precede lexical insertion.

The argument collapses, however, when one observes that the formulated principle (quoted above) is inadequate. Thus alongside of (32) we have such sentences as (34):

(34) (i)   Shaving himself seems to John like torturing himself.
      (ii) Shaving himself makes John think of torturing himself.
      (iii) Shaving himself brings to John's mind the idea of torturing himself.
      (iv) Shaving himself appears to John to be as pointless as torturing himself.

One would hardly argue that these derive from something like (30). Rather these sentences are formally analogous to (32) and indicate that the rule in question can apply quite freely to such structures, independently of their postulated transformational source (quite different, in these cases). In short, the rule in question, whatever it may be, gives no support to the analysis of *remind*, since it appears to apply to structures such as (34) which contain no verbs of saying or thinking in the required position.

In fact, the situation is worse. Compare the set (35):

(35) (i)   John reminds me of a gorilla.
      (ii) John's presence reminds me of an appointment I missed.
            (Mary's diamond ring reminds me of my poverty, etc.)
      (iii) John reminded me of an appointment I missed.

Sentence (35i), according to Postal's analysis (1970), derives from something like (24). Sentences (35ii), (35iii) derive from entirely different sources. It is merely an accident, from this point of view, that they share the same surface form. Furthermore, one cannot argue that some "output condition" on surface (or shallow) structure requires this similarity of form for the various cases of *remind*, since the regularity illustrated in (35) is stateable only prior to transformational rules (such as passive) that yield surface (or shallow) structures. In fact, it is a regularity stateable precisely at the level of deep structure in the sense of EST.

Furthermore, exactly the same range of interpretations is possible when we replace *remind* in (35) by other phrases such as *make [me] think of, bring to [my] mind*, etc. Hence from this point of view there is a double accident: first, in the case of *remind* there is a single syntactic form (stateable at the level of deep structure, but nowhere else) with a range of interpretations corresponding to totally different "underlying" structures; second, other phrases similar in meaning to *remind* share the same range of interpretation, with a fixed syntactic form (stateable only at the level of deep structure).

These observations suggest that *remind* is inserted at the level of deep structure and that the range of interpretation of *remind* (as well as the other phrases similar to it in meaning) is determined by general principles operating at this level of representation. The optimal solution, of course, would be the discovery of general rules, not restricted to the case of *remind*, that express the range of meaning noted without the *ad hoc* assumption that separate (and presumably unrelated) lexical entries are involved in the set (35) (as well as in the parallel sets involving phrases similar in meaning). To discover such principles is not a trivial matter. Several lines of investigation suggest themselves. Thus the distinction between (35iii) and (35ii) seems analogous to the distinction between *John opened the door* and *The key opened the door* (or to the ambiguity of *John broke the window*—i.e., he did it as an agent or as an object thrown through the window). Perhaps it follows, then, from the principle that an animate subject of a verb of action can be interpreted as an agent. Furthermore, as Jackendoff notes (personal communication), the relation between (35i) and (35ii) seems analogous to that holding between *John irritates me* and *John's presence irritates me*. Perhaps, then, (35i) can be regarded as a special case of (35ii) in sentences with a generic interpretation where the specific characteristic noted explicitly in (35ii) (namely, *John's presence, Mary's diamond ring*) is not mentioned. It remains to formulate such a principle precisely and to relate it to the principle involved in interpreting animate subjects as agents. Such an approach, if feasible, has the considerable advantage that it would overcome the double anomaly that is otherwise left unresolved.

In short, properties of *remind* seem to provide no support for relaxing the condition of the (extended) standard theory that lexical insertion precedes all rules of the transformational cycle. On the contrary, this hypothesis seems to provide the best hope of explaining the properties of *remind* and other phrases with a similar meaning. I know of no other example that suggests a contrary conclusion.[26]

6.5.0

I have mentioned several lines of argument that might yield counterevidence to the assumption that lexical-insertion operations precede all nonlexical transformations. None of them, at the moment, seems to provide any such evidence. Although the possibility obviously cannot be ruled out that such evidence will be discovered, it seems to me that what evidence is now available supports the more restrictive (and therefore preferable) assumption of the standard theory that lexical-insertion operations belong to the base, and that deep structures therefore exist as a significant linguistic level.

In discussing autonomous (taxonomic) phonemics, I noted that the observation that no generalizations are lost if rules are ordered so that such a level appears in derivations would, if correct, be an argument for the existence of this level. The hypothesis, then, would be that this is an essential, not merely accidental, property of human languages. As Halle (1959) showed, this argument fails in the case of autonomous phonemics, but there seems, at the moment, no reason to doubt that the analogous argument is correct in the case of deep structure. A still stronger argument for autonomous phonemics would be that certain generalizations and limiting conditions on derivations can be formulated in terms of the postulated level. In the case of deep structure, there is good reason to believe that this stronger argument also holds.

6.5.1

I have already noted one example, namely, the case of *remind*. In general, it seems to be true that the properties of lexical items are formulable in terms of a set of phrase-markers that are defined by the categorial rules of the base. If true, this is a remarkable fact, expressed as a fundamental principle in the (extended) standard theory. To my knowledge, the principle is well supported by the available evidence, though there is no *a priori* reason why languages should be so constructed.

6.5.2

There are many other considerations that lead to the same conclusion. One simple example is noted by Jackendoff (1969). Consider the sentences (36):

(36)   (i)   A beaver builds dams.
       (ii) That beaver builds dams.
       (iii) A beaver is building a dam.
       (iv) The fattest beaver is the builder.

The first sentence can be interpreted only as generic, the second and the third only as specific, while the fourth is ambiguous as between the two interpretations. Clearly, the possibility of generic or specific interpretation is not determined simply by the choice of subject or the choice of predicate, but in part by an interaction between the two. At the level of deep structure, there is a very simple generalization governing such sentences as (36): any noun phrase can be followed by any verb phrase.[27] But the semantic representations will vary with respect to such properties as generic-specific. Thus such sentences as (36) will have varied paraphrases, and if it is supposed that something like the correct paraphrase is the initial term of the derivation, it will merely be a curious accident that at a certain stage of derivation—namely, that illustrated by (36)—there is the simple generalization just noted. It would, in other words, be claimed implicitly that the grammar of English would be no more complex if this (accidental) regularity did not hold true.

Furthermore, as Jackendoff notes, a theory that somehow derives such forms as (36) from their semantic representations would not only not be able to express the syntactic regularity of such forms, but it will in fact have to rule out the simplest underlying structures for at least some of them. Thus (36iv) will have two quite different initial phrase-markers in its two derivations, one of them similar to the initial phrase-marker of (36i) and the other similar to the initial phrase-marker of (36ii,iii). By accident, later transformations happen to give the forms satisfying the simple regularity illustrated by (36). In addition, it is necessary to ensure that (36i) does not have an initial phrase-marker similar to those of (36ii,iii). If, say, the latter have the underlying form NP-VP, then rules must be added to guarantee that there is no such form that will lead, by transformation, to (36i).

Compare this observation with Halle's argument with respect to autonomous phonemics. Halle showed that some generalization is not formulable *if* autonomous phonemics exists as a well-defined level of derivation. Jackendoff's argument indicates[28] that some generalization is not formulable *unless* deep structure exists as a well-defined level of derivation—furthermore, as a level generated independently by base rules. [29]

6.5.3

As a second, more intricate example of a similar sort, consider English derived nominals.[30] These vary widely in interpretation, but are severely constrained in form, in several ways.

First, derived nominals correspond only to forms that exist prior to syntactically motivated transformations. Thus we have such forms as (37) but not (38).

> (37) (i) John's certainty that Bill will leave
>   (ii) John's eagerness to please
>   (iii) the gift of the book to Mary
>   (iv) the belief that John was killed
>   (v) John's surprise at Bill's antics

> (38) (i) John's certainty to leave
>   (ii) John's easiness to please
>   (iii) the gift of Mary the book
>   (iv) the belief of John to have been killed
>   (v) Bill's antics surprise of John[31]

Notice that the proper generalization concerning admissible derived nominals is expressed in terms of deep structure—i.e., the level prior to application of syntactically motivated transformations—a fact that provides evidence for the existence of this level of representation.

Secondly, the patterns in question must exist independently for noun phrases, quite apart from these nominalizations, as we see from such expressions as *the story of Bill's exploits, the message from John to Bill about money, a war of aggression against England, the secretary general of the UN, his advantage over his rivals, his habit of interrupting, the prospects for peace, prolegomena to any future metaphysics, my candidate for a trip to the moon, a nation of shopkeepers,* and many others.

Thirdly, these forms fall under a simple phrase structure schema that applies as well to verb and adjective phrases, which appear with approximately the same complement structure as nouns.

Fourth, derived nominals have the internal structure of noun phrases—that is, many of them pluralize and take determiners and internal adjectives (*John's several proofs of the theorem, John's uncanny resemblance to Bill, the remarkable proof of the theorem that John presented,* etc.).

Fifth, derived nominals do not contain elements that are unique to verb phrases and never appear in other noun phrases, specifically, aspect. There is, in other words, no derived nominal containing perfect or progressive.

In all these respects derived nominals differ from gerundive nominals such as *John's refusing the offer.* These are not subject to the wide-ranging, often idiosyncratic variation of meaning that is characteristic of derived nominals; rather, all are related in meaning to the corresponding sentence by simple and uniform principles. As far as form is concerned, gerundive nominals correspond not only to base structures but to derived structures as well (*John's being certain to leave,* etc.); they do not correspond in form to independently existing noun phrases; their forms do not fall under a more general phrase structure schema governing all lexical categories; they do not have the internal structure of noun phrases (**the refusing the offer, *John's sudden refusing the offer, *John's provings the theorem*); and they may contain aspect (e.g., *John's having refused the offer*).

The properties of gerundive nominals follow directly from the assumption that there is a transformational process of gerundive nominalization. The very different cluster of properties of derived nominals follows directly from the assumption that they are not transformationally derived, but rather that the base component of the grammar contains a phrase structure schema that applies to all lexical categories (i.e., noun, verb, and adjective), and that certain lexical items may appear in more than one lexical category.[32] These assumptions account for the observed convergence of formal properties—that is, the fact that derived nominals have one set of properties and gerundive nominals an entirely different set. Of critical importance, in the present connection, is the fact that the explanation for the convergence of properties in the case of derived nominals depends on the assumption that deep structures exist—the appropriate explanatory principle is formulated in terms of the properties of deep structures. If, on the other hand, we were to suppose that each nominal, gerundive or derived, is generated from an initial phrase-marker representing its semantic interpretation, we would fail entirely to explain why the gerundive nominals, with a regular semantic relation to the associated sentence, have the formal properties of sentences, whereas the derived nominals, which would have a variety of different sources, exhibit the convergence of formal properties just noted (i.e., in essence, the properties of noun phrases), differing from gerundive nominals in this respect. All of this would be simply a remarkable accident, from this point of view. The convergence of formal properties and the relation between range of meaning and correspondence to either noun phrase (in the case of derived nominals) or sentence (in the case of gerundive nominals) cannot be explained in terms of universal semantics or properties of transformations—the only devices available to generative semantics for expressing regularities at early stages of derivation—though it can be explained immediately in terms of some general conditions on deep structures. Notice that the failure is one of explanatory, not descriptive, adequacy. There is no doubt that the facts noted can be described in a grammar that derives all of these forms by transformation.

This problem has been noted by Lakoff (1969c). He suggests that the regularities noted "are instances of constraints on shallow or surface structure." As in the other cases discussed here, this proposal is untenable, since these regularities do not appear at the level of shallow or surface structure, but only at a more "abstract" level prior to the application of the syntactically motivated transformations, which destroy these regularities. There seems no way to avoid the conclusion that the class K of admissible derivations [see (2), Sec. 2.1] is defined, in part, by categorial rules of the base (phrase structure schemata and context-free phrase structure rules) that restrict the class of initial phrase-markers of derivations. Deep structures, then, are the structures formed from these by insertion of lexical items.[33]

Summarizing, I believe that these considerations again provide strong evidence in support of the (extended) standard theory, with its assumption that deep structures exist as a well-defined level with the properties expressed by base rules.

6.6.0

At this point, I would like to comment on arguments that have been offered against the analysis of derived nominals just reviewed—what I have called the "lexicalist hypothesis." I know of three that have appeared in print.

6.6.1

Ross (1969*b*) argues as follows. Consider such sentences as (39):

(39) Bill mentioned his plans to do away with someone, but he didn't mention whom.

Ross argues that the source for the second conjunct must be (40):

(40) Bill didn't mention whom he plans to do away with.

He concludes that this "provides evidence against any theory of grammar in which 'his plans to do away with someone' is not identical, at some stage, to 'he plans to do away with someone.' " But the lexicalist hypothesis denies that these two are identical at any stage of derivation. Consequently, the argument provides evidence against the lexicalist hypothesis.

Suppose that Ross's argument were valid. Now replace *his plans* in (39) by any of the following: *his plan, those plans of his, his several weird plans*, etc. By the same argument, it follows that all of the resulting phrases in (41) must be identical, at some stage of derivation, to *He plans to do away with someone:*

(41) Bill mentioned his plans (his plan, those plans of his, his several weird plans, etc.) to do away with someone.

Therefore, the various sentences of (41) must be identical with one another at some stage of derivation. Then either they are synonymous, if they are identical at the initial stage of derivation, or they may be different in initial phrase-marker, different in final structure, but all identical at some intermediate stage D. The question would then arise how the subderivations from initial phrase-marker to D are properly paired with their continuations to surface structure. Without pursuing the matter, I think it is sufficiently clear that in either case, we have reached an intolerable conclusion. Consequently, the argument is at best suspect—and, in fact, it is unclear what force it had even apart from these unacceptable consequences.

6.6.2

Ross presents a second argument against the lexicalist hypothesis in Ross (1970). Here he considers the following expressions:

(42) his shrug of displeasure
(43) he shrugged his displeasure
(44) he-showed (manifested)-his displeasure-by shrugging

He argues that (44) is converted to (43) by an operation that replaces the second term by the fourth, so that the nominalization (42) corresponds to a transform (43), contrary to the lexicalist hypothesis which requires that derived nominals correspond only to base forms.

This argument is extremely weak, even if we accept the idea that something like (44) underlies (43). Notice that *shrugging* in (44) can be replaced by many noun phrases (e.g., *an obscene gesture, an angry letter, a shrug*). Consequently, we could accept the hypothesis that the noun *shrug* is a lexical item, and derive both (42) and (43) by an operation that applies to a noun phrase or a sentence of the form (45), replacing the second term by the fourth:

$$
(45) \quad [\text{he} - \text{manifest(ation)} - \text{his displeasure} - \text{by} \begin{Bmatrix} \text{a gesture} \\ \text{shrugging} \\ \text{a shrug} \end{Bmatrix}]
$$

But even this much is dubious, and I question, therefore, that this is at all the correct approach. Consider the sentence (46):

(46) He manifested his displeasure by a shrug of annoyance (displeasure).

If we assume a rule giving (43) from (44), the structure underlying (46) must be something like *He manifested his displeasure by manifesting his annoyance (displeasure) with a shrug (by shrugging).* But this seems to give the wrong meaning: he didn't manifest his displeasure by manifesting some emotion, but by a shrug. In any event, the motivation for any such rule is extremely weak. One might just as well propose that all lexical items with some feature (call it [+manifestable]) can appear as nouns in the fourth position of (45) and as head noun or verb in (42) and (43), dispensing with all of these transformations, and the attendant problems.

6.6.3

The only other argument that I know of appears in Postal (1969). He considers the phrase (47) and notes that in it, *America* must be understood as the subject of *attack:*

(47) America's attempt to attack Cuba

This observation, he claims, is a counterargument to the lexicalist hypothesis since if "such nominalizations are not transformationally derived,. . . [then] . . . no general account of which NP controls complement subject deletion will be possible." The point is that in (48), we can say that the subject, *America*, controls complement subject deletion, but in (49), underlying (47) by the lexicalist hypothesis, some entirely different rule would be needed:

(48) [America – attempts [America attacks Cuba]$_S$]$_S$
(49) [America's – attempt [America attacks Cuba]$_S$]$_{NP}$

The appropriate generalization requires that we assign the same grammatical relation to the pair (*America, attempt*) in (48) and (49) (namely, *America* is subject of *attempt* in both cases). Then we could formulate the principle that the NP that controls complement subject deletion "must be the subject of the immediately dominating clause" (or in these terms, the immediately dominating S or NP).

Postal's counterargument is based on a misunderstanding. He overlooks the essential claim of the lexicalist hypothesis, namely, that grammatical relations must be generalized in such a way that the subject-verb relation holds of (*America, attempt*) in (49), as in (48), and perhaps even of the same pair in the phrase *the American attempt* [where *American* is what Postal calls a proper-pseudo-adjective (PPA)].[34] Hence nothing follows from Postal's observations, so far as the lexicalist hypothesis is concerned.

6.6.4

These are the only counterarguments that have been suggested in print, to my knowledge, to the lexicalist hypothesis.[35] Since the evidence for the hypothesis is quite strong, I think we must conclude, tentatively, that the hypothesis is well-supported, and consequently, that the assumptions of the (extended) standard theory with regard to deep structure, are well-supported as well.

6.6.5

Before turning to the next matter, let us pursue somewhat further Postal's discussion of PPA's, although this is not strictly relevant to the discussion here. He considers such phrases as (50), arguing that they must derive from the corresponding phrases of (51).

(50)   (i)   the American attack on Colombia
       (ii) the Markovian solution of that problem
       (iii) the Persian application for membership
       (iv) the American attempt to attack Cuba
       (v)   scholarly attempts to uncover the causes
       (vi) sociological studies

(51) (i)   America's attack on Colombia
      (ii) Markov's solution of that problem
      (iii) Persia's application for membership
      (iv) America's attempt to attack Cuba
      (v)   attempts by scholars to uncover the causes
      (vi) studies by sociologists

He argues that the paired phrases share grammatical and selectional relations, conditions on control, and deep structure constraints. Consequently, he concludes that (50) derive from (51).

The argument presented seems to me weak, however, The existence of these similarities is not in doubt, but they can be accounted for exactly as well by a lexicalist approach to PPA's which generalizes the subject-verb relation in the manner just noted and attributes the shared properties to the subject-verb relation itself, along the lines discussed in Chomsky (1970). Hence the facts that Postal presents seem to me to be quite neutral as between the assumption that (50) derive from (51) and the assumption that all are (essentially) base forms.

However, looking into the matter further, I think there is a good argument that the PPA's not only *need* not derive by transformation, but in fact that they *do* not. In fact, PPA's share some of the properties of derived nominals that argue against a transformational derivation, in particular, their semantic idiosyncracy.[36] Thus Postal's examples would be consistent with the transformational derivation of (50) from (51) that he proposes only if the paired phrases were synonymous.[37] This, however, is not the case. For example, the phrase *the Markovian solution* does not mean *Markov's solution* [see (50ii), (51ii)]. If I say that this problem has no Markovian solution, I mean that it has no solution along Markovian lines, not that it has no solution by Markov. The same is true in general of such phrases as *a Markovian analysis, a Fregean analysis,* etc. Similarly, the pairs (50v), (51v) are surely not synonymous (consider *The most scholarly attempts to uncover the causes were made by journalists*). A similar discrepancy appears in (50vi), (51vi) (consider *The best sociological studies are by anthropologists).* Other problems arise in the case of (i), (iii), (iv) of (50), (51). Thus (50iii) seems quite analogous in form and meaning to *Persian art* or *the Persian style,* which admits no transformational derivation from an analogue of (51iii). As to case (iv), consider *An American attempt to attack Cuba has been expected for many years.* It is difficult to see how this could arise from a source analogous to that postulated for (50iv). (Worse still, consider *Lots of American attempts to attack Cuba have failed*). In the case of (50i), there are, as Postal notes, several meanings. Thus consider (52):

(52) (i)   American offers to join a cane-cutting brigade
      (ii) Anglo-American difficulties over trade
      (iii) the Anglo-American commission

(iv) The Anglo-American refusal to aid Biafra

(v) the Caribbean alliance

In the case of (52i) the meaning is *offers by Americans*, not *America's offers*.[38] In (52ii) the meaning is *difficulties arising between England and America*. In (52iii) the meaning is *commission formed by England and America (or constituted of representatives chosen . . .)*. The phrase (52iv) means something like *the agreement by England and America that each refuse to aid Biafra* (i.e., their joint refusal individually to aid Biafra). In the case of (52v), there is no source at all. Not only do these phrases differ among themselves, but it is hard to see how any might have a reasonable underlying source from a possessive NP.

I think one must conclude, then, that at best the argument for derivation of PPA's from possessive NP's is shaky, and at worst, the facts show that there is no such derivation. This observation is of some interest, because Postal regards the conclusion that PPA's derive from NP's as "crucial for the subject of this paper." The reason is that this derivation gives the only strong argument[39] for the conclusion that transformations create "anaphoric islands," that is, phrases no part of which can appear in a relation of coreference (putting it loosely). It is clear that lexical items are such anaphoric islands. Thus to use Postal's example, we cannot say (53), meaning that Max misses his parents:

(53) Max is an orphan and he deeply misses them.

As Postal observes, this fact might serve as a *prima facie* argument against generative semantics, which would hold that *orphan* replaces some such structure as *person whose parents were dead*. One might ask, on these grounds, why pronominalization cannot have applied prior to the transformation which inserts the word *orphan*. To show that this fact does not count against generative semantics, it is crucial, Postal argues, to demonstrate that there are transformations that introduce anaphoric islands. Then the fact that lexical-insertion operations introduce anaphoric islands will not require a unique condition designed *ad hoc* to solve a problem that arises within the framework of generative semantics. Hence the importance of demonstrating that the PPA's (which, as Postal shows, are anaphoric islands) are introduced transformationally. Correspondingly, when the latter argument collapses, as I think it does, we are left with an argument (insignificant, in my opinion) against generative semantics: namely, it requires that lexical-insertion operations have the *ad hoc* property, not motivated by any other consideration, that they create anaphoric islands. Obviously, this is a problem that does not arise in the (extended) standard theory.

The correct generalization seems to be that items that have a lexical entry are "anaphoric islands." Thus nouns, verbs, adjectives, and idioms are anaphoric islands. There are no anaphoric processes "internal" to such expressions as *orphan, book, American, lighthouse keeper, kick the bucket,*[40] etc. No doubt refinements are needed, but this seems to be the basic principle. It is expressible easily in terms of the notion "lexical entry." Again, these considerations seem to me to add some slight support for a theory such as the (extended) standard theory that incorporates this notion in an essential way.

6.7

I have tried to show, in section 6, that there is no evidence against the narrower and more restrictive (hence preferable) assumptions of the (extended) standard theory with regard to lexical insertion. On the contrary, it seems that there are good reasons to suppose that all lexical-insertion rules precede any nonlexical transformation, so that the notion "deep structure" is defined and conditions on deep structure can be formulated to constrain derivations. These conditions are the rules of the base, including the lexical-insertion rules [which appear to meet the constraints on contextual features outlined in Chomsky (1965)] and the categorial rules that define the initial phrase-marker P_1 of a derivation Σ. The latter rules, in turn, can in part be generalized as schemata of the sort discussed in Chomsky (1970), so it seems. In these terms, we can account for striking regularities in form and convergence of properties that are expressible at the level of deep structure, though apparently not elsewhere.

6.8.1

The earliest work in generative grammar noted explicitly that the grammatical relations expressed in deep structure (as we are now calling it) do not correspond, one-to-one, to significant semantic properties, and the observation is, of course, familiar from traditional grammar. Within the framework of the standard theory or the proposed extension, rules must be formulated determining the semantic relations that hold of items in the deep structure, on the basis of the grammatical relations of the deep structure and specific properties of the lexical items themselves. To take a concrete example, consider the word *break* as it appears in the sentences of (54):[41]

(54)   (i)   The window broke.
        (ii) A hammer broke the window.
        (iii) The workman broke the window with a hammer.
        (iv) The window broke with a hammer.
        (v)   The child's toy broke against the tree trunk.
        (vi) The bully broke the child's toy against the tree trunk.

    (vii) The news broke (to the public).

    (viii) A doctor broke the news (to the public) (with a telegram).

    (ix) A telegram broke the news.

Following Matthews's terminology (1968), let us specify the semantic relations by assigning "cases" to the noun phrases as follows: animate agent is nominative; thing or person acted upon or toward is dative; thing used is instrumental; thing acted upon but not modified by the action is absolutive; place where is locative. Then in the examples (54), *window* is dative; *hammer* is instrumental; *workman* is nominative; *toy* is dative; *tree trunk* is locative; *bully* is nominative; *news* is absolutive; *public* is dative; *doctor* is nominative; *telegram* is instrumental. Suppose that the deep structures are similar to the surface structures in (54). Then the cases do not directly reflect deep structure grammatical relations.

    For example, the *window* is subject in (i) and object in (ii), but is dative in both cases; the subject is dative in (i) and instrumental in (ii), etc. Even on this assumption, we might, however, determine the cases by simple rules that use the grammatical relations of the deep structure and certain lexical properties of *break*. Suppose that *break* is entered in the lexicon with this specification:

    (55) *break* is intransitive or causative; it optionally takes locative and instrumental; the subject of the intransitive is dative or absolutive.

The terms "subject" and "intransitive" are defined in the obvious way in terms of deep structure; the term "causative" is so defined that a verb with the feature [+causative] appears in the context subject-object, where the object is the subject of the corresponding intransitive (see Chomsky 1965, 1970). Thus the lexical entry (55) specifies that *break* can appear in the contexts of (56), in deep structure, where NP_1 can be either dative or absolutive:

    (56) (i) NP_1 — (loc) (instr)

$$\text{(ii) } NP_2 \begin{bmatrix} - \\ +caus \end{bmatrix} NP_1 \ (loc) \ (instr)$$

A general rule specifies that the subject of a transitive verb of action—i.e., a verb such as *give* but not *receive*—can be an agent (nominative) if it is animate; otherwise, it is instrumental. Choice of dative or absolutive is contingent on concreteness vs. abstractness of the noun phrase.

    With these definitions and the specification (55), cases (i.e., semantic relations) are assigned properly in (54), and other possible examples are excluded.

6.8.2

Matthews suggests a different approach to this set of facts. He proposes that the central rule of the base grammar generate the structure (57):

$$(57) \quad it - \text{Aux} - [\text{V (NP) (NP)} \dots]_{\text{prop}}$$

The word *break* (similarly, every verb) imposes certain cases on the NP's that follow it in the proposition (prop). Thus *break* would be entered in the lexicon with the following specification:

$$(58) \quad break: - (\text{abs})_a(\text{dat})_b(\text{loc}) (\text{instr}) (\text{nom})$$
where either a or b must appear.

A general transformation rule takes an NP of prop in (57) and substitutes it for the subject *it*, under the following conditions:

(59) The rule applies to the final NP of prop when it is nominative, and optionally to the final NP of prop when it is instrumental: otherwise, it applies to the NP following the verb.

This approach, too, accounts for the phenomena of (54). Further refinements are possible in both cases, but the general ideas are clear. Both approaches are formulable within the (extended) standard theory. In fact, it might be questioned whether they are more than notational variants. Perhaps empirical differences can be determined. If not, we can think of them as alternative ways of assigning semantic functions on the basis of lexical properties and grammatical relations of the deep structure.

6.8.3

Matthews's systems is an expanded and modified version of some ideas of Fillmore (1968). Fillmore proposes a system with underlying case representations that are not phrase-markers at all. Thus he would interpret the proposition of (57) as an unordered set $(\text{V, C}_1, \dots, \text{C}_n)$, where the C_i's are various cases. A particular verb can be associated with V when its lexical entry and the cases of prop correspond; appropriate noun phrases can be associated with the C_i's. The grammar then contains two categories of rule. Rules of category I map case systems into phrase-markers.[42] For example, he would formulate a rule analogous to Matthews's (59) as a category I rule. The rules of category II are transformations which generate derivations in the usual way.

As Fillmore actually presents his system, it differs greatly from earlier versions of syntax. The basic differences, however, do not appear to be at the conceptual or theoretical level, but rather at the level of application to the particular grammar of English. Thus Fillmore takes the passive rule to be not a transformation of category II, but rather a rule of category I. It would be quite consistent with his theory of case grammar to regard passive as a transformation, rather than as a rule mapping case structure onto phrase-markers. There are clear empirical differences between these two proposals concerning the status of passive. I think that Fillmore's proposal is incorrect,[43] but this is a matter of choice of grammar, not choice of linguistic theory.

Fillmore argues that there are significant conceptual differences between case grammar and the standard theory. Specifically, he holds that

> it is likely that ... syntactic deep structure [independently motivated on syntactic grounds] ... is going to go the way of the phoneme. It is an artificial intermediate level between the empirically discoverable "semantic deep structure" [i.e., the case system] and the observational accessible surface structure, a level the properties of which have more to do with the methodological commitments of grammarians than with the nature of human language.

This conclusion has something of the flavor of generative semantics, in the sense discussed earlier. It is quite different from our tentative conclusion, a moment ago, that case grammar may not be empirically distinguishable from the standard theory, but may merely offer another notation for expressing the relation between deep structures and semantic relations.

Fillmore's assumption relies heavily on the hypothesis that the case systems express the meaning of the sentence, or in other words, that the rules of category I are meaning-preserving. He observes, however, that this hypothesis is not true in general. Consider his examples (60), (61):

(60)   Bees are swarming in the garden.
(61)   The garden is swarming with bees.

Clearly these are not synonymous. It might be that *Bees are swarming in the garden* [i.e., around their nest] *but most of the garden has no bees in it*, but replacement of (60) by (61) in this expression yields a contradiction. Yet (60) and (61) derive from the same case representation. Fillmore suggests that this is a matter of a "focussing difference" with some "cognitive content." The problem, however, seems to me more serious than his remark would suggest. Other examples, similar to Fillmore's, are noted by Dougherty (Forthcoming). I suspect that only rarely is there true synonymy among the various sentences that are derived by different rules of category I from a single case representation, and that the example (60), (61) is rather typical, not exceptional.

Fillmore's reference to a "focussing difference" suggests that the difficulty might be overcome, within his system, by adding rules of surface-structure interpretation that determine focus. Unfortunately, this is impossible. The distinction is not a property of surface structure, as we can see from such examples as (62):

(62)   (i) Bees are certain to be swarming in the garden.
        (ii) Bees were believed to be swarming in the garden.
        (iii) It is in the garden that bees are swarming.
        (iv) It is bees that are swarming in the garden.

These differ from one another and from (60) in surface structure, but all share the relevant semantic property; similarly, the different semantic property of (61) is shared by sentences with a variety of surface structures. The relevant distinction is stateable only at a more abstract level of derivation—in fact, at the level of deep structure in the sense of the (extended) standard theory. In Fillmore's terms, it is the structure formed by the rules of category I, prior to any syntactic transformation of category II, that determines the relevant semantic properties. The same is true in many other cases. Therefore, it seems to me that Fillmore's examples contradict his conclusion quoted above; they indicate, rather, that deep structure plays a significant role in determining semantic interpretation.

An even more critical example is provided in Fillmore's discussion of what he takes to be the explanatory power of case grammar. He argues that this theory makes it possible to capture the generalization (63):

(63) "The subject of an active transitive sentence must be interpretable as a personal agent just in case the sentence contains a *with* phrase of instrumental import."

The sentence (54iii) is an example, and such a sentence as *A hammer broke the window with a chisel* can only be interpreted as personification metaphor [note that (54vi) violates (63), however, since (63) asserts that containing a *with* phrase is a necessary condition for obligatory interpretation of the subject as personal agent].

Fillmore notes that the sentence (64) appears to constitute an exception to (63):

(64) The car broke the window with its fender.

In this case *car* certainly is not a personal agent; rather, it appears to be instrumental, in his terms. But, he argues, both (64) and (65) derive from the case representation (66), with *the window* specified as objective and *the car's fender* as instrumental:

(65) The car's fender broke the window.
(66) [V, *break*], [obj, *the window*], [instr, *the car's-fender*]

He suggests that the rules of category I that choose the subject "allow an option in this case: either the entire instrument phrase may appear as the subject [as in (65)], or the 'possessor' alone may be made the subject, the remainder of the instrument phrase appearing with the preposition *with* [as in (64)]" (numbering changed). He then concludes:

> The superficial nature of the notion "subject of a sentence" is made apparent by these examples in a particularly persuasive way, because in the possessor-as-subject cases, the "subject" is not even a major constituent of the sentence; it is taken from the modifier of one of the major constituents.[44]

It seems to me, however, that such examples do in fact show the inadequacy of (63). Much more important—these examples, contrary to the quoted conclusion, demonstrate the significance of the grammatical relations of deep structure. The phrase *the car* in (64) [but not in (65)] seems to function as a kind of an agent. Suppose, for example, that the laws of nature were changed in such a way that when a car is produced there is also, necessarily, a paired anticar produced along with it, called its "twin," the two then being independent of one another. Then from (67) we should, by Fillmore's rules, be able to form the synonymous pair (68):

(67) [V, *break*], [obj, *the window*], [instr, *the car's-twin*]
(68) The car broke the window with its twin [parallel to (64)].
       (ii) The car's twin broke the window [parallel to (65)].

Of course, these are not synonymous. The reason is that in some sense the car is performing the action in (64) and (68i), but not in (65) and (68ii). In other words, exactly as in the case of (60), (61), the grammatical relations expressed in the phrase-marker formed by the category I rules play a role in determining the meaning of the sentence.

We might seek to remedy this defect by restricting the operation of the category I rule of subject choosing to only certain kinds of possession—say, to possession of a part. To see the technical difficulties to which this suggestion would give rise, consider the case of two cars with radio antennas, one of the normal sort, one with an independent motor that raises and lowers the antenna. Consider the sentences (70) derived from the case structure (69):

(69) [V, *hit*], [obj, *the garage roof*], [instr, *my car's-radio antenna*]
(70)   (i) My car hit the garage roof with its radio antenna.
         (ii) My car's radio antenna hit the garage roof.

Sentence (70ii) has approximately the sense of (70i) in the case of the car with the normal antenna; but if the motor of the antenna independently caused the antenna to rise, hitting the garage roof while the car was parked in the garage, we could truly say (70ii) but not (70i). The reason, again, is that some sort of "agency" is associated with the subject position in (70).

Still a further difficulty is noted by Dougherty (Forthcoming). Consider the sentences (71):

(71) (i) Caruso broke the window with his voice.
     (ii) Caruso's voice broke the window.

These derive from (72), but (71i) also derives, independently, from (73):

(72) [V, *break*], [obj, *the window*], [instr, *Caruso's-voice*]
(73) [V, *break*], [obj, *the window*], [instr, *voice*], [agent, *Caruso*]

However, there is no ambiguity in (71i).[45] Thus an unambiguous structure derives from two distinct case representations. This can be reconciled with the assumption that case representation relates directly to meaning only if we accept the conclusion that the cases are not an independent set of semantic primitives, a conclusion that appears inconsistent with Fillmore's general assumptions. On the other hand, the observations noted are just what would follow from the assumption that the grammatical relations of the deep structure, taken together with the lexical properties of particular verbs, determine the semantically significant grammatical relations.

I think that these considerations show, fairly persuasively, that the very examples that Fillmore discusses to illustrate the explanatory power of case grammar and the "superficial" character of deep structure grammatical relations in fact demonstrate the opposite. The grammatical relations of the deep structure appear to play a central role in determining the meaning. The case representation appears to be nothing more than a notation to express what the standard theory would express in the form (55).[46]

Other examples that Fillmore discusses seem to me to lead to the same conclusion. To mention just one, consider the sentences (74):

(74) (i) Mary pinched John on the nose.
     (ii) Mary pinched John's nose.

Fillmore would derive these from (75), by a category I rule analogous to the rule of subject choosing just discussed:

(75) [V, *pinch*], [loc, *John's-nose*], [agent, *Mary*][47]

According to his analysis, either *John* or *John's nose* can be "promoted" to a major constituent by the category I rules, just as either *the car* or *the car's fender* could be promoted in (64), (65), and (66).

Here too, however, the analysis seems to me defective. Thus, suppose that *pinch* is replaced by *pull* in (75). Then we can have the analog to (74ii), but not (74i).[48] Surely the difference is related to the fact that the sentences of (76) are well-formed, but not those that result from replacement of *pinch* by *pull* in (76):

(76) Mary pinched John near the nose, behind his left ear, etc.

In short, *pinch*, but not *pull*, appears freely in the frame: − NP PP. The sentence (74i), then, is just one special case of this general deep structure pattern, while (74ii) is an instance of the pattern: − NP. The fact that *nose* bears a part-whole relation to *John* in (74i) is a general property of such phrases as *on the nose* (compare, e.g., the examples of note 47).

In this set of examples too it is the deep structure patterns that are crucial for determining form and meaning. The case representations are best understood as a notation for expressing the semantic relations determined by the interplay of deep structure grammatical relations and specific properties of particular lexical items. It seems to me that all of these considerations support the standard theory (or the proposed extension), rather than the conclusions that Fillmore draws.

6.8.4

Summarizing this discussion, it seems to me that presently available evidence leads us to accept the hypotheses of EST concerning lexical insertion, deep structure, and grammatical relations.[49]

7.0

Let us turn now to a different matter. As noted earlier, EST permits only base rules, transformational rules, a simple output condition on surface structures (and certain other conditions—see note 12), and rules of interpretation applying to deep and surface (and perhaps also shallow) structures. To be more precise, the latter rules apply to phonetically interpreted surface structures. Furthermore, there are general conditions on the application of transformations of the sort discussed in section 2.1. As already noted, recent work in generative semantics has suggested that there may be many other types of rules (derivational constraints). It would hardly come as a surprise to discover that this is true. Nevertheless, any such enrichment of linguistic theory must, of course, be empirically well-motivated and, furthermore, we shall naturally seek a narrow formulation of any richer devices, if they are empirically motivated, for reasons discussed in section 2.2. Let us consider a few concrete examples that have been proposed to illustrate the need to enrich the framework of linguistic theory by permitting new kinds of rules, and thus a much wider variety of possible grammars.

7.1.1

One concrete question that has been discussed in some detail concerns quantifiers and negation in English. Consider the sentences (77), (78):

(77) Many men read few books.
(78) Few books are read by many men.

Such sentences were suggested by Jackendoff (1969)[50] to illustrate the difference in meaning of paired active-passive sentences. Clearly the sentences do differ in meaning, and equally obviously, the difference is related to the order of the quantifiers in surface structure. Jackendoff proposed that the order and scope of quantifiers and negation is determined from the surface structure, in accordance with what I have here called the "extended standard theory."

Lakoff has suggested an alternative analysis (1969b), within the framework of generative semantics. He proposes that the underlying structures for (77) and (78) are essentially (77') and (78') respectively:

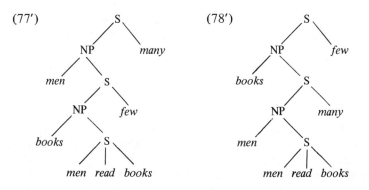

A rule of "quantifier lowering" is then formulated which, in (77'), first inserts *few* before *books* and then (on the next cycle) *many* before *men* [similarly, in (78'), with the order reversed]. A new derivational constraint guarantees that the "height" of the quantifier in deep structure corresponds to left-to-right order in surface structure, in the simplest cases, to which I will restrict attention.[51] Presumably, the relative clause condition will exclude such deep structures as (79):

(79)

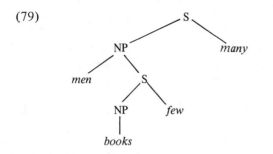

—i.e., (77′) with the most deeply embedded S missing.

Given this apparatus, we can say that deep structure (or P_1 of the derivation) relates directly to "logical form." Thus we could convert (77′) directly to a pseudo-quantificational form such as (80):

(80) for many $x \in$ Men, for few $y \in$ Books, x read y

Exactly the same is true if we drop the rule of quantifier lowering from the grammar, eliminate the derivational constraint, and take the deep structure of (77) and (78) to be (approximately):

(81)

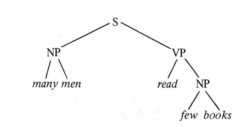

with (78) formed by the ordinary passive transformation. There is a trivial algorithm which, applied to the surface structures, gives the pseudo-quantificational forms such as (80).

Here then is a simple case where a rule of surface structure interpretation can be rephrased in terms of a derivational constraint, other well-formedness conditions, and a new transformation. Is there any point to this? I think not, for several reasons.

Notice first that the structures in which quantifiers appear as predicates have unique properties. For example, the structure (79) is admissible only if the embedded NP, *books*, has a relative clause attached to it; furthermore, this relative clause must contain both of the NP's that appear in (79). These conditions are without parallel among syntactically motivated structures. Furthermore, although (77′) appears to involve a "relative clause," this structure is unique in that its antecedent, *men*, does not appear within the "relative clause" of which it is the immediate antecedent.

Furthermore, NP's which appear in nonrelativizable positions can of course contain quantifiers, and will thus appear in these new pseudo-relative structures. Consider, for example, the sentence (82):

(82) Che's strategy of many Vietnams will succeed.

Presumably, in accordance with this theory, the structure underlying the NP subject is something like (83), just as the structure underlying *men read many books* is (84):

(83) [*Vietnams* [*Che's strategy of Vietnams*] *many*]
(84) [*books* [*men read books*] *many*]

But whereas in (84) *books* is in a relativizable position (compare *the books that men read are. . .*), in (83) *Vietnams* is not in a relativizable position (compare *Vietnams, Che's strategy of which, are. . .*). Yet both (83) and (84), or something like them, must be presupposed, and the rules of relativization (e.g., *wh*-movement) must apply in both, although general conditions on transformations (see sec. 2.1, above) preclude this in the case of (83). Further problems arise when we ask how (83) fits into the rest of the sentence, or if we consider such sentences as (85):

(85) Several strategies of many Vietnams will fail, but one will finally succeed.

Nevertheless, the unique properties of these new relative and predicate structures can be "isolated" from the remainder of the grammar. However the constraints on relativization are ultimately to be formulated, there is little doubt that they will be formulable so as to permit these particular cases of nonrelativizable relatives. The reason has to do with the operation of quantifier-lowering, which was formulated *ad hoc* for this case, and is itself quite unlike any syntactically motivated transformation in its properties. (Note that this is a further argument against, not a consideration in favor of, this theory.)

The rule of quantifier-lowering deletes the antecedent noun and moves the predicate of the matrix sentence into the embedded sentence. Thus applying to (84), it deletes *books* in the matrix structure and inserts *many* into the embedded "relative."[52] Neither of these operations has an analog within the syntactically motivated sections of the grammar. In particular, although there are a number of rules which extract items from an embedded sentence and move them into higher sentences, there is, to my knowledge, none that introduces an item into a phrase of an embedded sentence from outside this sentence. In fact, it has been proposed (see Chomsky 1965) that there is a universal condition blocking such rules.[53]

This was suggested as a possible way of explaining the familiar observation that reflexivization and "inherent coreference" (see Helke 1971) is impermissible in the case of embedded sentences, as in *John expected Mary to hurt himself, *John expected Mary to lose his mind. Dougherty (1968) observes, under an analysis that he develops in detail, that the same general condition would explain the fact that from (86) we can form (87), but from (88) we cannot form (89):

(86) Each of the men saw the others.
(87) (i) The men each saw the others.
     (ii) The men saw each other.
(88) Each of the men expected the police to catch the others.
(89) The men expected the police to catch each other.

Moreover, the rule of quantifier-lowering appears to violate the constraints suggested by Emonds (1969) for cyclic rules.

Thus the proposal under investigation sets up structures with unique properties and requires rules that violate otherwise plausible conditions on the application of rules. None of these arguments against this proposal is decisive—there is no such thing as a completely decisive argument in the present state of the field—but they do suggest that the proposal is incorrect, and specifically, that quantifier-lowering is not only a syntactically unmotivated rule of a unique character, but also perhaps an impossible rule, on general grounds.

These considerations, then, seem to me to support an approach rather like that of Jackendoff (1969), in which the syntax is left in the simplest possible form, and in which there is no rule of quantifier-lowering, no unique structures and rules, and no new sorts of derivational constraints. Rather, a rule of interpretation determines "logical form" from surface structure [just as in the alternative theory, a rule of interpretation might map (77') into (80), in some more "canonical" notation—see note 52]. This rule of interpretation, incidentally, need be formulated as part of a grammar only to the extent that it is language-specific.

7.1.2

Before we leave this topic, several other observations are in order. Lakoff notes that it is not just surface structure, but some structure prior to deletion operations that relates to "logical form." Consider, for example, the sentence (90):

(90) Jane isn't liked by many men, and Sally isn't either.

We must know, in interpreting this sentence, how *many* functions with respect to the second conjunct. This observation is correct, and would require a modification of Jackendoff's theory of semantic interpretation to permit also consideration of shallow structure (in the sense of note 6) if in fact there is a deletion operation involved in such sentences as (90). There are arguments for the latter hypothesis, but there are arguments against it as well. Consider, for example, the sentences (91), (92), and (93):

> (91) John hasn't been here for a month.
> (92) John has been here for a month.
> (93) John hasn't been here for a month, but Bill has.

The sentence (91) is ambiguous: it may be used to deny (92), meaning that John has not spent the entire month here; or, more naturally, it may be interpreted as meaning that there is no time during the past month when John was here, i.e., he hasn't been here even once. (This seems to me, furthermore, the only interpretation when *hasn't* is unstressed). But sentence (92) is unambiguous, having only the former interpretation: for all of the time during the last month, John has been here—i.e., he did not just appear now and then, but spent the month here.[54] Sentence (92) cannot have the meaning *John has been here at some time during the month*, i.e., the proposition denied under the second interpretation of (91). But now consider (93). Where the first conjunct is interpreted (in the natural way) to mean *It is not the case that John has been here at some time during the month* (i.e., *There is no time during the month when John was here*), the second conjunct means *Bill has been here at some time during the month*. Thus if (94) underlies (93), then the second conjunct in (94) has an interpretation which it cannot have in isolation:

> (94) John hasn't been here for a month, but Bill has been here for a month.

There are many similar examples, some of which even have syntactic residues; consider, for example, (95) and (96):

> (95) John won't leave until midnight, but Bill will.
> (96) *Bill will leave until midnight.

In the case of (95), (96), one might propose an "output condition" that excludes (96) in isolation while permitting it as an underlying conjunct of (95). To extend such a solution to (91), (92), and (93), one would have to say that (92) too is ambiguous, but that some sort of "output condition" eliminates one interpretation when it appears in isolation. Perhaps such a proposal can be given a coherent formulation. But such an enrichment of the theory of grammar seems to me a rather questionable move. More natural, I think, is the conclusion that (93) and (96) are not formed by deletion operations, and that "compositional semantics" must be abandoned (or at least restricted), with the semantic interpretation in such cases as (93) constructed along lines that have been explored by Jackendoff (1969) and Akmajian (1970).

There are other examples that suggest that rather complex aspects of semantic representation must be constructed from surface structure. Consider the sentence (97):

(97) It is being regarded as incompetent that disturbs John.

There are general principles determining focus and presupposition from surface structure which, applied to (97), specify the focus as (98) and the presupposition as (99):

(98) being regarded as incompetent
(99) something disturbs John

[See Chomsky (1971).] [The point is perhaps still clearer when (97) is negated.] These conclusions seem correct, but of course the property expressed by (98) is not associated with a deep structure phrase. The predicate *regard X as incompetent* expressed by (98) poses no problems of principle, but it is a predicate that is expressed only by a phrase of surface structure. The question that remains important, and essentially unanswered in any interesting way, is how such predicates are constructed and interpreted, given the full derivation Σ. Such considerations suggest that surface structure may contribute new predicates, as well as certain aspects of "logical form."

The problems posed by (90), and the general question of whether "shallow structure" must be considered along with surface structure in the revised theory, must, I think, be held in abeyance until these more general issues are resolved.

7.1.3

I think that a somewhat more careful look at the semantics of quantifiers and negation lends further support to an interpretive theory of the sort that Jackendoff has suggested. The examples (77) and (78) involved the quantifier *few*, which is inherently negative, meaning *not many*. This is crucial. If, in these examples, *few* is replaced, say, by *a few* or *several*, it is much less clear that there is a difference of meaning between the modified (77) and (78), or that left-to-right order in surface structure corresponds, in such a simple way, to order of quantifiers in a canonical notation such as (80). Looking at the matter more closely, consider Jackendoff's sentences (100), (101).

(100) Not many arrows hit the target.
(101) The target was not hit by many arrows.

Jackendoff and Lakoff have argued that these sentences are synonymous on one reading (they disagree as to whether the second is ambiguous, a matter that is irrelevant here), meaning *It is not so that many arrows hit the target*. Others have also accepted this conclusion (e.g., Chomsky 1971). However, I do not think that it is strictly true. There is a clear difference in presupposition. Sentence (100) (equivalently, *Few arrows hit the target*) presupposes that some arrows hit the target, but sentence (101) does not; (101), but not (100), is properly paraphrased as *It is not so that many arrows hit the target*. Imagine a situation in which no arrows hit the target and someone asserts that many arrows hit the target. We could deny his assertion by saying *It is not so that many arrows hit the target* or *The target was not hit by many arrows* [=(101); this interpretation perhaps requires stress on *not*], but we would not deny it, in this case, by saying *You're wrong, not many (few) arrows hit the target*. Such a response is inappropriate because of the expressed presupposition that at least some arrows hit the target.

There is a similar distinction in the analogous case of noncount nouns and their quantifiers. The sentence *Little enthusiasm was shown for that project* (equivalently, *Not much enthusiasm was shown for that project*) cannot be paraphrased as *It is not so that much enthusiasm was shown for that project* because it presupposes, as the proposed paraphrase does not, that at least some enthusiasm was shown. Thus if we know that no enthusiasm was shown, we would not deny the assertion that much enthusiasm was shown by saying *Not much enthusiasm was shown for the project*.

Discussion of presupposition is made difficult by the fact that there are a number of different kinds of presupposition that have not been distinguished with sufficient clarity. Thus consider the sentence (102):

(102) Two of my five children are in elementary school.

The statement of (102) presupposes that I have five children; if I have six children, the statement is without truth value. In quite another sense, (102) presupposes that three of my five children are not in elementary school. That is, it would be natural for the hearer to assume this, on the basis of the statement (102). On the other hand, if, in fact, three are in elementary school, (102) is not devoid of truth value; in fact it is true. Hearing (102), one is entitled to assume that three of my children are not in elementary school, perhaps by virtue of general conditions on discourse of a sort that have been discussed by Paul Grice in his work on "conversational implicature." However, it is easy to imagine conditions under which this assumption would be withdrawn and it would be perfectly appropriate to say *Two of my five children are in elementary school, and so are the other three*; but there are no circumstances under which the presupposition of (102) that I have exactly five children can be withdrawn.

The presupposition of (100) that some arrows hit the target seems to me of the latter sort. One might argue that insofar as presuppositions can be explained in terms of general "maxims of discourse" (in the Gricean sense), they need not be made explicit in the grammar of a particular language.[55] But the presuppositions associated with *few arrows* (or *not many arrows*, or *little enthusiasm*, or *not much enthusiasm*) or with *five children* in (102) do not appear to me to be of this sort, and it seems natural to require that a theory of grammar incorporate them. It would be of some interest to develop sharper analytic criteria in this area.

The matter is important, in the present connection, because of its bearing on the problem of "constituent negation," a central notion in Jackendoff's theory. In the sentence (100), the negative element is associated in surface structure with the first noun phrase. Similarly, in (103) it is associated with a noun phrase:

(103) John and Bill are arguing about nothing.

In the sentence (104), we can take the negative element to be associated with the verb, so that it means *John dislikes mushrooms*, or with the verb phrase, in which case it means *It is not so that John likes mushrooms*:

(104) John [(doesn't like) mushrooms].

In other words, either the parentheses or the brackets express a possible interpretation. Perhaps the same ambiguous interpretation is possible in the case of (101). It appears that interpretation as "sentence negation" without a specific presupposition is appropriate only when the negative element is associated with the predicate phrase. In the other cases, there seems to be a specific presupposition, as we have noted in the case of (100). Thus (103) presupposes that John and Bill are arguing, and asserts that there is no substance to their disagreement.[56] In (104), if we associate the negative element with the verb *like*, so that the meaning is *John dislikes mushrooms*, there is a presupposition that he has the relevant experience with mushrooms, but this is not the case when negation is associated with the entire predicate phrase. Thus if John has never tasted mushrooms and it is asserted that he likes them, I can deny the assertion by stating (104), interpreting the negation as associated with the predicate phrase, but not by stating *John dislikes mushrooms*, or (104) with the negation interpreted as associated with the verb.[57]

Though much remains unclear, it does seem that the actual position of the negative element in surface structure is quite critical, and that when it is not associated with the verb phrase, there are specific presuppositions that are otherwise lacking. These observations suggest that the position of the negative element plays a role in determining what is presupposed as well as what is asserted, and that "canonical paraphrase" in which negation is treated simply as associated with propositions, though perhaps possible with some artificiality, may well be an irrelevant sidetrack.[58]

7.2

Summarizing, a consideration of the properties of quantifiers and negations seems to support the view that syntactically motivated rules and the structures they involve suffice to account for whatever facts are clear, in a fairly natural way, and that the introduction of more abstract under lying structures and transformations with no syntactic motivation (such as quantifier-lowering) simply leads to new problems and complexity, while requiring that linguistic theory be enriched to incorporate a broader class of rules (derivational constraints).

To my knowledge, this case is typical, and it supports the working hypothesis expressed in EST. If we consider simply the problem of constructing grammars that generate surface structures with the devices of the standard theory (base rules and transformations), restricting ourselves to rules that are motivated in the sense that they permit the fullest expression of significant generalizations, we are led to the construction of deep structures that do not, in their formal configurations, express directly all of the semantic properties of sentences. I know of no clear cases, however, where these properties cannot be expressed by fairly general and natural rules applying to the motivated deep and surface (and perhaps shallow) structures. Of course, there are so many unclear cases (on any grounds) that one can only be extremely hesitant about putting forward a general hypothesis. Furthermore, there are serious conceptual questions that can be raised, for example, regarding the question what are "significant generalizations." In the cases so far discussed, however, and in others to which I will turn directly, postulation of more abstract structures to express semantic content and rules designed *ad hoc* to incorporate these more abstract structures in derivations offers at best a notational alternative, and at worst leads to new complications. It is for this reason that I believe that EST should, tentatively, be adopted as the framework for grammatical research.

7.3

Let me consider another case which illustrates fairly clearly what I believe to be the typical situation in this regard. Consider English modals, in particular, the modal *may*. It is well known that there is an ambiguity in such sentences as (105):

(105) John may leave tomorrow.

Sentence (105) may be interpreted as meaning that it is permitted that John leave or that it is possible that he will leave. Lyle Jenkins, in unpublished work, has pointed out that there is a somewhat different range of interpretation that appears in interrogatives. Compare (106) and (107):

(106) May John leave the room?
(107) May I (please) have the ashtray?

To (106), the natural response is *Yes, he may,* or *No, he may not.* To (107), the appropriate response is something like *Here, take it,* or simply the action of giving the ashtray. A mere affirmative response would be inappropriate. Sentence (106) is a question as to whether something is permitted (i.e., *may* is used in the permission sense), whereas (107) is a request for the ashtray.

Furthermore, this interpretation of a questioned *may* as a request for action depends in part on the surface subject. Thus consider the sentences (108) - (111):

(108) May I please examine you, Dr. X?
(109) May I please be examined by you, Dr. X?
(110) May you please examine me, Dr. X?
(111) May you please be examined by me, Dr. X?

Sentences (108) and (109) are requests, in the sense of (107), but (110) and (111) are not so interpretable, if they are well-formed at all.[59] The sentences (108) and (109) do not involve either the permission sense of *may* or the possibility sense. The interpretation as a request for action is impossible in cases (110) and (111), exactly as it would be if *I* were replaced by *you* in (107). It is the item that appears as surface subject of the sentence that determines whether this interpretation is possible in the case of (108) - (111).

Thus in declaratives, *may* has the sense of possibility or permission, whereas in interrogatives, it may have the sense of permission or a kind of request. The interpretation, in interrogatives, depends in part on the person of the surface subject. In this case, the semantic properties seem relatively straightforward, and should be formulable in a simple way. The underlying structures are characterized in terms of simple base rules, and the transformations involved are also quite simple and straightforward. But the interpretation depends on a property of the surface structure, as is quite generally the case with modals. There is absolutely no point in introducing further transformational apparatus, or phrase-markers unmotivated by independent considerations, into the description of these phenomena. There is no need for new derivational constraints (i.e., rules) to determine the sequences of phrase-markers that constitute derivations. We can use the term "derivational constraint" to refer to the rules that relate the surface structure to the semantic representation, but this is merely a terminological point—and a misleading one, if it serves as an avenue for the introduction of much richer descriptive devices into linguistic theory.

For many other examples of this sort, see Culicover (1971).

7.4

Are there "derivational constraints" other than the rules that relate surface (or shallow) structure to semantic representation? For example, are there examples of transformational rules that cannot be formulated as mappings of phrase-markers onto phrase-markers, but require rather some reference to earlier stages of derivation? Several such cases have been suggested, some in print. Generally, the "earlier stage of derivation" is the deep structure or semantic representation; a case in point was noted in the references of note 5, where a general condition on transformations appears to be involved.

It is clear that only certain types of examples of this sort are relevant to the (extended) standard theory. Suppose, for example, that the transformation T maps P into P′ just in case P meets both the syntactic condition C on phrase-markers and the semantic condition C′. We may ask whether the following reformulation is empirically equivalent: T applies freely to phrase-markers meeting condition C, but the resulting surface structure must be interpreted by a semantic rule that incorporates C′. This alternative will not always be available, in principle. To my knowledge, it is available in every case that has been suggested. If so, these cases fall under the narrower condition just suggested; they exemplify the filtering effect of semantic interpretive rules and have no bearing on the correctness of the standard theory.

An example is cited in Lakoff (1969c) from Labov. He claims that in certain dialects, the rule of subject-auxiliary inversion can apply only when the sentence in question describes or is a request for information; equivalently, we can say that the rule applies freely, and the result must be interpreted as such a request—it will be excluded as semantically anomalous if for some reason this interpretation is impossible. As noted earlier (see p. 115), the interpretation of interrogatives in general depends upon surface structure.

Note the analogy to the discussion of well-formedness in section 1.

7.5

This discussion does not exhaust all of the examples that have been proposed to try to show the necessity for richer devices than those permitted by EST. In a sense, any unsolved problem, any collection of phenomena that remain unexplained, constitutes a potential example of this sort, and there are, needless to say, many such cases. However, of the arguments that seek to establish some specific positive conclusion, I know of none more compelling than those that have been reviewed here.

8.1

To summarize briefly, the standard theory has been shown to have certain defects. Two general proposals for remedying these defects have been discussed: EST and generative semantics. When unclarities are removed, it seems to me that these approaches differ in three essential ways: with respect to (a) lexical insertion, (b) derivational constraints, and (c) the ordering of lexical and nonlexical transformations.

As to (a), EST keeps to the assumption of the standard theory that lexical items enter into deep structures in positions dominated by lexical categories, where each lexical item contains an intrinsic account of meaning of a sort that is little understood in detail. I have no doubt that the lexicon itself has an internal structure (for example, in the case of "semantic fields"). The semantic characterization of lexical items and the structures in which they appear can be given in terms of phrase-markers and transformations, for the uninteresting reason that virtually anything intelligible can be presented in these terms. This is of course a weakness, not a strength of this mode of expression, to be overcome, one hopes, as more insight is gained into the detailed structure of the lexicon.

In contrast, generative semantics maintains that lexical items replace phrase-markers that express their meaning. This is an attractive idea, and if it were tenable, there would be good reason to take it very seriously as one approach to the description of meaning. Unfortunately, it does not seem tenable. As noted earlier, the "phrase-markers" that are replaced in lexical-insertion operations vary in form without discernible limit, and no comprehensible proposal has been put forth about such a simple matter as how a lexical item in an embedded sentence can be associated with its semantic representation (in particular, the presuppositions expressed, in the case of verbs). Therefore, this thesis, for the moment, seems to be at best a notational proposal with little motivation or support.

With regard to (b), there are two kinds of constraints to be considered. As to constraints internal to derivations, EST maintains that there are none (beyond transformations and general conditions on transformations), whereas generative semantics, in the formulations considered here, suggests that further conditions are permitted (freely, at least so far as the published literature indicates). Since there seem to be no plausible cases to justify richer devices, the narrower theory is to be preferred. As to constraints relating semantic representations and derivations, EST holds that there is only one category of such "constraints" — namely, certain specific aspects of surface (or shallow) structure are relevant to semantic interpretation. Generative semantics again permits richer devices. Every rule of interpretation mapping surface (or shallow) structure into some aspect of meaning can be described as a "derivational constraint" (i.e., a "rule of grammar"), but not conversely. Unless examples are presented to justify the extra wealth of theoretical devices permitted in generative semantics, the narrower theory is again to be preferred, for reasons discussed in section 2.2. There seems to me to be no such justification.

The ordering of lexical and nonlexical transformations seems to me to be probably the most interesting outstanding issue. For the moment, I see no empirical reason to reject the more restrictive, hence preferable, theory that restricts the ordering to lexical followed by nonlexical, uniformly. Furthermore, there seem to be strong empirical reasons in favor of this narrower hypothesis—namely, the syntactic and semantic generalizations that are formulable in terms of deep structure, but not, apparently, otherwise.

In short, it seems to me that in the few areas of substantive difference, generative semantics has been taking the wrong course. But to a certain extent, the differences between these two approaches are hardly more than notational, hence of no serious concern.

8.2

The basic property of transformations is that they map phrase-markers into phrase-markers. Each transformation applies to a phrase-marker on the basis of the formal configurations expressed in it, and quite independently of the meanings or grammatical relations expressed by these formal configurations. Thus such sentences as *John received the book, John read the book, John expected the book to be good, John gave Bill the book,* and so on, undergo the passive transformation in exactly the same way. The transformation applies blindly to any phrase-marker of the proper form, caring nothing about meanings or grammatical relations. This situation is typical; I know of no exceptions, and no counterarguments that amount to more than terminological revision, although some intriguing proposals have been put forward and should obviously be explored.

These formal operations meet fairly restrictive conditions of the sort I have mentioned. As far as I know, the trivial output conditions of the standard theory suffice (but see note 12). Furthermore, the initial phrase-markers of syntactically motivated derivations meet the conditions of a context-free grammar which is "projected" from the basic categories N, V, A by phrase structure schemata. I see no reason to weaken the condition of the standard theory that lexical insertion precedes all such transformations; rather, the evidence supports this assumption. Thus it seems to me that deep structure is a well-defined level which meets the phrase structure conditions of the base rules, defines the proper contexts for lexical insertion, and provides the appropriate grammatical relations for interpretation in terms of "semantic relations" or "conceptual structures."

There seems to me to be no justification for any enrichment of the theory to permit other devices for "constraining derivations," i.e., other kinds of rules. Specifically, there seem to me to be no persuasive examples of "global derivational constraints," beyond those permitted in EST. Many aspects of meaning (scope and order of logical elements, coreference, focus and certain types of presupposition) seem to involve surface (and perhaps shallow) structure in an essential way.

A central idea in much of structural linguistics was that the formal devices of language should be studied independently of their use. The earliest work in transformational-generative grammar took over a version of this thesis, as a working hypothesis. I think it has been a fruitful hypothesis. It seems that grammars contain a substructure of perfectly formal rules operating on phrase-markers in narrowly circumscribed ways. Not only are these rules independent of meaning or sound in their function, but it may also be that the choice of these devices by the language learner (i.e., the choice of grammar on the basis of data) may be independent, to a significant extent, of conditions of meaning and use. If we could specify the extent precisely, the working hypothesis would become a true empirical hypothesis. Such an effort may be premature. It does, however, seem noteworthy that the extensive studies of meaning and use that have been undertaken in recent years have not—if the foregoing analysis is correct—given any serious indication that questions of meaning and use are involved in the functioning or choice of grammars in ways beyond those considered in the earliest speculations about these matters—say, in Chomsky (1957).

There is, of course, no doubt that language is designed for use. The study of language form will ultimately find its place in a broader framework that will incorporate considerations of meaning and use, just as the study of grammar will ultimately find its place in a richer investigation of how knowledge of language is acquired. I believe that the work that I have been discussing here will prove to be of lasting impact and importance, whether its general hypotheses turn out to be correct or not, in that it has redirected the attention of linguists to a wide range of semantic considerations that must be integrated into the general theory of language. These questions have been disregarded for far too long, and the study of language can surely be advanced and enriched by serious concern for these topics, as is illustrated by much of the work that I have reviewed.

Very roughly, this seems to me a fair assessment of the state of the theory of transformational generative grammar—at the moment. Obviously, any such assessment must be quite tentative and imprecise at crucial points. I will be very surprised if in a similar review several years from now, or perhaps next week, I will not want to present a rather different picture—surprised, and not a little disappointed as well.

NOTES

I am indebted to Ray Dougherty, Ray Jackendoff, Morris Halle, Jay Kesser, and John Ross for very useful comments.

[1] Of the latter two, the first deals with German, and the second is based on some general observations about word order by Greenberg. Arguments concerning the German auxiliary bear on English only if one is willing to make some general assumptions about translatability of rules that seem to me unwarranted. Ross argues that Greenberg's data could be explained on the assumption that auxiliaries are main verbs. Evidently, the force of the explanation will depend on the independent evidence for the assumption. In this paper, at least, little is presented.

[2] It is misleading to put the matter in this way, because the notion "feature" had not been developed for syntax at that time. What was proposed was a notational device that would now be interpreted as a feature. I have restated Ross's proposal, treating his category V as a feature [+V]. Nothing turns on this in the present connection.

[3] I will not go on here to discuss Ross's specific arguments. I find them unconvincing. To cite just one case, he argues if *have* and *be* are [+ stative] (hence verbs), we can account for the fact that they are embedded after *seem* by simply requiring that the latter requires a [+ stative] complement. But there is a still simpler way to account for the facts, namely, to place no condition at all on *seem*: structures that can be sentences in isolation can be embedded as sentential complements of *seem*, a conclusion which is natural enough if one interprets *seem* semantically as a predicate having a proposition as argument.

Point by point, the other arguments seem to me equally inconclusive.

[4] The assumption is not uncontroversial, but I will not discuss the matter here. For a strong argument that it is false, see Bresnan (1971).

[5] For some discussion, see Ross (1967) and Chomsky (1968), particularly chapter 2, note 11). The first reference to the possibility that history of derivation may be relevant to deletion is in Lees (1960).

[6] More precisely, "shallow structures," to use a term first suggested by Postal. I use the term here to refer to the structures that appear prior to the application of what Emonds (1969) calls "root transformations." Overlooking details, the term refers to structures that appear prior to the application of the last cycle of transformational rules—i.e., in English, prior to such operations as auxiliary inversion, interpolation of parenthetical expressions, and other operations that do not appear to meet the narrow constraints on cyclic rules (if Emonds's theory is correct).

[7] Insofar as the concern for discovery procedures can be reformulated in these terms, American structuralism of the 1940's was surely on the right track, in principle—see Chomsky (1968) for discussion.

[8] We may, nevertheless, be forced to this regression on empirical grounds, by the discovery that this additional latitude is required for descriptive adequacy.

[9] Or other counterarguments of the sort discussed in Chomsky (1964), Postal (1968).

[10] To be sure, general metatheoretic considerations of "simplicity," "plausibility," and so on might count against him, but it must be emphasized that these are so little understood as to be hardly operative.

[11] One sometimes hears a similar argument put in this way: true, there is no general notion of "simplicity of linguistic theory" to which we can appeal,

but surely if we have a theory with a certain range of theoretical apparatus, and another with all of this and more in addition, the first is preferable. This sounds plausible, until one begins to ask how "theoretical apparatus" is measured. Suppose we have a theory stating that grammars contain rules, and a second, more elaborate theory is proposed holding that they have transformational and phonological rules, with their particular properties. There is no doubt which of the two theories is to be preferred, but which has "more theoretical apparatus"?

[12] Similarly, $\triangle$ cannot appear in a surface structure. Since # and $\triangle$, as defined, are in complementary distribution, they can be identified. I will not consider here some important studies of output conditions the results of which must surely be incorporated into syntactic theory. I have in mind what appear to be graded acceptability conditions involving surface form as discussed in Ross (1967) and conditions on word (and perhaps sentence) structure of the sort investigated in Perlmutter (1968).

[13] Actually, he maintains rather that they are deviant, but less so than (8). The question is not relevant here. What is at issue is only whether in determining (degrees of) deviance we refer to presence of # only in the surface structure, or alternatively, to its presence anywhere in the derivation as a feature of the category X that is deleted. Thus the issue is one that belongs to the theory of interpretation of deviant structures.

[14] This will be sharpened in a moment.

[15] To be sure, the semantic representation could, trivially, be represented as a phrase-marker, e.g., by defining a new symbol σ and forming the phrase-marker $P_1 \sigma$ PR σ Top σ F σ ... (assuming, that is, that PR, Top, F, ..., are represented as phrase-markers). As noted earlier, the notion "phrase-marker" can accommodate an enormous range of possibilities. I return to this matter below.

[16] In one sense; there are several senses that have appeared in the literature, as noted (though inadequately) in Chomsky (1971).

[17] Or perhaps shallow structure—see note 6.

[18] Inconsistently, as just noted, since elsewhere he states that semantic representations are phrase-markers—indeed, this is held to be the fundamental innovation of generative semantics. Lakoff discusses the notion of focus in (1969c), but incorrectly identifies his version of some remarks of Halliday's with the quite different formulation in Chomsky (1971).

[19] Here too, Lakoff's terminology may be misleading. He states that a transformation is a "local constraint," relating two successive terms of a derivation, and that general conditions on application such as those mentioned in sec. 2.1 are "global constraints." This leads him to the conclusion that "global constraints" of a much more general kind would be quite natural. However, the conditions on application are, in fact, not "global constraints" in the general sense, but rather conditions that constrain any pair of successive terms of a derivation, i.e., conditions on local constraints.

Though this has no bearing on the present discussion, it should be noted that Lakoff's definition of "transformation" is incorrect. It would not, for example, distinguish between the identity transformation and a permutation of two nodes of the same category; the pair of "tree conditions" (A-B-A, A-A-B) would define two distinct transformations; etc.

[20] Morgan tries to give some further content to this assumption by arguing that rules forming constituents Q for lexical insertion meet the general conditions on application of transformations (see sec. 2.1, above). Thus he claims that there cannot be a verb *sneep* with a meaning such that *John saw Mary laying a wreath at the grave of the unknown hippie* is a paraphrase of *John*

sneeped Mary laying a wreath at the grave of the unknown, since these conditions prevent *hippie* from being moved out of this position and attached to *see*. But if this were the reason for the impossibility of *sneep* in this sense, then there should be a possible *John sneeped taking a picture of* meaning *John tried taking a picture of a hippie*, since *hippie* is extractable from this context. The latter, however, is equally bad, so that this argument collapses.

On the relation of *kill* to *cause to die*, see Fodor (1970). Notice that the situation with respect to *uncle* is worse than as stated here. If a child were born to a brother-sister marriage, the father would not be its uncle. Laws against incest are no part of the meaning of "uncle." Therefore, Q must contain the information that an uncle is distinct from the father, a fact that requires still more elaborate collapsing rules.

²¹ See Langendoen and Savin (1971) for a discussion of the question of how presuppositions of sentences are determined from assertions and presuppositions of embedded structures.

²² I have discussed this argument in some detail in Chomsky (1971). Lakoff (1969c) claims that the position I tried to reconstruct from McCawley's scattered argument is actually a position that McCawley rejects, rather than the one he proposes. Since Lakoff gives no argument at all for this claim (specifically, no reference to McCawley's text) and does not indicate in what respect my reconstruction, which was based on cited comments from McCawley's text, is inaccurate, I cannot comment on his claim—though it may be correct, for as I noted there explicitly, it is quite difficult to reconstruct McCawley's argument. But the whole matter is irrelevant, since as Lakoff himself admits, "McCawley does not propose a characterization of the necessary operation [i.e., the generalization he claims to be inexpressible, given the assumption of deep structure]. He merely points out that there is a generalization to be stated here, and some such unitary operation is needed to state it." That is, he does not give an argument of the type that Halle presented against taxonomic phonemics, which was precisely my point. Lakoff appears to interpret McCawley's argument as an attempt to show that semantic representations must be given in the notation of phrase-markers. Further interpretation of Lakoff's argument, in this respect, is impossible without some explanation of the limitations he believes to exist in the expressive power of phrase-markers, specifically some explanation of his claim that Katz-style semantic representation could not be translated into this notation. This seems to be his central point, but I find it totally obscure, even apart from the inconsistency noted above (note 18).

²³ Lakoff seems to me in error in his assertion that *dissuade* is synonymous with *persuade not*, for reasons noted earlier (p. 78). The presuppositions differ. This question, however, is not material to the argument, since he assumes that lexical insertion requires reference to presuppositions—see sec. 6.2, above.

²⁴ He suggests the "deeper" source *cause to become not alive*, but this has no bearing on the present argument.

²⁵ Lakoff's argument follows Postal (1970). As far as I can judge, Lakoff correctly extracts the essence of the argument. Postal presents much further evidence which I will not discuss. It seems to me less strong than that which Lakoff presents, involving rather questionable judgments and many interesting but inconclusive observations. For further discussion see Kimball (1970), Bowers (1970), Katz (Forthcoming).

²⁶ Lakoff mentions one argument (attributed to D. Perlmutter) which he

he claims "seems to provide clear and incontrovertible evidence" that lexical insertion must follow certain transformations. In Spanish, we have normal noun-adjective agreement in *Mi madre y mi padre son respectivamente alta y bajo* ("My mother and my father are tall [fem.sg.] and short [masc.sg.] respectively"). He claims that in certain dialects the corresponding form with *padres* ('parents') would be *Mis padres son respectivamente alta y bajo* ("My parents are tall [fem.sg.] and short [masc.sg.] respectively"). He concludes, therefore, that the rule inserting *padres* for *madre y padre* must follow the transformational rule of adjective-noun agreement.

The argument is based on the assumption that such *respectively*-constructions are derived by transformation from conjunctions, e.g., the above from *Mi madre es alta y mi padre es bajo.* This assumption, however, untenable. Consider, for example, the problem of deriving in this way: *The successive descendants of my fruit fly will be heavier, respectively, than the successive descendants of yours,* or any case involving an infinite set or finite set of unknown size. Many other arguments are given in Dougherty (1968, 1970). Thus the gender assignments noted by Lakoff are not explained in his terms in any event. If his empirical observations are accurate, it would appear that gender agreement may be a matter of surface interpretation, perhaps similar to determination of coreference. This would seem not unnatural.

[27] Obviously, this is only a first approximation and further refinements are necessary. Thus certain phrases—for example, *any beaver with teeth*—can appear only with one interpretation. This fact is irrelevant to the point at issue, since it requires comparable qualifications in both of the approaches being compared. If we choose to preserve the simplest syntax, with free choice of subject and predicate, the deviance of *Any beaver with teeth is building a dam* (etc.) would be attributed to the filtering effect of the semantic rules.

[28] To prove the point it would be necessary to demonstrate that there does not exist a way to capture the relevant generalization within the alternative framework. The formulations are, for the moment, too loose to permit a demonstration of any such proposition.

[29] Jackendoff's point is strengthened by the observation that determination of such properties as generic-specific seems to depend in part on late, perhaps surface, structure (consider, e.g., such examples as *John is hunting a tiger, There is a tiger that John is hunting; John writes poems, There are poems that John writes;* etc.). Notice also that the regularity exhibited by (36) cannot be a matter of "output conditions" on surface or shallow structures, even if such conditions exist, since it holds only prior to the application of such transformations as passive—i.e., it holds of deep structures.

[30] For detailed discussion, see Chomsky (1970).

[31] Case (v) presupposes that *John is surprised at Bill's antics* is, in effect, involved in the structure underlying *Bill's antics surprise John.* For discussion, see Chomsky (1970), where it is suggested that the latter is a causative of the former. An apparent counterexample to the generalization just formulated is that there are nominals such as *the destruction of the city by the enemy* and *the city's destruction by the enemy* that correspond to passives. However, there are good independent reasons to suppose that the passive is applied to the nominal rather than nominalization being applied to the passive in such cases. See again Chomsky (1970) for discussion. As noted there, the two components of the passive transformation apply to noun phrases independently of whether these noun phrases correspond to sentences (are nominalizations). Emonds (1969) gives a motivated explanation for the fact that in the case of the nominal, either

one or both of the two components of the passive transformation may apply, whereas in the case of sentences, both must apply. Thus there is no passive sentence corresponding to *the destruction of the city by the enemy.*

[32] For details, see again Chomsky (1970). It is suggested there that there may be still more general similarities in the internal structure of noun phrase, verb phrase, and adjective phrase, reflected in higher-order schemata. Interesting arguments in support of this speculation are presented by Bowers (1968, 1969), Selkirk (1970), who point out syntactic relations between qualifiers of adjectives and determiners of nouns [specifiers, in the terminology of Chomsky (1970)]. There are also certain semantic similarities among specifiers. For example, the generic-specific property of sentences is partially determined by choice of determiners and verbal auxiliaries (specifiers of nouns and verbs, respectively, in this framework), and it has often been noted that tense systems share certain of the referential functions of determiners—see, for example, McCawley's discussion (1971) of respects in which auxiliaries have a quantifier-like structure.

If these proposals stand, we can formulate an abstract condition on the base component of any grammar, namely, that it generate structures which, in a well-defined sense, are projected from the basic lexical categories N, V, and A, with only certain variation possible (e.g., in range of complements, in order of elements). Furthermore, there is reason to believe that each of these lexical categories is to be taken as a bundle of syntactic features (two features would provide the categories: N, V, and A, everything else, where N and A share a feature, and V and A share a feature). It seems plausible that such abstract conditions form part of universal grammar, and that they determine the range of potential variation in base structures.

[33] And leading to surface structures meeting the output condition of (4c). It should be noted that there is no evidence that there exist output conditions of the sort presupposed by Lakoff's suggestion. Hence, even if, contrary to fact, it were tenable, it would require new and otherwise unmotivated syntactic devices.

[34] See Chomsky (1970) for discussion. PPA's are not discussed there, but the necessary extension is fairly clear. The generalization of grammatical relations is necessary quite apart from the question of control of complement subject deletion, as is the assumption that NP and S function as the domain of transformations. Observe that trivial modifications are required in the rule of complement subject deletion, under this analysis.

[35] Others have been proposed orally, but I know of none that have any force, and since they have not been presented publicly, I will not take the time to discuss them.

[36] This characteristic argues against the transformational derivation for reasons noted earlier in connection with derived nominals. That is, on the latter assumption it would merely be an accident that the PPA constructions share formal properties stateable by simple phrase structure constraints, given that they arise by transformation from very different sources. On the other hand, the argument for a lexicalist approach is far stronger in the case of derived nominals because of the clustering of properties noted earlier.

[37] Given, that is, his assumption that meaning is determined by the initial phrase-marker of a derivation. Notice that the distinction in meaning suffices to undermine Postal's inference from sharing of formal properties (selectional relations, etc.) to identity of source. At best, this line of argument is extremely weak [see Chomsky (1970) for some discussion], and as these examples show, is untenable in the present instance.

[38] Postal discusses such cases, arguing that they show that "generic" NP's such as *Americans* or *machine-guns* "involve the names of sets," so that PPA's are derived from the "natural class" of proper nouns and generic NP's. However, it is unclear how the name of a set is involved in (52i), or in *Americans offered to go to Cuba*, or even in the example that Postal gives to illustrate the point (namely, *Machine-guns are so-called because they fire automatically*—here, as in *Machine-guns misfired*, the phrase *machine-guns* is not used to name a set).

[39] Others are suggested, but as Postal would surely agree, they do not carry much weight.

[40] That is, one cannot say *John kicked the bucket and Bill kicked it too*, meaning both died. It should be noted, incidentally, that idioms would appear to be a difficult problem for generative semantics in the first place. An interpretive system can simply provide interpretive rules for certain well-formed phrases, but the generative semantics approach will leave unexplained the fact that, characteristically idioms have normal grammatical structures: e.g., if *kick the bucket* is introduced by transformation from an underlying phrase-marker *die* or *become not alive*, why does it have the internal structure of a normal verb phrase? The problem is analogous to several that we have discussed earlier.

Notice, incidentally, that however *lighthouse keeper* enters a derivation, it must be assigned its meaning by an *ad hoc* rule, since it is not synonymous with *person who keeps a lighthouse*—i.e., *keep* in this idiom does not, strictly speaking, have exactly the same meaning as in *John kept the gift, keep house*, etc.

[41] The examples are from Matthews (1968). He notes that such sentences as (54iv), though perhaps dubious in isolation, are motivated by other examples, such as *The window won't break, even with a hammer, The window broke easily with a hammer*, etc.

[42] It appears that he construes this as a one-step mapping, not decomposable into iterated rules of category I.

[43] For several arguments, see Dougherty (Forthcoming). In particular, Dougherty shows that Fillmore's rules of preposition-insertion, when properly extended, require a condition that amounts to an independent reformulation of the passive transformation, and he discusses other difficulties as well. Ross has noted other problems (personal communication). Thus the assignment of the correct passives to such sentences as *John argued with Bill about money (about money with Bill)* leads to considerable complexity, on Fillmore's assumption.

[44] As further support, Fillmore claims that when the possessor is extracted by the subject-choosing rule, the possessive pronoun *its* must be left as a residue. Thus we cannot say *The car broke the window with a fender*. I doubt the accuracy of this observation; we can surely say *The car hit the window with both fenders*. In any event, the force of the observation is unclear, even to the extent that it may be accurate. Thus if something like (65) is taken as deep structure, the choice of *its* will be determined by general rules that are independently needed, as in *John lost his way, John hit the window with his head*, etc. See note 45.

[45] Furthermore, the derivation of (71i) from (73) shows that *his* must be introduced quite apart from the rule of selection of possessor of the instrument phrase.

[46] Fillmore cites only one other example of the "explanatory force" of case grammar, namely, in connection with certain restrictions on conjunction. Dougherty (Forthcoming) shows that at the very least, more cases will be needed to account for the restrictions on conjunction. I suspect that the restrictions on conjunction do not involve cases at all; rather, there is a gradation of acceptance

case grammar, namely, in connection with certain restrictions on conjunction. Dougherty (forthcoming) shows that at the very least, more cases will be needed to accout for the restrictions on conjunction. I suspect that the restrictions on conjunction do not involve cases at all; rather, there is a gradation of acceptance of conjunction depending on a variety of properties of conjoined elements.

[47] Actually, a further analysis is suggested for *John's nose*, but this is irrelevant here.

[48] There is, of course, the sentence *Mary pulled John by the nose*, but this surely must have a very different source, if meaning is to be expressed correctly. Similarly, compare *Mary pulled John's hair, Mary pulled John by the hair, Mary pulled John on the hair*, etc.

[49] For some very interesting discussion of how semantic relations can be determined from deep structure, and some possible semantic and syntactic consequences, see Jackendoff (1969, pp. 74ff), developing some ideas of Gruber (1965).

[50] See also earlier work of his cited there.

[51] For the purposes of comparison of theories, nothing is lost by this restriction. Comparable complications arise in the alternative theories as further complexity is introduced.

[52] The only function of the antecedent is to identify the noun to which the quantifier is attached. Thus we could just as well eliminate the antecedents *men* and *books* in (77'), (78') (79) and assign appropriate indices to the two predicates *many* and *few*, and the words *men* and *books*, in the most deeply embedded sentence. Then the rule of quantifier lowering can be simplified, since it need not delete the antecedent. Taking the argument one step further, we can eliminate the rule and the indices entirely by assigning the quantifier to the noun phrases with which it shares an index. With these relatively slight modifications we return to a deep structure of a familiar sort, rather like the surface structure. As already noted, it can be related directly to the pseudo-quantificational form (80).

Lakoff notes that in some cases the quantifier appears in the predicate (*The men who read books were many*), though of course in some cases it cannot (**The men who read the book were a lot, *The enthusiasm that he showed me was little*). I see no way to construct an argument, one way or another, on the basis of these observations. It is worth noting that when the quantifier appears in predicate position, its semantic relation to the subject is quite different from any other subject-predicate relation.

[53] To formulate such a condition precisely and completely is no easier than in the case of the other general conditions on transformations, most of which have unexplained inadequacies. But, as in the other cases, the general lines of a formulation can be stated, subject to further sharpening.

[54] I overlook, as irrelevant to this distinction, a more precise statement of what *to be here for a month* means.

[55] Observe that there are two questions intermingled here, one having to do with the universality of the maxims, the second with the question whether they belong to "grammar" or to some other study, perhaps a theory of performance.

[56] Note that *nothing* must receive main stress in (103), as distinct from *something* in *John and Bill are arguing about something*, which is normally unstressed. Some connections between position of main stress and presupposition (in one sense) are discussed in Chomsky (1971).

[57] Again, the matter of stress placement is critical. Consider, in the same connection, the presupposition and assertion of the negation of (97).

[58] Lakoff and Ross (1969) argue that a paraphrase with sentence negation always exists, and conclude that constituent negation is therefore an unnecessary notion. The argument has no force. By the same logic, we could show that sentence negation is an unnecessary notion, since there is always a paraphrase in terms of constituent negation (i.e., *not*-S can always be paraphrased as *It is false that S* or *It is not the case that S*, where we interpret *not the case* (=*false*) as "constituent negation" (noting that *It is not the case that S* can be denied by *It is* not *not the case that S*). Neither argument proves anything. The interesting question has to do with the rules and principles that determine the interpretation of the syntactic forms, and the possibilities of paraphrase in one or another canonical notation tell us virtually nothing about this.

[59] I leave open the question whether they are syntactically ill-formed, or syntactically well-formed but ruled out by the filtering function of semantic interpretive rules.

REFERENCES

Published items are identified by date of publication, Mimeographed items by date of appearance. Therefore, the dates do not always indicate order of original appearance.

Akmajian, A. 1970. On deriving cleft sentences from pseudo-cleft sentences. *Linguistic Inquiry* 1:149-68.

Bowers, J.S. 1968. Adjectives and adverbs in English. Mimeographed.

_____.1969. Surface structure interpretation in English superlatives. Mimeographed.

_____. 1970. A note on "remind." *Linguistic Inquiry* 1:559-60.

Bresnan, J. 1971. Sentence stress and syntactic transformations. *Language* 47:257-81.

Chomsky, N. 1957. *Syntactic structures*. The Hague: Mouton.

_____. 1964*a*. Current issues in linguistic theory. In *Proceedings of the Ninth International Congress of Linguists*, ed. H. Lunt. The Hague: Mouton.

_____. 1964*b*. Current issues in linguistic theory. In *The structure of language: readings in the philosophy of language*, ed. J. Fodor and J. J. Katz. Englewood Cliffs, N. J.: Prentice-Hall.

_____. 1964*c*. *Current issues in linguistic theory*. The Hague: Mouton.

_____. 1965. *Aspects of the theory of syntax*. Cambridge: M.I.T. Press.

_____. 1968. *Language and mind*. New York: Harcourt, Brace.

_____. 1970. Remarks on nominalization. In *Readinsg in English transformational grammar*, ed. R. Jacobs and P. Rosenbaum. Boston: Ginn.

_____. 1971. Deep structure, surface structure, and semantic interpretation. In *Semantics: an interdisciplinary reader in philosophy, linguistics, anthropology, and psychology*, ed. D. Steinberg and L. Jakobovits. London: Cambridge University Press.

_____, and Halle, M. 1968. *The sound pattern of English*. New York: Harper & Row.

Culicover, P. 1971. Syntactic and semantic investigations. Ph.D. dissertation. Cambridge: M.I.T.

Dougherty, R. C. 1968. A transformational grammar of coördinate conjoined structures. Ph.D. dissertation. Cambridge: M.I.T.

_____. 1970. A grammar of coördinate conjoined structures: I. *Language* 46: 850-98.

_____. Forthcoming. Review of E. Bach and R. Harms (eds.), *Universals in linguistic theory. Foundations of Language*.

Emonds, J. E. 1969. Root and structure-preserving transformations. Ph.D. dissertation. Cambridge: M.I.T.

Fillmore, C. J. 1968. The case for case. In *Universals in linguistic theory*, ed. E. Bach and R. T. Harms. New York: Holt, Rinehart.

_____. 1969. Verbs of judging: an exercise in semantic description. *Papers in Linguistics* 1:91-117.

Fodor, J. 1970. Three reasons for not deriving "kill" from "cause to die." *Linguistic Inquiry* 1:429-38.

Gruber, J. 1965. Studies in lexical relations. Ph.D. dissertation. Cambridge: M.I.T.

Halle, M. 1959. *The sound pattern of Russian*. The Hague: Mouton.

Helke, M. 1971. The grammar of English reflexives. Ph.D. dissertation. Cambridge: M.I.T.

Jackendoff, R. S. 1969. Some rules of semantic interpretation for English. Ph.D. dissertation. Cambridge: M.I.T.

Katz, J. J. 1966. *The philosophy of language.* New York: Harper & Row.

_____ . 1967. Recent issues in semantic theory. *Foundations of Language* 3:124-94.

_____ . Forthcoming. Some things Kuhn never told us.

_____ , and Postal, P. M. 1964. *An integrated theory of linguistic descriptions.* Cambridge: M.I.T. Press.

Kimball, J. 1970. "Remind" remains. *Linguistic Inquiry* 1:511-24.

Lakoff, G. 1968. On instrumental adverbs and the concept of deep structure. *Foundations of Language* 4:4-29.

_____ . 1969a. Presuppositions and relative grammaticality. In *Studies in philosophical linguistics*, ed. W. Todd, series 1.

_____ . 1969b. On derivational constraints. In *Papers from the fifth regional meeting of the Chicago Linguistic Society*, ed. R. I. Binnick et al. Chicago: University of Chicago, Department of Linguistics.

_____ . 1969c. On generative semantics. Mimeographed.

_____ , and Ross, J.R. 1969. Another case of propositional negation. *Phonetics laboratory notes*, vol. 4. Ann Arbor: University of Michigan.

Langendoen, D. T. and Savin, H. B. 1971. The projection problem for presuppositions. In *Studies in linguistic semantics*, ed. C. J. Fillmore and D. T. Langendoen. New York: Holt, Rinehart.

Lees, R. B. 1960. *The grammar of English nominalizations.* The Hague: Mouton.

Matthews, G. H. 1968. Le cas échéant. Mimeographed.

McCawley, J. D. 1968a. The role of semantics in a grammar. In *Universals in linguistic theory*, ed. E. Bach and R. T. Harms. New York: Holt, Rinehart.

_____ . 1968b. Lexical insertion in a transformational grammar without deep structure. In *Papers from the fourth regional meeting of the Chicago Linguistic Society*, ed. B. Darden et al. Chicago: University of Chicago, Department of Linguistics.

_____ . 1971. Tense and time reference in English. In *Studies in Linguistic semantics*, ed. C. J. Fillmore and D. T. Langendoen. New York: Holt, Rinehart.

Morgan, J. L. 1969. On arguing about semantics. *Papers in Linguistics* 1:49-70.

Perlmutter, D. 1968. Deep and surface structure constraints in syntax. Ph.D. dissertation. Cambridge: M.I.T.

Postal, P. M. 1968. *Aspects of phonological theory.* New York: Harper & Row.

_____ . 1969. Anaphoric islands. In *Papers from the fifth regional meeting of the Chicago Linguistic Society*, ed. R. I. Binnick et al. Chicago: University of Chicago, Department of Linguistics.

_____ . 1970. On the surface verb "remind." *Linguistic Inquiry* 1:37-120.

Ross, J. R. 1967. Constraints on variables in syntax. Ph.D. dissertation. Cambridge: M.I.T.

_____ . 1969a. Auxiliaries as main verbs. In *Studies in philosophical linguistics*, ed. W. Todd, series 1.

_____ . 1969b. Guess who? In *Papers from the fifth regional meeting of the Chicago Linguistic Society*, ed. R. I. Binnick et al. Chicago: University of Chicago, Department of Linguistics.

_____ . 1970. On declarative sentences. In *Readings in English transformational grammar,* ed. R. Jacobs and P. Rosenbaum. Boston: Ginn.

Selkirk, L. 1970. On the determiner systems of noun phrase and adjective phrase. Mimeographed.

Weinreich, U. 1966. Explorations in semantic theory. In *Current trends in linguistics*, vol. 3, ed. T. A. Sebeok. The Hague: Mouton.

Chapter 4

THE BEST THEORY

Paul M. Postal

I. STRANDS OF AGREEMENT

Beyond the multifarious disagreements which, as of the present, divide even those investigators of linguistic structure who regard themselves as operating within the framework of generative grammar, one may, I think, safely pick out at least the following general points of agreement:

(1) (a) A language includes an infinite set of representations of meanings: call them *semantic representations*.
   (b) A language includes an infinite set of representations of pronunciations; call them *phonetic representations*.
   (c) A language includes an infinite set of representations of bracketed strings of words: call them *surface structures*.

To the extent that (1) does indeed represent part of what is agreed on, there is acceptance within the generative camp that in the most general terms a language must be regarded as a system containing at least three distinct levels of structure:

(2) Semantic representation
|
Surface structure
|
Phonetic structure

No doubt the solidest accomplishments in generative work[1] deal with the specification of the relations between surface structure and phonetic structure, that is, with phonology and morphophonemics. But I will ignore that subject almost totally in this discussion. I am concerned rather with what can be said about the relations between semantic representation and surface structure. This area is currently subject to pervasive controversy, controversy which is deep enough and fundamental enough to call into question most *substantive* assumptions which have over the last dozen years or so been accepted within generative grammatical work.

I said in the preceding sentence "most." One thing which I think all agree on is:

(3) In the overall mapping mediating between semantic representations and surface structures, rules of the type developed by N. Chomsky and called "grammatical transofrmations" play a significant role.

In the period since the publication of his *Syntactic Structures* (Chomsky 1957), an immense amount of research involving such rules has been carried out and, phonology aside, they represent the most highly elaborated and conceptually articulated type of linguistic apparatus. These rules can be characterized briefly as operating on certain kinds of structures, *trees,* or single-rooted well-formed labeled bracketings of elements, mapping one tree into another. Thus transformations have, as output, structures formally of the same type as their input.

It is agreed that surface structures are the final output of the set of transformational rules, hence that surface structures are trees. It follows from this that a subpart (*N. B.*, not necessarily a *proper* subpart, hence much of what follows) of the mapping between semantic representation and surface structure is given by a sequence of transformational rules generating for each sentence S_i a sequence of grammatical trees $(G_{i_1}, \ldots, G_{i_n})$, where G_{i_n} is the surface structure of S_i and where G_{i_1} is the input to the transformational rules for S_i. Let us refer, in a way which is here neutral, but historically loaded, to G_{i_1} as the *deep structure* of S_i. In this terminology, then, the deep structure of a sentence is no more and no less than that tree which is input to the first transformational rule which applies in the derivation of that sentence.

It seems to follow from (1) and (2) that there is agreement that a *grammar* of some language can be regarded as a finite system[2] which generates the correct triples of semantic representations, surface structures, and phonetic representations. However, given the restriction of topic here, let us use the term *grammar* to refer to a finite system whose function is to generate pairs of semantic representations and surface structures. Notice that a system which generates the correct set of such pairs also necessarily generates the correct class of semantic representations and the correct class of surface structures. That is, a system of the type in question defines for a language L all of

(4) (a) the class of well-formed semantic representations of L;
    (b) the class of well-formed surface structures of L; and
    (c) the class of well-formed surface structure-semantic representation pairings of L.

Furthermore, given (3), there is inferrable agreement that a subpart of the mapping between semantic representations and surface structures is carried out by a sequence of transformational rules. Thus:

(5) Semantic representation

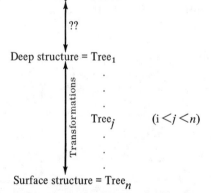

Such a diagram leaves open then just what kind of operations relate the deep structure of a sentence—that is, the input to the first transformational rule applied in the generation of that sentence—and the semantic representation of that sentence.

II. AN IMPLICATION FROM THE AGREEMENT:
THE BEST THEORY, VERSION I

Diagram (5) represents an outline of a certain system, part of whose structure is agreed on, part of whose structure is not. Given what is agreed on, together with the accepted goals—that is, constructing a system which accomplishes (4)—one is in a position to ask certain *a priori* questions. Namely, independent of any factual matters beyond those already implicit in (1) through (5), what is, conceptually and logically, the best possible formulation of the nature of grammar which replaces (5) by something without question marks? In other words, given the constraints imposed by what is already accepted about grammar, what would be the best possible overall theory of a system which generates pairs of semantic representations and surface structures? The answer to this question is, I think, clearer than one might assume.

We agree that a system which generates semantic representations and surface structures must contain a subset of mappings which are grammatical transformations, generating sequences of structures, each of which is a formally defined object known as a tree. The most conceptually elegant, and hence *a priori* most desirable, theory would be one which replaced the question marks in (5) not by new, distinct kinds of operations or rules, but rather *which took this part of the mapping also to be carried out by transformations.* The consequences of this step are, minimally, that it is necessary to regard semantic representations as consisting formally of the same kind of tree representations as surface structures, deep structures, and the structures intermediate between them, and, further, that deep structure, as defined above (but not as traditionally defined, of course)[3] becomes identical to semantic representation, or possibly to a subpart of this.[4]

Hence one replaces (5) by:

(6) Semantic representation = (Presuppositions ?) + [Deep structure = Tree$_1$]

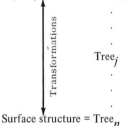

Surface structure = Tree$_n$

Diagram (6) is thus the outline of a theory of the following type. It contains a set of *base rules* of some here-unspecified type, which generate an infinite set of semantic representations in tree form. And it contains a set of transformational rules which successively deform (subparts of) the base semantic trees into surface structure trees. It thus contains two types of rule and one type of basic structural representation entity—namely, trees.

A view like that just outlined is, of course, not at all unreal. Just such a conception of grammar has been proposed by Bach, Gruber, and most extensively, McCawley, and a significant modification to which I return below has been discussed by G. Lakoff,[5] all under the unfortunate rubric of "generative semantics." I say "unfortunate" because this terminology does not really highlight what is special to (6). Indeed, it wrongly suggests to the unwary and naive the idea that a crucial notion of this theory has something to do with directionality of mappings, when in fact such directionality is meaningless. What is crucial, of course, is that, as against other views of generative grammar which have been proposed, this schema assumes that the full mapping between surface structure and semantic representation is *homogeneous*, i.e., carried by a sequence of rules of one type, transformations, with no point where some other type of operation plays a role. A consequence is the view that semantic representations and surface structures are formally homogeneous – i.e., that they are trees—and that the base rules have as output semantic representations per se rather than some kind of semantically or phonetically arbitrary deep structures. It follows that no sharp line between "syntax" and "semantics" is drawn. Because of these properties, I will refer to the framework outlined in (6) as *Homogeneous I.*[6]

It is not my intention or goal at this point to try to justify any single part, still less any extended portion, of the Homogeneous I framework in *empirical* terms. What I wish to suggest briefly is that because of its *a priori* logical and conceptual properties, this theory of grammar—or rather, a significant though limited revision of it which I will discuss in the next section—is the basic one which generative linguists should operate from as an investigatory framework, and that it should be abandoned, if at all, only under the strongest pressures of empirical disconfirmation. In short, I suggest that the Homogeneous I framework has a rather special logical position *vis-à-vis* its possible competitors within the generative framework, a position which makes the choice of this theory obligatory in the absence of direct empirical disconfirmation. The reasons for this are quite simple, and in effect already touched on.

I do not wish to pose as an expert on the philosophy of science, nor to suggest that theoretical disputes in linguistics can in general find solutions in the philosophy of science. Still, certain points are relatively clear. Given two distinct theories of the same domain, one may make a clear choice between them if certain logical relations hold between these theories. In particular, if the theoretical machinery of one theory is included in that of the second, but the second has, in addition, certain additional theoretical machinery, then, all other things being equal, the first, most conceptually restricted theory is to be chosen. That is, the conceptual elaboration[7] of the second theory can only be justified on the basis of direct empirical arguments showing the need for this extension. In general, this support will take the form of evidence showing that certain facts in the domain cannot be explained using only the original apparatus provided by the first theory, but that the facts in question do receive a formulation in terms of the additional theoretical apparatus provided by the second.[8]

With everything held constant, one must always pick as the preferable theory that proposal which is most restricted conceptually and most constrained in the theoretical machinery it offers. One obvious reason for this is that, given any theory which seems adequate for some domain, it is always possible to construct a new theory, identical to the old except that it has an additional component of perfectly useless conceptual apparatus. To take an extreme example, given any biological account of human body structure, one can propose a new theory whose verifiability is not distinct as follows. The new theory consists of the original theory plus a set of claims that every normal human has two heads, with the proviso, however, that the second, hitherto ignored, head has certain special properties which render it unamenable to direct perception by either human senses or the best instruments now available. It can be suggested that the second head has its locus in other dimensions. Clearly, the new theory explains everything the old theory did and yet is logically incompatible with it. Some principle is thus required to choose between them. Since all of the empirical facts which support the old theory support the new one as well, and there are no known empirical facts which distinguish them, the choice must be made on theoretical rather than narrow empirical grounds. The relevant principle is the one which requires the minimal conceptual elaboration consistent with the domain of facts, that is, the principle which says in effect that each piece of theoretical machinery needs to be justified.

From this point of view, one can see that, given certain competing theories of a particular domain, some have, from the point of view of theoretical value, a privileged position. Namely, to just the extent that theories can be aligned logically in such a way that they are commensurable and one is, as it were, included in another, the theoretically more impoverished is always more highly valued. Among such theories, the conceptually most restricted is, other things being equal, the best theory.

Returning now to linguistic questions proper, the fact is that Homogeneous I is, in these terms, the best grammatical theory *a priori* possible, given the accepted goals of generating semantic representation-surface structure pairs and the accepted (as of now)[9] empirical fact that part of this pair producing mapping is mediated by transformations. Under these conditions, any theory distinct from Homogeneous I must be conceptually more elaborate, and hence, as we have seen, on *a priori* theoretical grounds, inferior from the point of view of potential truth. Such alternatives must contain additional *types* of rule, additional *types* of linguistic structure, or both. In fact, such *a priori* theoretically inferior theories are quite prevalent and some have the irrelevant apparent virtue of being either or both historically antecedent to or in some sense more widely spread socially than any formulation of Homogeneous I.

For example, the various revisions of a general linguistic theory proposed over the last six years by J. Katz and his sometime collaborators[10] involve not only the conceptual apparatus of Homogeneous I—i.e., base rules, trees, and transformations,—but, in addition, hypothesized semantic representations which are not trees,[11] a unique distinguished level called *deep structure*, and a special class of rules, so-called *projection rules*, which are distinct from grammatical transformations and which serve to relate deep structures to semantic representations. This class of theories, consisting in essence of Katz's revised semantic theories welded onto the earlier nonsemantic transformational syntax of Chomsky, might be called the standard overall view of grammar within the generative framework over the last half-dozen years. A conceptually still more elaborate, and hence *a priori* even less highly valued, theory or set of related theories have been proposed recently by Chomsky, Jackendoff, Dougherty, Akmajian, and others.[12] These writers now conceive of a system which has not only the apparatus of Homogeneous I, the apparatus of deep structure,[13] and the projection rule apparatus of Katz's theories, but, in addition, further types of so-called interpretive rules of, to me, an unclear sort.[14] I emphasize again that I am not *here*[15] raising the question of the empirical adequacy of any of these theories or the subproposals about various aspects of linguistic structure which they contain. What I am trying to stress is that these linguistic theories are not all equal competitors and that on *a priori* methodological grounds some are in need of more justification than others.

As argued above, given the same empirical base, on general grounds one must choose that theory which has the most restricted theoretical makeup. With respect to all competitors, such a theory must be held to be privileged, only to be abandoned in favor of some conceptually more complex alternative in the face of direct empirical evidence showing the need for such additions. But, with respect, for example, to Katz's theories, or those of Chomsky, Jackendoff, etc. mentioned above, Homogeneous I bears just such a relatively superior position with respect to theoretical elaboration. Thus the analogy drawn by McCawley (1968c) between grammatical theories and phonological theories is directly *apropos*. McCawley observed that the theory claiming the existence of a level of autonomous phonemic structure in addition to the obviously required levels of systematic phonemic and phonetic structure is not an equal competitor with a theory advocating only the latter two forms of representation. Special empirical arguments are needed to justify the additional level of structure and the otherwise unnecessary bifurcation of phonological rules which this requires.

Just so, with any theory which claims the existence of special levels of structure beyond surface structure and semantic representation in grammar, or the existence of any special types of rule beyond the base rules and transformations required in a minimal grammatical theory, of which Homogeneous I is a primitive formulation. But the theories of Katz and Chomsky, Jackendoff, etc. are just such theories since they posit at least a special level of deep structure and special kinds of rules over and above the apparatus of Homogeneous I.[16] With respect to this latter theory, then, any of these theories require special empirical justification, as would any other theory with the same logical properties. In other words, from this point of view one can see that one does not, given acceptance of (1) and (3) above, need to provide special justification *for* acceptance of the Homogeneous I framework. One needs rather, if one is so inclined, to provide special justification for *not* accepting it, that is for advocating a conceptually more elaborated view.

A further analogy might help. At the beginning of work on generative grammar, Chomsky and others compared the theoretical adequacy of two competing theories, one a pure phrase structure grammar theory, the other a theory with a phrase structure component supplemented by a transformational overlay. *A priori*, the choice between these two is clear. Since the latter is conceptually far more elaborate and complicated, it must be rejected in the absence of direct empirical evidence showing the need for the posited elaborations.[17] It was thus not at all surprising that there was felt a strong need to show in considerable detail just to what a great extent such evidence was forthcoming. Indeed, much of the early literature on transformational grammar is concerned with just this point, an emphasis which can seem a little odd given the situation today, when the need for transformational rules has come to be largely taken for granted.

III. FILTERS: THE BEST THEORY, VERSION II

Despite its relatively privileged character methodologically, Homogeneous I, like the similarly relatively privileged pure phrase structure theory, can, I think, be definitively shown to be incorrect. As stated, this theory countenances two types of rules, base rules generating underlying semantic trees, and transformations. It has, however, been shown that such a restricted framework cannot, regardless of assumptions about the form of the base rules, generate the correct class of semantic-surface pairs. It is known that in addition a proper theory of grammar must contain a class of rules I shall refer to here as *filters* and which G. Lakoff, in the revision of Homogeneous I referred to above, has discussed in terms of the general notion of *derivational constraint.*

Notice that, in terms of Homogeneous I, one can define the notion *sentence* in one way as any one of the infinite class of sequences of trees generated by the base rules and transformations. Each such sequence will have a semantic representation as initial member and a surface structure as final member. By a filter, I refer to a type of rule which is defined on such sequences and which has the function of marking as ungrammatical or ill-formed sequences which may be perfectly well-formed as far as the base rules and transformations are concerned. Such sequences are marked as ill-formed just because they fail some structural condition which defines the relevant filter.

The best known and no doubt most widely accepted types of filter are those which have generally been called *output conditions* or *surface-structure constraints*. These were apparently first suggested by Ross (1967) and have been most intensively studied and justified by Perlmutter, particularly in his work on clitic sequences in French and Spanish.[18] Briefly, a surface-structure constraint is some structural condition which marks as ill-formed a class (typically infinite) of tree sequences whose surface structures fail some condition definable on a subpart of the grammatical form specified in surface structures. Surface-structure constraints thus have several notable properties:

(7) (a) They are defined on a single level of structure.
  (b) They have an exclusively filtering function rather than the "creative"[19] function of either base rules or transformational rules.
  (c) They are defined on surface structures.

Of these three, (7c) has probably received as much emphasis as any when in fact it is the least significant feature.[20]

Other types of filtering apparatus have not been absent from transformational work over the last several years. For example, the proposals of G. Lakoff and the present writer[21] to use Chomsky's phonological device of rule features to handle lexical exceptions to transformational rules is a proposed filter type with more than passing plausibility. It is also one which cannot be defined on surface structures.[22] However, possibly this filtering device can be defined on a single level of structure if this is specified with logical variables rather than by constants as in the case of the level specification of so-called output conditions. Similarly, it has been proposed that there are deep-structure constraints,[23] that is, filters which specify certain outputs of the base rules as ill-formed. Most notably, the set of constraints on variables in transformational rules of movement, deletion, and feature marking proposed by Ross (1967) form a significant set of filters. Ross's coordinate-structure constraint, for example, throws out derivations in which movement rules operate across the boundaries of true coordinate structures. An initial formalization of this constraint in terms of his general notation for derivational constraints is provided by G. Lakoff (Forthcoming). Other proposals for grammatical filters also exist.[24]

These varied, scattered, unorganized proposals about grammatical filters have led G. Lakoff (1969*b*, Forthcoming), in what is, I believe, a fundamental theoretical clarification, to suggest as a fundamental aspect of linguistic theory the existence of a component of filter rules. Hitherto such rules, while being proposed, have tended to be regarded as desperation devices needed to patch up a sinking description or theory. At this time, then, filters must be taken seriously as a fundamental type of grammatical rule. Most crucially, Lakoff has uncovered a significant empirical basis to show that the class of filters is not limited to single-level types, but, rather, that there exist global filters, those whose statement requires reference to multiple levels of structure within a derivation, that is, to more than one tree. One can hope that a restriction to a maximum of two would suffice.

In fact, a more or less disguised set of multiple-tree filters is in a sense implicit in the rather unconstrained theory of *syntactic features* initiated by Chomsky's proposals in *Aspects of the Theory of Syntax* (1965). For this theory, in conjunction with a view that there are *arbitrary* syntactic features available, allows the coding of properties of early trees into later trees by transformational feature marking. I made use of just such a device in a recent paper (1971), positing a feature [Doom] whose function is exactly to mark in later trees a contrast between certain properties of earlier trees that is otherwise obliterated by intervening cyclically applied rules.[25]

Given the existence of explicit multitree filters, such arbitrary syntactic features can be eliminated, and there are theoretical advantages gained thereby. In particular, such features render more or less contentless the claim that each transformation takes account of only the structure in the immediately preceding tree generated in the sequence of transformationally derived trees. This "don't look back" property of transformations makes an interesting empirical claim which can be rendered substantive again with the elimination of features which code early tree properties into late ones in the absence of structural deformations. That is, under the newer proposals, transformations retain a "semi-Markovian" character, but it is explicitly asserted that filters do not have this property and that these can state "discontinuous" restrictions across noncontiguous trees in a derivation.

In these terms, then, one can propose a reformulation of Homogeneous I as follows. The class of structural descriptions is maintained as before (although no doubt ultimately there will be a radical decrease in the class of possible arbitrary syntactic features,[26] for reasons like those in part described just above, that is, the structural description of a sentence is a sequence of trees. However, the class of grammatical rules is widened to include a set of derivational constraints or filters whose function is exclusively to mark as ill formed a subset of the set of all tree sequences generated by the base rules and transformations alone. As against Homogeneous I, Homogeneous II makes the empirical claim that in general the set of derivations (tree sequences) generated by a theory containing only base rules and transformations is too wide, and that to really characterize a natural language this set must be pared down by filters.

One should add further that a rich set of filters has been implicitly part of transformational theory since the beginning. I refer to what has been called *rule ordering*. One can regard rule ordering as consisting of a set of filters which throw out all derivations, thought of as generated by randomly ordered rules, whose trees are not aligned by a sequence of rules which meet the ordering conditions. A formal account of rule ordering in these terms is given by G. Lakoff (Forthcoming). I note only that this point of view brings out clearly *that ordering statements must be regarded as actual grammatical rules,* a right conclusion, I think, since in many cases ordering statements compete with other types of grammatical apparatus as we shall shortly see. I see no reason whatever for assuming, as in the past, that ordering statements are freely available while other types of statements require justification. This asymmetry has, as far as I know, never been justified.

I would like now to illustrate further the need for filters by discussing briefly a number of cases from English grammar. These will, I hope, reveal something of the scope and variety which such devices seem to manifest.

It was observed many years ago by Fillmore (1965) that indirect object NP based on *for*-prepositional phrases in general behave differently under passivization than indirect object NP based on *to*-prepositional phrases. Hence:

(8) (a) Lou gave a deathray to Celia.
    (b) Lou gave Celia a deathray.
    (c) A deathray was given to Celia by Lou.
    (d) Celia was given a deathray by Lou.

(9) (a) Lou bought a deathray for Celia.
    (b) Lou bought Celia a deathray.
    (c) A deathray was bought for Celia by Lou.
    (d) *Celia was bought a deathray by Lou.

As the contrast between (8d) and (9d) shows, *for*-indirect object NP cannot serve as the basis for passivization. The only solutions ever offered for these facts involve filters. Fillmore's solution was to posit two distinct indirect object movement rules to derive forms like (8b) and (9b) from, respectively, (8a) and (9a). Call these rules To-IO Shift and For-IO Shift. He then proposed that these be ordered with the rule which forms passives as follows:

(10) (a) To-IO Shift
     (b) Passive
     (c) For-IO Shift

Thus, shifted *for*-indirect objects were prevented from being input to Passive by virtue of the ordering. Fillmore's solution hence makes use of five grammatical rules, three transformations, and two filters of rule ordering, one of which specifies that (10a) precede (10b), the other of which specifies (10b) precede (10c). This was very likely the only solution available at the time, 1962, when Fillmore first encountered this problem, since the only filters countenanced at that time were rule-ordering statements.

The overly narrow character of such a limitation is brought out, I think, by the unsatisfactory character of the solution (10). In particular, the existence of two almost identical rules with distinct order is more than dubious. In terms of a richer set of filter rules, one can provide a more natural solution. One need recognize, in addition to Passive, only a single rule of indirect object shift—call it IO Shift—and no relative order of these two rules need be specified. Further, let us refer to the rule features [see G. Lakoff (1965)] assigned by application of these rules in a clause as respectively [Passive] and [IO Shift]. I assume [see G. Lakoff (1965)] that application of these rules in a clause with main verb V_i leads by general principle to assignment of the features [+ Passive] and [+IO Shift] to V_i. Given these assumptions, the facts can be represented by addition to the grammar of a filter rule:

(11) Throw out all derivations in which a single verb V_a both:[27]
  (i) occurs in an underlying structure with a *for*-indirect object; and
  (ii) occurs in a derived structure marked $\begin{bmatrix} +\text{Passive} \\ +\text{IO Shift} \end{bmatrix}$.

This newer proposal thus involves only three rules as against the five of the ordering solution; Passive, IO Shift, and the filter (11). The latter says directly that no verb which has a *for*-indirect object can undergo both Passive and IO Shift. Although (11) is far from precise, the advantages over a description like that in (10) are obvious.[28]

These advantages grow, it seems to me, when it is recognized that there are dialects which lack the restrictions noted by Fillmore. For these dialects, in terms of an ordering solution, one must provide a description involving only a single rule of indirect object shift, ordered before Passive. This then claims that in these dialects indirect object shift must be described in a way quite distinct from that in the standard dialect. But such an extreme grammar differentiation on the basis of relatively minor factual differences seems incompatible with a reasonable theory of dialect differentiation. Given the description proposed here, though, all dialects involve the same transformations, the difference being attributed to the presence or absence of the *ad hoc* filter (11). This would be consistent with a general account of syntactic dialect differences as due in significant part to the presence or absence of filters, and further to a claim that "standard" dialects tend to differ from "lower-class" or "uneducated" ones in having a larger number of filters, that is, in having more irregularities.

For a second case, consider the expressions:

(12) (a) Mary and Arthur Mulligan (both) have jobs.
     (b) Mary Mulligan and Arthur Mulligan (both) have jobs.

Each of these sentences refers to two different individuals named Mulligan and in most ways the sentences seem equivalent semantically. Given what is assumed about coordination in general, one might well wish to derive (12a) from a structure like that underlying (12b) by way of the general rule of Coordination Reduction, which is thought to relate as well such pairs as:[29]

(13) (a) Mary and Arthur are (both) famous.
      (b) Mary is famous and Arthur is famous.

Observe, though, that the semantic properties of (12a) and (12b) differ in one significant respect. In (12b) two individuals are each said to be named Mulligan but there is no presupposition that this fact either is or is not a consequence of their being related. That is, (12b) could be used by a speaker either to describe individuals who he believes to be related or to describe persons who he believes coincidentally in possession of the same last name.

In (12a), however, it must be the case that the speaker believes the individuals to have the same name because of some kinship relation, either consanguineal or affinal. Thus the semantic representations of (12a) and (12b) must differ with respect to the presuppositions specified as believed by the speaker. It follows that there is a constraint on derivations involving the rule of Coordination reduction such that when this rule applies to expressions which are names of (human) individuals,[30] there must exist in the semantic representation a presupposition that the individuals bearing the names do so because of relationship. This restriction is not naturally stateable as part of the rule Coordination reduction due to the relevance of semantic information and to the fact that the rule is general enough to operate on constituents of quite different types. Thus its own description will not contain any specific constituents at all but rather variables over constituents.[31] Rather, the constraint is naturally stated as an *ad hoc* filter which is not part of Coordination reduction as such, a filter which throws out all derivations in which there is a semantic representation *with* the relevant names but *without* the relevant presupposition and a later tree in which the names have been smashed together by Coordination reduction. Although I am obviously far from knowing how to state this filter precisely,[32] the need for reference to two different trees in a derivation which are more or less obviously not contiguous is clear. It is also clear that one of the levels referred to is semantic representation. Finally, this case falls into the mold to be expected of facts which could support the need for filters. This is a situation where base rules and generally stated transformations such as Coordination reduction will yield too rich a set of derivations. In particular, in this case, the set will include a derivation for sentences like (12a) in which the semantic representation incorrectly contains no presupposition about relatedness.

The third filter illustration concerns the fact that in many contexts verbs like *seem, appear, happen, turn out, strike,* etc. cannot occur in grammatical structures which *have not undergone* the rule Extraposition:

(14) (a) It seems to me that Greta is getting meaner.
     (b) *That Greta is getting meaner seems to me.
(15) (a) It appears to me that Schwarz will win.
     (b) *That Schwarz will win appears to me.
(16) (a) It happens that I am going to Chicago.
     (b) *That I am going to Chicago happens.

What is peculiar here is that application of the rule which throws *that*-clauses to the end of the next most inclusive clause is in almost all other cases optional:

(17) (a) It is odd that Betty can't fly.
     (b) That Betty can't fly is odd.
(18) (a) It is well known that Osenaufer is the world's greatest living bookie.
     (b) That Osenaufer is the world's greatest living bookie is well known.

A general statement of Extraposition must thus specify this rule as optional, regardless of how optionality is to be characterized formally. Therefore, a grammar containing this general rule will incorrectly generate well-formed derivations for sentences like (14b), (15b), and (16b).

A first idea is to add to the grammar a filter based on the rule feature mechanism mentioned earlier, a filter which requires application of Extraposition[33] "to" verbs like *seem, appear, happen,* etc., that is, which throws out all derivations in which such verbs occur with unextraposed subjects. That this is, however, not sufficient is indicated first by examples like:

(19) (a) Johnson seems to have been evil.
     (b) That seems to have annoyed you.
     (c) The wind seems to bother you.
(20) (a) Melvin happens to like seafood.
     (b) Richardson happened to be in Hong Kong.
     (c) Apples happen to make her sick.

For in these, the relevant verbs occur without ill-formedness in spite of the fact that Extraposition has not applied. In these cases, it has not applied because it is not applicable, the possibility of applicability having been removed by earlier (cyclical) application of the rule Raising. This rule takes the underlying "subject" of the embedded clause and raises it up to become an "object" of the main clause verb. Schematically, such sentences can be characterized as follows, making use of McCawley's (1970*a*) important insight that there is underlying V-S-O order in English:[34]

(21) (a)

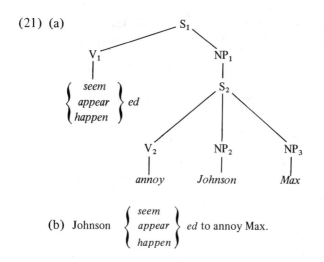

(b) Johnson $\left\{\begin{array}{l} seem \\ appear \\ happen \end{array}\right\}$ *ed* to annoy Max.

When Raising applies to such structures, NP_2 will be lifted up into the main clause as a new "object" of V_1:

(22)

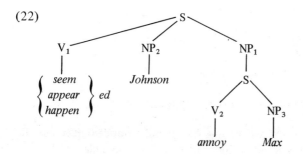

Consequently, when the rule Subject formation applies, it will permute NP_2 around V_1 yielding the surface order. No sententially complex NP ever becomes a subject, and Extraposition never becomes applicable. Consequently, on these grounds alone it is incorrect to claim that all instances of verbs like *seem* must undergo Extraposition. It might be assumed, however, that it is correct to say that if Extraposition is applicable in the clauses of such verbs, it must apply. This would explain its obligatoriness in examples like (14), (15), and (16), leaving Raising cases like (21) irrelevant.

That even this is insufficient is, however, indicated by the typical *optionality* of Extraposition with these verbs in sentences of the form:

(23) (a) It seems strange that Betty can't type.
     (b) That Betty can't type seems strange.
(24) (a) It appears (to be) true that Louis is dating Bertha.
     (b) That Louis is dating Bertha appears (to be) true.

The well-formed (b) sentences here show that the relevant verbs need not undergo Extraposition even when the latter rule is applicable.

The contrast between (23b) and (24b) versus (14b), (15b), and (16b) remains. The closest I have been able to reach to a solution depends on distinguishing the former class of examples from the latter class in terms of application of the rule Raising, and in making use of a suggestion of G. Lakoff (personal communication). He proposes that the facts can be expressed in terms of the incompatibility for the relevant class of verbs of nonapplication of Extraposition and applicability of the rule or rules which mark a complement as a *that*-clause (in contrast to infinitival or gerundive marking). A first attempt at such a rule could be expressed in terms of rule features roughly as follows, assuming that the features associated with Extraposition and the *that*-marker phenomenon are respectively [Extra] and [That]:

(25) Throw out all derivations in which the verbs *seem, appear, happen*, etc. occur with the feature markings $\begin{bmatrix} \text{-Extra} \\ \text{+That} \end{bmatrix}$.

This filter rule then marks as ill-formed examples like:

(26) *That Max is a vampire seems (to me).

while allowing the extraposed versions:

(27) It seems (to me) that Max is a vampire.

since, as noted earlier, we assume on general grounds that nonapplication of a rule R to a clause leads to the marking of the main clause of that rule with a minus value for the feature [R]. Consequently, the verb in (26) will be marked [-Extra]. But this verb will also be marked [+That], since its complement has been marked by this rule. In (27), on the other hand, the output is [+Extra] and (25) does not mark the derivation as deviant.

Reference to the feature [+That] in (25) of course guarantees that sentences like (19) and (20) will not be excluded. The question must arise, however, how (25) fails to mark as deviant examples like (23b) and (24b). The main verbs of these are under our assumptions certainly marked [-Extra]. Therefore, if they are marked [+ That], (25) should exclude them. In fact, however, they are not marked [+ That]. As mentioned above in introducing Lakoff's suggestion, Raising is relevant here. The *that*-clauses in such examples are not underlying "objects" of *seem, appear,* etc., but rather underlying NP's of the embedded verbs which are raised into the main clause. Thus the underlying structure of (23b) would be roughly:

(28)

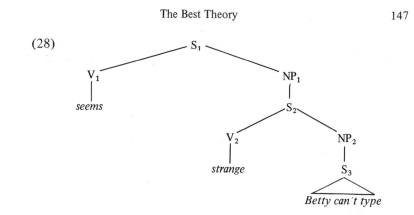

Hence *that*-marking is determined is S_2 and it is the main verb of this clause, *strange* in this case which receives the marking [+That]; *seems* in this structure thus remains throughout [- That] and no violation of (25) ensues, NP_2 is moved into the main clause here by Raising, ultimately becoming main clause subject.

Thus the applicability of (25) to sentences like (14b), (15b), (16b), but nonapplicability to sentences like (23b) is strong evidence for the Raising analysis of the latter type of construction, an analysis which provides the necessary differentiation which (25) requires.[35]

Unfortunately, while the analysis proposed seems adequate for the facts touched on so far, it does not stand up when a wider class of facts is considered. In particular, given the assumption that application of a rule R in a clause C_i marks the main verb of C_i with the feature [+ R], (25) is only adequate if it is true that all cases of the obligatory Extraposition restriction are limited to obligatory application in the clause of the verb where the potentially extraposable NP starts out. But this is not the case. Consider:

(29) (a) *That Harry threw the game is likely to seem.
     (b) It is likely to seem that Harry threw the game.

Examples like (29) show that even when the relevant verb, *seem, appear*, etc. is embedded, and has its subject NP raised,[36] Extraposition is still obligatory. Since it is known that Extraposition must be last cyclical [see Ross (1967)], in such cases Extraposition could not apply until the cycle of the adjectival verb *likely* (ignoring the *be*-form). Consequently, the occurrences of *seem* in both (29a) and (29b) will remain with the feature [-Extra], and (25) predicts, *wrongly*, that both of them should be ill-formed. Evidently then, (25) must be replaced by a formulation which can simultaneously cover both the examples treated correctly by (25) and those like (29). There are several ways to approach this problem, none of them seem very happy, and I shall not attempt a formulation here. My aim after all is to suggest that a grammar must contain a set of filter rules, it is not to claim that there exists now much knowledge about how to formulate these (see sec. V).

The fourth case to be discussed concerns the curious element *such* of anaphoric sentences like:

> (30) Harry needed an invisible cape but has been unable to find any such cape.

It was pointed out to me by D. Perlmutter (personal communication) that the element *one* of sentences such as:

> (31) Harry needed atomic ray guns and George sold him many used ones.

involves a special incompatibility with the form *numerous*. Clearly, *ones* drops when it has no post nominal elements in its NP:

> (32) (a) *Harry needed atomic ray guns and George sold him many ones.$\Longrightarrow$
> (b) Harry needed atomic ray guns and George sold him many.

But, as Perlmutter observed:

> (33) *Harry needed atomic ray guns and George sold him numerous (ones).

Compare this with the perfectly fine analog to (31) with *numerous*:

> (34) Harry needed atomic ray guns and George sold him numerous used ones.

It is thus the sequence *numerous ones* which becomes surface structure *numerous* that must be blocked.

Next note that one finds sentences like:

> (35) (a) Harry needed twin-barreled atomic ray guns and George sold him many such atomic guns.
> (b) Harry needed twin-barreled atomic ray guns and George sold him many such $\Longleftarrow$ (*ones).

We thus expect to find both:

> (36) (a) Harry needed twin-barreled atomic ray guns and George sold him numerous such atomic ray guns.

(b) *Harry needed twin-barreled atomic ray guns and George sold him numerous such ⟸ (*ones).

But this expectation is only half-fulfilled. It appears that *such* is incompatible with a directly preceding *numerous* when nothing follows in the NP. We thus see that both the anaphoric *one(s)* and *such* manifest a peculiar and *ad hoc* restriction on occurrence with the adjective *numerous*. Statement of such a restriction once in a grammar would be odd enough; twice is unbelieveable. Fortunately, the two facts can be reduced to one restriction by deriving the *one* forms from *such* forms.[37] That is, one observes that:

> (37) (a) *such a one
>   (b) *such ones

It is thus natural to derive sentences like (38b) and (39c) from more remote sources like (38a) and (39a) respectively:

> (38) (a) John was looking for a telepathic fox but he couldn't find such a one. ⟹
>   (b) John was looking for a telepathic fox but he couldn't find one.
> (36) (a) John was looking for telepathic foxes but he couldn't find any such ones. ⟹
>   (b) John was looking for telepathic foxes but he couldn't find any such. ⟹
>   (c) John was looking for telepathic foxes but he couldn't find any.

Thus the restrictions in both examples like (33) and examples like (36b) are reduced to an exclusion between *numerous* and *such*.

It is pretty clear now that this must be stated as a filter. No non-*ad hoc* way of preventing generation of the underlying structures appears to exist, especially in view of the normal distribution of the closely related form *many*.[38] A rough approximation of the required rule might be:[39]

> (40) Throw out all derivations in which the substructure NP[numerous such ones]NP occurs.

Interesting properties of (40) include the fact that it refers to only a single tree. But this tree clearly *cannot* be the surface structure since (40) must cover examples like (33) in the surface structure of which no word *such* occurs, and examples like (36b) in which no form *ones* occurs. Hence (40) applies to some level or levels of intermediate structure. It can be taken as showing that single-level filters are not restricted to the surface structure, or to semantic representation, or to just these.

A fifth case of the need for filter rules is provided by the "anaphoric island" phenomena discussed in Postal (1969). There many arguments are presented showing that *pseudo-adjectives* like the italicized forms in

(41) (a) the *Chinese* attempt to destroy the world
    (b) the *governmental* claim that the men were spies
    (c) the *imperial* attack on the outlying islands

must be derived from underlying NP's like those in

(42) (a) China's attempt to destroy the world
    (b) the government's claim that the men were spies
    (c) the empire's attack on the outlying islands

Part of the reason for this is the fact, illustrated by (41a), that the surface structure pseudo-adjective serves as the "controlling" antecedent element for the rule Equi, which deletes complement subject NP under conditions of coreference. This shows that the ancestors of such pseudo-adjectives partake of coreference relations in sentences. Yet, there is a restriction blocking most types of expression of this coreference, partly illustrated by contrasts like those in

(43) (a) China's attempt to destroy itself
    (b) *the Chinese attempt to destroy itself
(44) (a) the government's justification of itself
    (b) *the governmental justification of itself
(45) (a) the empire's$_i$ claim that the democracies were trying to destroy it$_i$
    (b) *the imperial$_i$ claim that the democracies were trying to destroy it$_i$

Comparing phrases like (41a), where a pseudo-adjective participates in underlying coreference relations without ill-formedness, with (43b), (44b), and (45b), where pseudo-adjectives cannot grammatically express this relation, we see a generalization. Namely, in the latter ill-formed cases, the coreference manifests itself in the surface structure in terms of actual pronominal NP, while in (41a), the rule of complement subject deletion eliminates the element which would otherwise show up as a pronominal NP in surface structures. One can begin to handle these facts in a natural way with a filter roughly along the following lines:

(46) Throw out all derivations in which both:

(i) the semantic representation contains a pair of NP's, NP_a and NP_b, which are stipulated coreferents;[40] and

(ii) [a] the surface-structure correspondent of NP_a is a pseudo-adjective;[41] and

   [b] the surface-structure correspondent of NP_b is a pronominal NP.

As evidence for a formulation roughly along these lines, observe that in contrast to examples like (43b), (44b), and (45b), sentences such as

(47) (a) American self-justification is disgusting.
   (b) Chinese self-defense depends on public morale.

are well-formed. But what has happened in these cases is that the elements which normally show up as pronominal NP's have been incorporated into noun compounds, losing in the process[42] their NP character. Unlike the ill-formed examples, sentences like (47) then do not violate the filter rule (46). Compare:

(48) (a) *American justification of itself is disgusting.
   (b) Chinese defense of itself depends on public morale.

Hence (41a) and (47) show that quite different types of operation which prevent underlying coreferent NP's from showing up as surface-structure pronouns preclude violation of the filter which rules out examples like (43b), (44b), and (45b).

A sixth illustration of the existence of a component of filters in a grammar is provided by one of the cases discussed in Postal (1970b). In particular, the (a) and (b) examples of the following forms differ in that the (a) forms undergo the rule Raising, while the (b) forms do not, but do undergo Extraposition:

(49) (a) Jerry seemed to me to like Lucille.
   (b) It seemed to me that Jerry liked Lucille.
(50) (a) Jerry struck me as liking Lucille.
   (b) It struck me that Jerry liked Lucille.
(51) (a) Jerry was claimed by the government to have attacked the secretary.
   (b) It was claimed by the government that Jerry attacked the secretary.
(52) (a) Jerry was found out by the police to be living with Margaret.
   (b) It was found out by the police that Jerry was living with Margaret.

The examples in (49) and (50) are the result of application of the rule Psych movement, those in (51) and (52) of the rule Passive. These rules are parallel, indeed probably identical, in effecting the interchange of NP's destined to become subjects and objects.

In sentences which undergo either Psych movement or Passive and Raising, there is a peculiar constraint on coreferent pronouns. Compare:

(53) (a) *Jerry seemed to me to like me.
      (b) It seemed to me that Jerry liked me.
(54) (a) *Jerry struck me as liking me.
      (b) It struck me that Jerry liked me.
(55) (a) *Jerry was claimed by $Pete_i$ to have attacked him_i.
      (b) It was claimed by $Pete_i$ that Jerry attacked him_i.
(56) (a) *Jerry was found out by the $police_i$ to be criticizing $them_i$.
      (b) It was found out by the $police_i$ that Jerry was criticizing $them_i$.

Reformulating the statement given in Postal [1970b, see statement (55) there], one can express these facts in terms of a filter roughly along the following lines:

(57) Throw out all derivations which have both:
     (i) an underlying structure[43] of the form:

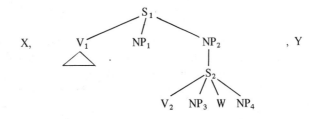

where NP_1 and NP_4 are stipulated coreferents; and

     (ii) a later derived structure of the form:

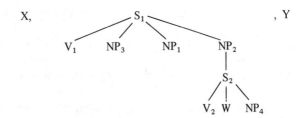

The filter (57) will be violated by just those derivations in which the NP_3 of

(i) is moved into the main clause by Raising and then interchanged in position by either Passive or Psych movement with NP_1, such that NP_3 ultimately becomes main clause subject. Thus it will mark as ill formed derivations like schematically:

(58) (a)

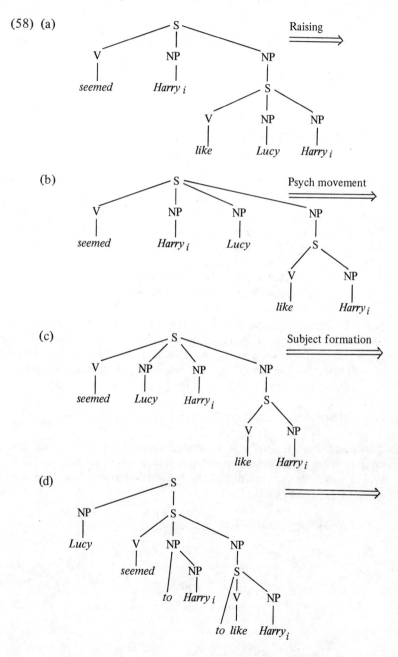

(e) *Lucy seemed to Harry$_i$ to like him$_i$.

Another example, especially clear, of the role of filtering in grammatical description is provided by such relatively trivial facts as the following:

(59) (a) John and the doctor drove away.
     (b) The doctor and John drove away.
(60) (a) I arrested John and the doctor.
     (b) I arrested the doctor and John.
(61) (a) John and I drove away.
     (b) *I and John drove away.
(62) (a) The police arrested John and I.
     (b) *The police arrested I and John.

That is, while in general constituent NP's can occur in any order in coordinate constructions, there is a constraint on the first person form *I*. The constraint is not clear from the examples so far. We might conclude either that *I* must not occur as the first element of a coordination, or must occur as the last element. In fact, the latter seems right, as shown by:

(63) (a) *John, I, and Max drove away.
     (b) John, Max, and I drove away.

Since in (63a) *I* is not the first element and yet the structure is still ill formed, one cannot require only that *I* not be thy first element. The requirement then seems to be that if *I* occurs as one element of a coordination, it must be the last element. A further note is required, however, since examples like the following seem well formed:

(64) *John* and *I* (and *Betty* and *Lou*) played tennis.

The point here is that the four underlined NP's are not homogeneously conjoined in a quaternary structure; rather, there is internal bracketing, a fact signaled by the presence of the second *and* after *I*. Thus the structure of the subject in (64) would be:

(65)

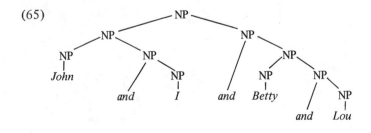

while the subject NP in (63a), for example, would be:

(66)

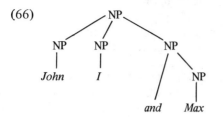

The ill-formedness of the latter in contrast to the satisfactory form of the former shows that the requirement that I be last in a coordination only holds with respect to those NP's which are sister constituents of I under the same coordinate node. Hence we can tentatively express this restriction as the filter rule:

(67) Throw out all derivations containing a tree with an n-ary coordinate node NP_0 of the form:

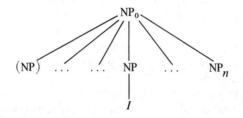

The question arises whether the tree mentioned in (67) can be the surface structure. There is at least one argument to the negative. Namely, if stated on presurface trees, (67) can be assumed to apply to structures before *and* or *or* has been inserted in front of conjuncts. If stated on the surface structure, (67) would have to be slightly more complicated, since the restriction holds for conjuncts with I regardless of whether these are preceded by a conjunction particle.

I can see no way of handling the restrictions in (61), (62), and (63) without filters. Clearly, the general rules of conjunct formation, whatever they are, will generate all combinations of NP order, and it is only in a tiny handful of cases that there are restrictions.

It should be mentioned that apparently something like the reverse constraint holds for the word *me*:

(68) (a) Me and John will go to Detroit.
     (b) *John and me will go to Detroit.
(69) (a) The cops arrested me and John.
     (b) *The cops arrested John and me.

I recognize the *a*-forms here as well-formed in a colloquial style of speech, while the *b*-forms have no use at all. Similarly:

(70))a) *John, me, and Max will go to Detroit.
     (b) Me, John, and Max will go to Detroit.

Hence there is apparently a filter parallel to (67) where *me* replaces *I* and the optional constituent follows while the obligatory one precedes. This will assert then that while *I* can only occur last in a coordination, *me* can only occur first.

The last set of facts I want to discuss is illustrative of a point which needs considerable airing at this juncture. Namely, once it is granted that a component of filter rules exists, many facts *can* be stated in terms of filters which formerly had to be built into restrictions on particular trans-formational rules. But in many such cases there is no compelling reason to do so. This raises the question of how one is to choose between building particular restrictions into transformational rules and stating them as separate filters in cases where both are possible.

A case in point is the fact that genitive NP's in English do not seem to occur with appositive relative clauses:

(71) (a) Johnson's term was marked by disorder.
     (b) *Johnson's, who was power-mad, term was marked by disorder.
(72) (a) I talked to a friend of Harry's.
     (b) *I talked to a friend of Harry's, who was a monk.

The star on (72b) is meant to indicate, obviously, that the relative must be construed with the whole NP, rather than with *Harry*. Appositives in such cases seem little better if the genitive-marker is after the relative:

(73) (a) *Johnson, who was power-mad's term was marked by disorder.
     (b) *I talked to a friend of Harry, who was a monk's.

Now, assuming that appositives are derived from conjoined sentences, in a way schematically indicatable as:

(74) (a) Johnson had an unhappy experience and he was normally gay. $\Longrightarrow$
     (b) Johnson, and he was normally gay, had an unhappy experience. $\Longrightarrow$
     (c) Johnson, who was normally gay, had an unhappy experience.

It is the step from (a) to (b) here that is impossible in the case of genitive NP's. Clearly, this restriction could be built into the rule which accomplishes this deformation of the conjoined clause into a parenthetical constituent. Equally clearly, we could formulate the restriction as a filter throwing out constituents of the form:

$$(75) \qquad \left[\begin{bmatrix} NP \\ X + \text{Genitive} \end{bmatrix} , \; S, \right]$$

where the commas here represent the typical comma intonation of appositives.

     Which of these solutions is correct? What considerations in general determine the choice in such cases? I cannot claim to have answers to these and related problems. But the following line of argument seems relevant. We hope to be able to construct the most extensive substantive theory of universal grammar consistent with the facts. Restrictions of the sort just noted tend to be language-particular. In these cases, then, representation of the restrictions in a separate filter leaves the relevant transformational rule in a more general, less *ad hoc* form. Just such properties, however, increase the probability that a rule can be stated as part of universal grammar. I take it, then, that one type of argument which may be possible in such cases is that statement of *ad hoc* restrictions in the form of filter rules is consistent with a stronger statement of universal grammar, permitting as it does many *ad hoc* restrictions to be extracted and stated separately in the form of language-particular (dialect-particular) filters.

     One can conclude, then, that there is a body of evidence of different types strongly suggested that a theory involving base trees and transformations must be supplemented at least by a component of rules which are filters. There is every reason to think that the class of filters is quite rich and varied. An impressionistic guess is that the greater part of a natural language grammar may be made up of members of the class of filter rules. Naturally, filter rules being a relatively new addition to grammatical theory, the properties of such remain vague and unclear, and the number of questions about such devices which can be answered precisely at the moment is small. This seems to me neither surprising nor upsetting. For what is clear is that filters offer the hope of providing a way of stating a vast number of restrictions and generalizations which generative linguists have discovered over the last years, but which have proved incapable of incorporation in a grammar containing base rules and transformations alone.

IV. HISTORICAL ACCEPTANCE OF NONOPTIMAL THEORIES

     I have tried to suggest that Homogeneous II is a kind of minimal linguistic theory. Given what is known and accepted about linguistic structure, it is not possible, I think, to conceive of a theory which involves *less* conceptual elaboration. At the same time, extra elaborations can be justified only by providing direct empirical grounds for any proposed additions. For instance, a theory which claims the existence of a unique level of deep structure distinct from semantic representation requires such empirical justification. It is clear to me, however, that no such evidence is known in this case.[44] More generally, I am aware of no evidence whatever which would justify any general conceptual complication beyond that provided by Homogeneous II. It is significant that the historical development of the generative grammatical framework in which transformational studies began was such that questions of justifying the independent existence of deep structure never had cause to arise and in fact did not arise. Chomsky's original studies were based on the position—which he has never, I think, totally abandoned, despite a weak acceptance of a different view for a time under Katz's influence—that semantic structure cannot be taken seriously. That is, the position is that the semantic domain of language is so obscure, mysterious, and unamenable to serious description that no conclusions about its overall nature, still less any inferences for other aspects of language, can be safely drawn. In any event, there was assumed to be a well-defined syntax, independent of any semantic considerations, hence, automatically given transformational ideas, a level of deep structure which is independent of any semantic representation. The question of justifying the distinction between deep structure and semantic representation just could not arise.

When, largely under Katz's influence from 1963 on, transformational grammarians were led to take seriously the idea that there is a well-defined level of semantic structure,[45] the notion of an independent syntax was apparently too well established, and the distinction between deep structure and semantic representation went unquestioned. Katz incorporated such a fundamental distinction as a basic element of his overall view and apparently maintains it strongly up to the present. Hence he was led to develop a theory of the relation between deep structure[46] and semantic structure which was entirely distinct from the theory relating deep structure to surface structure—that is, entirely distinct from the theory of transformational grammar. Again, however, conditions were such as to suggest no need for arguments justifying the difference between syntactic structure and semantic representation, hence justifying the need for two distinct theories of mapping (i.e., transformations in syntax, projection rules in semantics).

Since it was not seen that logically such a theory is less than optimal, as compared with a homogeneous view like Homogeneous II, up till the present no arguments have been given to justify the extra theoretical machinery of a theory which incorporates a distinct level of deep structure and a special class of projection rules. The more recent further complication of linguistic theory suggested by Chomsky, Jackendoff, et al. is, in my view, naturally even less justified[47] and requires additional justification above and beyond that required for even the extra degree of complication found in Katz's "standard" interpretive theory. Since all of these theories require all of the apparatus of Homogeneous II,[48] each theoretical addition they involve requires special justification. The burden of justification remains therefore entirely with the supporters of these theories.

I think this cannot be stressed too much. Because of the historical development, in which *logically nonoptimal* theories arose first within the overall transformational framework, the relative logical relations and priorities among theories have become confused. Thus some have tried to give the impression that advocates of a view like Homogeneous II are maintaining an incredibly radical, implausible, and generally extremist position. They have tried, I believe, to suggest that such a radical departure cannot be taken seriously at the moment. In fact, however, considered from a logical point of view, the situation is, if anything, quite the reverse. Homogeneous II is the most *conservative* possible position in generative linguistic theory. It embodies no types of structural element and no types of grammatical rule which are not more or less agreed to be indispensable to linguistic description. All of its possible competitors, on the other hand, insist on some further conceptual elaborations.

If these elaborations can be regarded as cautious or conservative, it is probably only in historical terms.[49] And the importance of this is reduced, very nearly to nil in my opinion, when it is seen that the historical conditions were such as to never have required these elaborations to be justified as against the homogeneous position. Where, for example, is there work showing that the job putatively to be accomplished by projection rules cannot be accomplished by rules of transformational form — that is, by mappings of trees into trees by operations which meet the conditions on "syntactic rules" (i.e., Ross's coordinate-structure constraint, prohibition of rules which move a constituent exactly three clauses up, etc.)? Where is there work showing that the initial input to transformational rules is distinct from a subpart of semantic representation? Where is there work showing that lexical items provide a hard-and-fast boundary between organization of one sort, syntactic, and organization of another sort, semantic? Where, in short, is there any work at all which shows that the framework of Homogeneous II needs to be replaced by one which is conceptually more elaborate in one or more ways, in particular, by one which involves distinct levels of grammatical organization like deep structure? I am aware of no such work.

But, if the argument of this paper is not wholly mistaken, until direct empirical evidence of the need to complicate the framework of Homogeneous II is provided, this minimal theoretic schema is the one that must be chosen. In the absence of such evidence, every linguist has a stake in attempting to preserve the homogeneous, conceptually most restricted theory and in attempting to describe the incredible variety and vast expanse of grammatical facts within its terms, since Homogeneous II seems to be, on general theoretical grounds, the best theory now imaginable of the subject matter of grammar.

V. THE POVERTY OF PRESENT UNDERSTANDING

I think what was said in sections I-IV is basically right and it defines for me the proper attitude toward competing linguistic theories of the mapping between semantics and surface structure insofar as such theories can be taken very seriously. But how far is this? I think not too far. It can have escaped no one that the theoretical description in sections I-IV was so abstract and general as to provide very little substantive content. In part, this is an artifact of space limitations and of my assumptions that anyone interested in these questions is in a position to supply a certain amount of content for himself.

But surely the better part of the contentlessness in my description of linguistic theory is necessary no matter what a writer assumes, simply because when we turn to empirical facts in detail so little is understood of linguistic structure that one adds content to linguistic theory only at the cost of considerable arbitrariness. For the chief – and to my mind most valuable–result of a dozen years or more work on generative grammar is the sharp and steadily deepening demonstration that natural languages are fantastically vast, complex, and mysterious systems whose principles have so far largely eluded specification. It is worth remarking, for example, that after more than a dozen years of generative study of English grammar by dozens and dozens of people, we remain with hardly a single reasonably articulated analysis of any component of the grammar which even approaches relative stability or unchallengeability. Proposal after proposal, from the auxiliary analysis, to selectional features, to noun-phrase conjunction, to cyclic pronominalization, to cross-over constraints, has collapsed or slid into the murk of competing claims and contradictory evidence. Generative transformational work in grammar has thus demonstrated the vastness, intricacy, and underlying obscurity of the system involved, a result which reveals in its light the primitiveness and semicontentlessness of any conception of grammar worked out so far.

To many this result seems depressing, and its truth is often no doubt resisted on no other ground. In fact, there is no reason to regard it as depressing. It can be taken as a real and important contribution, albeit not one of the sort that was envisaged in the early days of transformational study. Then we naively assumed that it was actually possible at the time to construct generative grammars for human languages, and people set about seriously attempting just this. These efforts have unquestionably taught us a great deal. It is a fact, however, that actual grammar construction in the sense of early works like Chomsky's *Syntactic Structures* (1957), Lee's

Grammar of English Nominalizations (1960), etc. probably stopped at least by the mid-sixties, and, in any event, certainly does not go on at the present.[50] If the pursuit of generative grammar has not led to the construction of viable generative grammars, it has led to a deepening appreciation of just what a fantastic system each human has articulated within him. The pursuit of a precise formulation of grammar, although it has not brought precise formulations which are valid, has created a correct attitude, an attitude which previous work did not engender.

Thus the great traditional grammarians, who were aware of and documented a vast array of facts, never seem to have come to any feeling that these facts were the visible reflection of some underlying mystery whose essential nature they hardly touched. They lacked the sense, which spreads today, that there is, underlying the mass of facts, as intricate but only dimly perceived structure. That is, they lacked the sense that the array of grammatical facts provides a bewildering puzzle. They could not see the problem. Quite the contrary, they seem to have felt that essentially grammar was well understood, at least the grammar of "well-known" languages. Modern grammarians of pregenerative and nongenerative varieties have also, I believe, been far from sensing the vast mystery inherent in the documentable and in part documented welter of grammatical detail. One result—but only one—of this lack has been the ease with which, over time, writers on language have been able to put forward the most simplistic and superficial accounts of language "learning," accounts which have a germ of plausibility only in the absence of a perception of the underlying system of grammar.

In my opinion, this failure to perceive the meaning of the factual documentation of grammatical variety and complexity which was made prevented any serious deepening of grammatical understanding. The goals of generative grammar, on the contrary, have made it possible for us to see this welter of linguistic fact in its correct light, as the tracks of an uncaught prey. We have moved in the direction of a deeper and more serious understanding of grammar, despite our inability to construct actual generative grammars, by seeing the successive demolishment of a variety of what seemed at the time not only powerful and sophisticated, but even empirically highly supported, pieces of theoretical machinery. To take just one example, the argument given by Ross (1969a) for the transformational cycle as a basis for English pronominalization is a brilliant analysis, one which simply seems to demand immediate agreement. It has, however, quite typically collapsed and no one can now take seriously the idea that pronominalization is governed by a transformational rule as there described or believe that the cyclic principle explains the facts there noted. The point is that not just bad ideas or poor, unsupported analyses fall down. The system seems to resist the best work as well as the rest.

Thus as the documentation of the factual enormity of, for example, English grammar continues and expands—and of course we have probably uncovered since the early sixties more new facts than could be put in a dozen works like Jespersen's biggest—we can, thanks to the underlying generative goals, see with increasing clarity the quite incredible scope of human grammar and correspondingly the limitations of any set of principles that can be posited today to reconstruct this system. Even the best theory is none too good. One must, I think, be led to an increased respect for the subject under study and, ultimately, for the unknown forces which brought it into existence.[51]

NOTES

I would like to thank G. Lakoff and J. R. Ross for valuable criticisms of the manuscript.

[1] There are, of course, a number of solid accomplishments of a negative sort in other areas, e.g. demonstrations of inadequacy of finite-state devices, context-free grammars, etc.

[2] I feel compelled to point out that the argument usually given to show that each speaker must have internalized within him a generative grammar is logically unsound. The argument, the conclusion of which we have typically taken as a kind of necessary truth, goes like this:
 (i) Each speaker knows (in some specific sense) an infinite set of sentences.
 (ii) Each speaker is a finite organism.
 (iii) Ergo, each speaker must have internally represented a finite system (generative grammar) which specifies (generates, recursively) enumerates) the infinite class of sentences.

Regretably, as one can easily see by writing down (i) and (ii) in some explicit form, the consequence (iii) is not logically entailed by the conjunction of premises (i) and (ii). Moreover, in order to make the argument valid, one must evidently add a premise something like the following:
 (iv) The *only* way a finite object can know (in the specific sense) an infinite set of objects is to have represented in it a finite device which recursively enumerates that set.

However, (iv) is not self-evidently true.

[3] Traditionally, the account of deep structure includes at least the following assumptions:
 (i) Deep structures are the output of the base rules.
 (ii) Deep structures contain the information needed to define "logical" grammatical relations.
 (iii) Deep structures are the locus of statement of "selectional restrictions."
 (iv) Deep structures are the locus of insertion of lexical items.

[4] In particular, a large class of what can be called *presuppositions* must be part of the semantic representation but probably not part of the input to the rules which form surface structures. For illustration of this point see sec. III below, and G. Lakoff (Forthcoming).

[5] See Bach (1968), Gruber (1967), G. Lakoff (1969a, 1969b, Forthcoming), McCawley (1967, 1968a, 1968b, 1968c, 1968d, 1969, 1970a, 1970b). 1970b).

[6] The role of the lexicon is one of the obvious places where Homogeneous I differs from theories which draw a sharp line between "syntax" and "semantics." In particular, unlike earlier views, Homogeneous I claims that lexical items are inserted *after* a non-null number of transformational applications. Positive evidence in favor of this assumption and against the more traditional one that lexical insertion is pretransformational has already been brought forward. See G. Lakoff (1969a, b), Morgan (1968), Postal (1969, 1970b).

[7] *Elaboration* in the sense of the text here must be sharply distinguished from another kind of linquistic positing which is also often referred to by this term. Thus Ross's suggestion of various constraints on rules (1967) can be regarded as an elaboration of transformational theory. However, observe that

elaborations in this sense *restrict* either or both the class of structural descriptions or the class of rules, and thus *narrow* linguistic theory. Such elaboration is quite necessary because linguistic theories are typically stated initially in a much too unspecified, overly general form. While such restrictive elaborations need empirical support, the logic of this support is quite different from that required by the "opposite" sort of elaboration discussed in the text, that in which the class of descriptive devices is *expanded*.

[8] Of course, this counterevidence seldom reaches the level of proof in the mathematical sense.

[9] Naturally, if one rejects now or in the future the assumption that transformational rules play a role in grammar, then the argument of this paper cannot be given. However, it will have a more general version even in this case. Namely, one will always prefer a homogeneous theory of semantic representation-surface structure relations.

[10] See Katz and Fodor (1963), Katz and Postal (1964).

[11] Katz (Katz and Fodor 1963) originally referred to readings as *paths* of semantic markers, later more typically as sets of semantic markers, where the latter are either atomic elements or molecules with a possibly quite complex internal structure.

[12] See Chomsky (1971), Jackendoff (1968a, b, 1969), Dougherty (1968a, b,), Akmajian (1968).

[13] In addition, it seems to me that such writers are committed to the existence of other kinds or levels of linguistic representation, namely, those that are the output of a subset of their "interpretive" rules. This follows, since not all of these rules can have the final semantic representation as output and since these rules do not generate intermediate tree representations which are part of the transformational derivation.

[14] To take just one illustration, Chomsky (1971) speaks of "surface-structure rules of interpretation" throughout, suggesting a type of rule which takes surface structures as input. However, he discusses the phenomenon of "focus" in this paper and proposes an analysis under which this presumed "interpretive" property is assigned to sentences on the basis of the placement of main stress. At the same time, he maintains his past position that stress is assigned by rules which operate on the surface structure, which, as such, contains no stress markings. It follows that the "surface-structure rule of interpretation" in this case cannot operate on the surface structure. At the same time, it is clear that the proposed rule cannot operate on the *phonetic representation* alone, which would have the appropriate stress levels indicated but not other relevant information, such as constituent boundaries. Hence the input to the rule which putatively assigns "focus" is obscure.

[15] For initial arguments against the theories mentioned in this paragraph, see G. Lakoff (1969a, b, Forthcoming), McCawley (1968c), Postal (1969, 1970b), Ross (1969b).

[16] It is crucial to observe that each of the three unquestioned levels which Homogeneous I accepts is subject to direct empirical inspection by native speakers. That is, speakers have direct intuitions about what their sentences mean, how they are pronounced, and how they are organized into words. There are, however, no intuitions at all about the level of deep structure in the traditional transformational sense, i. e., in the sense where this is a level of structure distinct from (a subpart of) semantic representation.

This point is relevant to the terminology of "abstract syntax," which has sometimes been used (G. Lakoff 1968) to describe the more and more semanticlike syntactic analyses which have been proposed in recent years, and which were one motivation for the final development of theories like Homogeneous I. This terminology is relevant insofar as one understands "abstract" to mean "abstract from the surface structure." But it is quite misleading if it is interpreted, as many have wrongly interpreted it, I think, to mean "abstract from empirical fact." For, since such analyses are closer to the empirical data of facts about meaning than other analyses, they are not *more* but *less* abstract in this sense. From this point of view, it is the traditional transformational analyses which make use of semantically arbitrary deep structures, relatively remote from semantic facts, which are abstract along this dimension. I thus suggest that *abstract syntax* be replaced by the term *concrete syntax*, and that the former term be restricted to describe the work of those who posit semantically arbitrary underlying structures. A vague, sloganlike statement of the claims of Homogeneous II thus might be: human syntax is concrete syntax.

[17] The point is that the best of n theories in the sense being discussed here may very well be false, while a worse theory may turn out to be true.

[18] See Perlmutter (1968).

[19] The import of a distinction between "creative" rules and "filters" is called into question in part by G. Lakoff's observation (1969*b*, Forthcoming) that even transformations and base rules can be regarded as filters. That is, they can be so regarded by relegating all "creativity" to random formation of trees and tree sequences out of a fixed alphabet or set of alphabets. Although the distinction is vague at the moment, I believe there is a real difference to be characterized.

[20] It is not clear that the output conditions so far suggested either must be, or can be, in fact defined on surface structures. For example, they may be definable in terms of all representations in which word boundaries are specified.

[21] See G. Lakoff (1965).

[22] Relevant data here would include cases where the locus of exception-type ungrammaticality marking still induces ill-formedness even though it is not present in the surface structure. Such cases exist, though. For example, the verb *lack* seems to control the obligatoriness of a minor rule which deletes the form *any* directly before a noun. Hence the contrast:

(i) Johnson lacked any real courage ⇒ Johnson lacked real courage

(ii) *Johnson lacked any courage ⇒ Johnson lacked courage

But the ill-formedness is preserved even when the verb has been deleted – say, by being gapped:

(iii) *Johnson lacked any real courage and Rusk any honesty.

(iv) Johnson lacked any real courage and Rusk honesty.

[23] See Perlmutter (1968).

[24] See Postal (1969, 1970*b*).

[25] See the discussion in G. Lakoff (Forthcoming).

[26] Arbitrary features—that is, those which are neither semantic nor determined by particular transformations [i. e., rule features in the sense of G. Lakoff (1965)]—now seem valid to me in a very limited class of cases, chiefly where they are associated directly with irregular pronunciations, as in suppletion.

[27] The careful reader will realize that speaking of a single verb, or any other constituent, as occurring in two different trees is literally senseless. What is needed both in this case, and in general in multitree filters, is the notion of *corresponding constituents*, where this keeps track of the descendents of a particular constituent in the initial tree through the succeeding trees. This notion will be the basic new predicate required of a theory of multitree filters. For

initial discussion of this question, see G. Lakoff (Forthcoming). These comments are relevant to many of the examples of filter rules which follow in the text.

[28] I said earlier that the only descriptions for these facts ever offered involved filters. In the oral discussion after a reading of this paper, a solution was proposed by N. Chomsky which apparently makes no use of such. Chomsky proposed that if passive sentences have an underlying *by+dummy* element-marker in their predicates, the restrictions can be stated as part of a single rule of IO Shift. Namely, this rule is blocked for *for*—indirect objects when *by+dummy* is present. Such a solution does seem to build all the restrictions into base rules and transformations and thus to avoid filters (other than rule ordering). However, this claim seems almost empty in such cases. The filter required—namely, (11) in the text, or the like—mentions the rule feature [+ Passive], a feature which uniquely indicates that the rule Passive has applied. If then one assumes that the base structure involves a unique marker of Passive application, it is hardly surprising that the restrictions can be stated without a filter, since the filter has in effect been built into the base. The whole question then devolves on whether the appropriate method of keeping track of rule application is with rule features or with *ad hoc* devices like Chomsky's *by+dummy* element. It seems to me that a variety of arguments suggest the former. In particular, such *ad hoc* devices are incompatible with a set of *natural* constraints on base structures, in particular incompatible with the claim that base structures are (subparts of) semantic representations. We might say then that filters like (11) permit—while *ad hoc* markers like Chomsky's do not—restrictions like those observed by Fillmore to be stated while maintaining *natural* base structures. And, more generally, the claim that filters are required in a theory of grammar is properly stated in terms of a notion of *natural* (hence possibly universal) underlying structures.

[29] At a still deeper level, the sentences of (12) might have representations like *Mary Mulligan has a job and Arthur Mulligan has a job*.

[30] Actually, this process is only relevant for last names. First names do not collapse in English:

    (i) (a) Paul Jones and Arthur Jones
         (b) Paul and Arthur Jones
    (ii) (a) Paul Jones and Paul Mason
         (b) *Paul Jones and Mason

Other grammatical differences between these two types also exist:

    (iii) (a) You saw Melvin who?
          (b) *You saw who (what) Petersen?

[31] Hence, technically, such a rule is not a "transformation" in the most narrow formal sense since these must refer only to actual constituents. For an initial formulation of such a rule in these terms see Petrick, Postal, and Rosenbaum (1969).

[32] Remarks like this should become unnecessary. It is obvious that no one knows how to state any grammatical rules precisely. Full precision can be purchased today only at the cost of wholesale arbitrariness.

[33] An attempt to build such restrictions into the rule runs into the difficulty that Extraposition itself can be stated generally enough so that the constituent verb need not be mentioned at all for all regular cases. One suspects the existence of a principle which excludes exceptional items from affecting the form of a rule. Building the restrictions into rule features runs up against the problem of *government* [(G. Lakoff 1965)]. That is, typical exception cases are such that exceptional behavior of a rule in a clause is determined by the main verb of that clause. This leaves the contrast between examples like (14b) and (19b) unrepresentable.

³⁴ I ignore in this structure the fact that verbs like *seem* and *appear* actually occur with an additional underlying NP, that which designates the individual who experiences the mental content which the verb and its sentential "object" NP describe. This additional NP, called the *Experiencer NP* in Postal (1970b) shows up with the preposition *to* in sentences like *Johnson seemed to me to annoy Max*.

³⁵ Moreover, the fact that (25) is not applicable to structures like (23b) is counterevidence to any superficial analysis of such constructions in terms of an underlying structure like

$$\begin{array}{c} \text{VP} \\ \diagup \quad \diagdown \\ \text{Verb} \quad \text{Adjective} \end{array}$$

as suggested in Chomsky (1965, pp. 94-96). Such an analysis provides no general way of distinguishing structures like (23b) from those like (14b) with respect to the obligatoriness of Extraposition.

³⁶ Notice that this NP can move very far away from its original position by successive applications of Raising and other rules:

    (i) *John claimed that Bill threw the game was likely to seem.

    (ii) *That Bill threw the game was claimed to be likely to seem.

    (iii) *That Bill threw the game was discovered to have been claimed to be likely to seem.

Yet no matter how far it moves, if the *that*-clause is the underlying "object" of *seem*, it remains subject to obligatory application of Extraposition, as the ill-formedness of (i), (ii), (iii) reveals.

³⁷ This derivation can, I think, be developed into a powerful argument showing that lexical nouns have a source in restrictive relative clauses. See Postal (Forthcoming).

³⁸ The impossibility of blocking the underlying structures is clearer if one recognizes that sequences like

    (i) *Harry needed yellow mothballs and so Pete bought numerous (such) (ones).

derive from structures like

    (ii) Harry needed yellow mothballs and so Pete bought numerous such mothballs.

which in turn derives from

    (iii) Harry needed yellow mothballs and so Pete bought numerous mothballs which were such that they were yellow.

For arguments in favor of such derivations see Postal (Forthcoming).

³⁹ There appear to be speakers who not only do not accept *numerous such,* and *numerous such ones,* but who also block forms like *numerous such meatballs.* For them, then, the relevant filter might be formulated by replacing *ones* in (40) by a variable.

⁴⁰ I use the term *stipulated coreferents* as an equivalent to what I have previously (Postal 1969, 1970b, 1971) referred to as *presupposed coreferents.* Such NP's contrast with, among other things, *asserted coreferents* like those in:

    (i) *The one who rang the bell was the boy with green eyes.*

The newer terminology is required, I think, because unlike true presuppositions, one cannot imagine a statement of coreference of the type in sentences like

    (ii) *Harry shot himself.*

being false. The fact that the underlined NP's in (ii) designate the same individual is not a statement of fact which could be wrong but simply a stipulation by the speaker.

⁴¹ I do not know how to characterize the properties which will formally distinguish pseudo-adjectives in surface structures. Perhaps there is no such notion and a pseudo-adjective is simply a surface-structure adjective whose

underlying correspondent constituent is an NP. If so, (46) will have to be reformulated accordingly.

[42] While the relevant rule of incorporation is far from clear, it seems to share properties with the rules which form elements like *lionhunter, lionhunting*. No one would claim that *lion* is an NP in such surface forms, although the underlying structure must obviously be a generic NP.

[43] With this terminology, I leave open whether (i) is to be regarded as part of the semantic representation. If not, then the mention of stipulated coreferents, which refers to semantic representation, would mean that (57) involves three distinct trees in a derivation.

[44] Moreover, there is the counterevidence mentioned in note 15.

[45] This contribution of Katz's will, in my opinion, remain fundamental regardless of how the issues discussed in this paper are ultimately resolved.

[46] Actually, the claim that only deep structure was relevant for interpretive semantics came later (Katz and Postal 1964).

[47] No doubt some of the facts motivating this development are relevant to the difference between Homogeneous I and Homogeneous II, that is, are relevant to the fact that a grammar must contain a rich component of filters. The views mentioned in the text are in part prior to, in part simultaneous with, a clear recognition of the need for extensive filtering. Many arguments taken to support this development can be seen to assume (implicitly, of course) the absence of the possibility of relevant filters.

[48] While I know of no explicit statement by the authors of these views recognizing the need for filters, I see no possibility of their doing without such in the face of facts like those of which the cases in sec. III are a small sample.

[49] Perhaps they can also be regarded as conservative if it is taken to be conservative to maintain only very weak theories. Homogeneous II is a relatively strong theory in claiming the adequacy of a relatively restricted array of grammatical devices. As a general principle, though, one always seeks to have the strongest theory compatible with the known facts.

[50] If generative research does not consist of the construction of generative grammars, it is important to ask what it does consist of. In a no doubt never-to-be-written paper, Lakoff, Postal, and Ross (Forthcoming) argue that today such research consists in the construction and validation of arguments supporting this or that claim about particular grammars, or the general theory of grammar. This carries on a strand of activity which dates to the beginning of generative work. For example, Chomsky's demonstration of the inadequacy of finite-state devices was work of just this sort. For a time, this kind of activity was pushed into the background by the goal of pursuing here and now the construction of actual grammars. As the latter goal has come to be seen as more and more unrealistic, the other has naturally expanded to fill the gap.

[51] Perhaps nothing illustrates more clearly the gap between the conception of the problem of grammar which emerges from generative work and much past thought than the idea, expressed sometimes by "anthropological" linguists, that language is an invention of man. The research of the last dozen years has shown, if previous work did not, that so far are we from having invented language that, even with massive research by dozens of people armed with the hindsight of generations of previous work, we can hardly begin to understand it. Or, according to a little-known saying: "Science makes a good business but a bad religion."

REFERENCES

Akmajian, A. 1968. An interpretive principle for certain anaphoric expressions. Mimeographed. Cambridge: M.I.T.

Bach, E. 1968. Nouns and noun phrases. In Bach and Harms (1968).

_____, and Harms, R., eds. 1968. *Universals in linguistic theory.* New York: Holt, Rinehart.

Binnick, R. I., Davison, A., Green, G. M., and Morgan, J. L., eds. 1969. *Papers from the fifth regional meeting of the Chicago Linguistic Society.* Chicago: University of Chicago, Department of Linguistics.

Chomsky, N. 1957. *Syntactic structures.* The Hague: Mouton.

_____. 1965. *Aspects of the theory of syntax.* Cambridge: M.I.T. Press.

_____. 1971. Deep structure, surface structure, and semantic interpretation. In Jakobovits and Steinberg (1971).

Dougherty, R. C. 1968a. A comparison of two theories of pronominalization and reference. Mimeographed. Cambridge: M.I.T.

_____. 1968b. A transformational grammar of coordinate conjoined structures. Ph.D. dissertation. Cambridge: M.I.T.

Fillmore, C. J. 1965. *Indirect object constructions in English and the ordering of transformations.* The Hague: Mouton.

Gruber, J. 1967. Functions of the lexicon in formal descriptive grammars, TM 3 776/000/00. Santa Monica, Calif.: System Development Corporation.

Jackendoff, R. S. 1968a. An interpretive theory of pronouns and reflexives. PEGS paper 27. Washington, D.C.: Center for Applied Linguistics.

_____. 1968b. Speculations of presentences and determiners. Mimeographed. Cambridge: M.I.T.

_____. 1968c. An interpretive theory of negation. Mimeographed. Cambridge: M.I.T.

_____. 1969. Some rules of semantic interpretation for English. Ph.D. dissertation. Cambridge: M.I.T.

Jakobovits, L. A., and Steinberg, P. P. 1971. *Semantics: An interdisciplinary reader in philosophy, linguistics, anthropology, and psychology.* London: Cambridge University Press.

Katz, J. J. 1964a. Analyticity and contradiction in natural language. In Katz and Fodor (1964).

_____. 1964b. Semantic theory and the meaning of "Good." *Journal of Philosophy* 61.

_____. 1966. *The philosophy of language.* New York: Harper & Row.

_____. 1967a. Recent issues in semantic theory. *Foundations of Language 3.*

_____. 1967b. Some remarks on Quine on analyticity. *Journal of Philosophy* 64.

_____. 1968. Unpalatable recipes for buttering parsnips. *Journal of Philosophy* 65.

_____. Forthcoming. *Semantic theory.*

_____. and Fodor, J. A. 1963. The structure of a semantic theory. *Language*

_____, and Fodor, J. A. 1964. *The structure of language.* Englewood Cliffs, N. J.: Prentice-Hall.

_____, and Postal, P. M. 1964. *An integrated theory of linguistic descriptions.* Cambridge: M.I.T. Press.

Lakoff, G. 1965. *On the nature of syntactic irregularity.* Cambridge: Harvard University, Computation Laboratory, Math. Ling. and Auto. Trans. Report NSF-16.

————. 1969a. Repartee. *Foundations of Language 5.*

————. 1969b. On derivational constraints. In Binnick, Davison, Green, and Morgan (1969).

————. Forthcoming. *On generative semantics.*

————, Postal, P.M., and Ross, J. R. Forthcoming. What to do until the rules come.

Lakoff, R. 1968. *Abstract syntax and Latin complementation.* Cambridge: M.I.T. Press.

Lees, R. B. 1960. *The grammar of English nominalizations.* The Hague: Mouton.

McCawley, J. D. 1967. Meaning and the description of languages. *Kotoba No Uchu* 2, nos. 9-11.

————. 1968a. Lexical insertion in a transformational grammar without deep structure. In *Papers from the fourth regional meeting of the Chicago Linguistic Society.* Chicago: University of Chicago, Department of Linguistics.

————. 1968b. The role of semantics in a grammar. In Bach and Harms (1968).

————. 1968c. The annotated respective. Unpublished paper. Chicago: University of Chicago.

————. 1968d. Concerning the base component of a transformational grammar. *Foundations of Languages* 4.

————. 1969. Semantic representation. Paper read at Cognitive Studies and Artificial Intelligence Research, March 2-8, 1969. Chicago: University of Chicago Center for Continuing Education.

————. 1970a. English as a *VSO* language. *Language* 46.

————. 1970b. Where do noun phrases come from. In *Readings in English Transformational Grammar,* ed. R.A. Jacobs and P.S. Rosenbaum. Boston: Blaisdell-Ginn.

Morgan, J. L. 1968. Remarks on the notion "Possible Lexical Item." Paper read at the winter meeting, Linguistic Society of America, New York.

————. 1969. On the treatment of presupposition in transformational grammar. In Binnick, Davison, Green, and Morgan (1969).

Morgenbesser, S. 1967. *Philosophy of science today.* New York: Basic Books.

Perlmutter, D. 1968. Deep and surface structure constraints in syntax. Ph.D. dissertation. Cambridge: M.I.T.

Petrick, S. R., Postal, P.M., and Rosenbaum, P. S. 1969. On coordination, reduction and sentence analysis. *Comm. ACM* 12.

Postal, P. M. 1969. Anaphoric islands. In Binnick, Davison, Green, and Morgan (1969).

————. 1970a. *Cross-over phenomena.* New York: Holt, Rinehart.

————. 1970b. On the surface verb *Remind, Linguistic Inquiry* 1.

————. 1971. On coreferential complement subject deletion. In Jakobovits and Steinberg (1971).

————. Forthcoming. On the derivation of nouns.

Reibel, D. A., and Schane, S. A. 1969. *Modern studies in English.* Englewood Cliffs, N. J.: Prentice-Hall.

Ross, J. R. 1967. Constraints on variables in syntax. Ph.D. dissertation. Cambridge: M.I.T.

————. 1969a. On the cyclic nature of English pronominalization. In Reibel and Schane (1969).

————. 1969b. Guess who? In Binnick, Davison, Green, and Morgan (1969).

Chapter 5

THE PROJECTION PROBLEM:
HOW IS A GRAMMAR TO BE SELECTED?

Stanley Peters

Introduction of the concept "generative grammar" into linguistics stimulated many changes in the field. As significant numbers of linguists adopted the program of constructing grammars which specify in a finite, fully explicit fashion the linguistic intuition speakers will have about each of the infinity of possible phonetic sequences, certain new sorts of questions naturally came to be asked. One such question is how a person's rather limited experience with language in childhood enables him to arrive at the intricate and subtle judgments he is able to make about sentences. What is the relation between the data necessary to language learning and the linguist's model of the tacit linguistic knowledge that a person eventually acquires (i.e., a generative grammar of his language)? It was proposed in the middle fifties that linguistic theory answer this question. I will here examine motivation for adopting this goal, how to formulate it more precisely, progress toward achieving it, whether it is appropriate as a guide for future research, and its current indications for research directions.

Revival of a concern for explaining linguistic phenomena has had consequences at least as far-reaching as the pursuit of those elusive generative grammars. One facet of explaining the nature of language clearly involves showing how a representative sample of data from a language gives rise in the minds of speakers to a grammar of the complete language. A truly explanatory theory of language must indicate much in addition to this, of course—among other things, that certain modifications of a grammar are possible diachronic changes while others are not, that certain collections of grammars represent collections of dialects that can be commanded by a single speaker while others do not, etc. Matters such as the latter are only beginning to receive study within the framework of generative grammar, but the problem of "projecting"[1] from presented data to acquired grammar began to be the subject of serious inquiry in the early fifties (e.g., Chomsky 1955), well before the term "explanatory adequacy"[2] was introduced (Chomsky 1964b) to cover this goal. Thus we are motivated to solve the projection problem by two of the most central features of present linguistic theory, the search for generative grammars and the search for an explanatory theory.

In addition, this problem in effect asks us to provide an objective basis for selecting the correct grammar of a language in a general, principled manner on the basis of a sample of data regarding that language. Concern with such requirements is a natural outgrowth of certain features of structural linguistics in both America and Europe, namely, of the effort to provide objective *procedures* of analysis. Clearly, if a procedure could be devised which would allow any linguist to construct the correct grammar of a language by analyzing a corpus drawn from that language, then this would constitute a solution of the projection problem. Acceptance of the projection problem as a guide for research amounts to a lowering of goals from that of providing an analysis procedure to that of specifying grammars in a possibly *nonconstructive* fashion.[3] At the same time, of course, it raises the standard of "correctness" for the resulting grammar from observational adequacy to descriptive adequacy. One further motivation for seeking to solve the projection problem can be more clearly stated after we have more precisely defined what the projection problem is and will therefore be deferred until that time.

Every mature speaker of a natural language acquires his linguistic competence by virtue of certain aspects of his experience with language. Let us term the relevant aspects his *basic data*, deferring until later the question of what they are. For each possible natural language, whether it has ever been spoken or not, there is at least one set of basic data from which a human could learn it. By the *projection problem* I mean the problem of providing a general scheme which specifies the grammar (or grammars) that can be acquired by a human upon exposure to a possible set of basic data. To avoid misunderstanding, let me explicitly note that all mention here of language learning or grammar acquisition has reference to the process by which children learn a language naturally and without tutelage, not (necessarily) to the (possibly) different process by which adults master one.

More precisely, let D_1, D_2, D_3, ... be a recursive enumeration of all sets D_i, of basic data (represented in some formal way) such that each could form the basis for acquisition of a grammar by humans. Let G_1, G_2, G_3, ... be a recursive enumeration of (formal) grammars such that the descriptively adequate grammars of all possible natural languages appear in the enumeration (i.e., representations of all possible human linguistic competences appear). The human capacity for language acquisition induces a mapping π of indices of data sets D_i to sets of indices of grammars which could be acquired on the basis of them. That is, there is a function π such that $j \in \pi(i)$ if and only if some human could acquire G_j if exposed (at the appropriate age, etc.) to D_i, for every i and j. It may be that each D_i actually gives rise to a unique G_j, in which case we could just as well define π to map data-set indices to grammar indices. But, as has often been remarked, it is still quite an open empirical question whether there are some sets of data which fail to uniquely determine the acquired grammar, so that some humans learn one, some another grammar on the basis of these data. Thus our choice of formulation.[4] Now it is possible to state the projection problem with precision: it is to provide a finite, completely explicit specification of the function π.

We are now in a position to describe the additional motivation mentioned above for seeking a solution to this problem. We can best approach it indirectly. Note that the projection problem is nontrivial because every class of grammars we know of which offers reasonable promise of containing the correct grammar(s) for each possible natural language has the property that for each set D of what we think to be basic data many grammars in the class could account for D. If there were only one grammar for each set of data, then the projection problem would be automatically solved without any further mechanism. Now this same state of affairs obtains with respect to the full set of facts regarding any language. That is, even when we consider the infinite set containing all linguistic intuitions that a speaker's knowledge of his language provides about every possible phonetic sequence, there are still multiple grammars in any reasonable class which are consistent with the facts.[5] As a result, there is a difficulty in determining which grammar(s) really constitute a correct account of the speaker's linguistic competence. Given enumerations of grammars and sets of basic data as before, let us define the function π' by the condition that for every i, $\pi'(i)$ is the set of all indices of grammars that are compatible with the full set of linguistic intuitions of a person who learned his language on the basis of data D_i. By definition $\pi(i) \subseteq \pi'(i)$ for every i. Now it has been suggested, in effect, that there will be only one function for which we can provide a finite, explicit specification such that it maps each data-set index i into a nonempty subset of $\pi'(i)$. If this is the case, then we can be fairly confident that for every i, correct grammar(s) are selected by that function for the language learned on the basis of data D_i and, therefore, that that function is in fact the projection mapping π.[6] According to this view, solving the projection problem is a necessary as well as, obviously, a sufficient condition for specifying the correct grammar(s) for every natural language. This reason for tackling the projection problem is perhaps the most important one at the present stage of linguistics. The difficulty presented by the existence of alternative descriptions of a given language all equally in accord with the facts of that language (which is not to say that any of them is even approximately in exact accord) is no less a problem today than it was in the mid-fifties. Thus any means of selecting between accounts on an empirically significant basis ought to be pursued vigorously.

Before turning to the progress which has been made toward a solution to the projection problem, I will pick out for comment two points about this definition. First, observe that while the problem deals only with the relation between a complete set of basic data and a grammar, we have not in any way assumed that these data are presented to language learners all at once or that language acquisition is an "instantaneous process."[7] As has frequently been remarked, the temporal order of events providing the basic data for language acquisition may play a role in determining the particular grammar that is ultimately acquired.[8] Obviously, experiences which form the basis for language acquisition occur in a temporal sequence; however, I have characterized the notion "basic data" in such a way that information about this sequence forms a part of these data if it is relevant to what grammar is ultimately acquired. Thus the basic data might turn out to be very much unlike a *corpus* (an *unordered set* of well-formed utterances) in that it specifies an order of exposure to utterances—and possibly in many other ways. But our way of stating the problem does not preclude the possibility of solving it, even if order of exposure turns out to be significant.

Secondly, a solution to the projection problem as here stated need not concern itself with the tentative grammars an individual develops on the basis of partial exposure to the experiences that eventually determine his basic data. That is, we have posed a simpler problem than that of accounting for the sequence of intermediate hypotheses (grammars) that a child temporarily entertains but ultimately rejects in learning his native language; simpler because any solution to the latter problem is a solution to the projection problem, but not conversely. Perhaps one can best relate basic data to ultimately acquired competence by considering preliminary steps along the road,[9] but such a solution is not excluded by our formulation of the projection problem. Thus the basis for choice between the goal of solving the projection problem and that posed by this more ambitious problem is an estimate of which is the more likely to be significantly approached at the present stage of linguistic inquiry, not the possibility that only one of them admits of solution. I think that the projection problem is really simpler[10] and is sufficiently ambitious to guide fruitful research for some time to come.

I have tried to formulate the projection problem in a way which follows as closely as possible the discussions of this matter by Chomsky (1957, pp. 14-15, 50; 1962, pp. 530-31, 534-35; 1965, pp. 30-47). It may be useful to digress briefly at this point and discuss what I believe to be an error that is relevant to the points just made. McCawley (1968, pp. 559-60) objects to Chomsky's familiar proposal (1957, pp. 50-55) for solving the projection problem on the grounds that children acquire language by continually "constructing and revising" their grammar as new data are presented to them "rather than by the accumulation of a large body of unanalyzed data." But, as we have seen, this objection does not find the mark because Chomsky only attempts to present a general scheme for projecting from finite sets of data to the grammars that would be acquired on the basis of them, as distinguished from a point-by-point model of the process a child actually goes through in learning his language. That is, Chomsky's model is concerned only with the total effect of all the basic data on the grammar ultimately acquired. As we have seen, there is nothing *a priori* wrongheaded about investigating this question. If it is true that a solution to the projection problem which concerns itself with intermediate stages in the language-learning process is superior to one which does not, this needs to be demonstrated on the basis of empirical evidence rather than just being assumed, as in McCawley's review.

This confusion of the sort of model Chomsky has proposed for language acquisition with a model for the hypothesis-forming, -testing, and -rejecting steps a child makes in the process of language acquisition is not unlike the confusion, at one time common, which construed a grammar (i.e., a model of a speaker's linguistic competence) as a model of actual or potential linguistic performance. But just as a grammar merely specifies a pairing of phonetic representations with sets of structural descriptions, a finite, explicit description of the function π merely specifies a pairing of sets D_i of basic data with sets $\{G_{j_1}, \ldots, G_{j_k}\}$ of grammars which are the end product of the language-acquisition process.

Some conception of the nature of the basic data for language acquisition is essential to making progress on the projection problem. Much of what happens in the environment of a child learning to speak clearly does not influence what grammar he will ultimately internalize. Just which aspects of his linguistic experience are influential is unfortunately very hard to determine. We may plausibly suppose that a child needs to know that certain utterances are grammatical. How he could get such information is not altogether clear, however. As has often been remarked, one rarely hears a fully grammatical sentence of any complexity. How then can a child who does not yet know the rules of grammar tell which of the utterances he hears are grammatical? One strategy open to him is to put the greatest confidence in short utterances, which are likely to be less complex than longer ones and thus more likely to be grammatical. Which grammatical utterances a child hears seems to affect the grammar he acquires in two ways. First, it clearly affects the precise formulation of the grammar's rules: a child who grows up hearing people say (1) will learn a different modifier-preposing transformation than one who hears (2):

(1) Here is a picture ready to color.
(2) Here is a ready picture to color.

Second, it apparently determines whether or not a rule is in the grammar, as the following thought-experiment indicates. Consider a person whose native language is some standard variety of English, who learned English by projecting from some set D of basic data. Modify D now just by excising all grammatical sentences whose derivation involves, say, the passive transformation of our English speaker's internalized grammar, and imagine that the resulting set of data is the basis for language acquisition by some other person. Does the grammar that the latter person will internalize contain the passive transformation? It seems most unlikely. Why should passive (or indirect object inversion, or any other transformation) be so predictably a part of the grammar of English that one need only have data justifying the other rules to know that the passive transformation is necessarily in the grammar too? Is it an impossible diachronic change for English to lose the passive transformation but remain unchanged in other respects?

Less clear is whether negative information—e.g., that *John elapsed* is ungrammatical—is part of the basic data for language acquisition. One problem here is just how a child could obtain such information. McCawley contends that the basic data "must include not only things that the 'informants' say, but things that the learner himself says and his observations of the results which follow upon his saying them" (1968, p. 560). This suggests that a child might obtain negative data when he says something that is understood either incorrectly (from his point of view) or not at all, or that results in someone correcting him. If this is how negative information becomes available, then such information is not necessary for language acquisition. Lenneberg has studied a child who evidently learned to understand English despite a congenital defect resulting in an inability to produce intelligible sounds (1962; 1967, pp. 305-9). The child reportedly has no trouble understanding spoken English, so his linguistic development is apparently normal except for the inability to coordinate his vocal tract muscles. Of course, his basic data did not include anthing he said or the consequences of his saying anything, so this could not be a source of negative information for him.

Another question about the nature of basic data is how much information about meaning it contains. Since one thing a person acquiring a language learns is the meaning of each lexical item, it is clear that some semantic data is essential. Conceiveably, however, information about reference is sufficient, when used in conjunction with linguistic universals, to determine the sense of lexical items. For example, it is plausible that the meaning of at least some nouns like *cow, man, table*, adjectives like *tall, red, smart*, and verbs like *bite, walk, throw* are learned simply on the basis of ostention. To show that information about sense must appear in the basic data, we might consider syntactic constructions like restrictive vs. nonrestrictive relative clauses and yes-no vs. alternative questions. Nonrestrictive relatives are distinguished from restrictives by certain nonsemantic characteristics, e.g., the well-known intonational features and occurrence as a modifier of ordinary proper nouns; while only restrictive relative clauses may utilize the complementizer *that* in place of a relative pronoun and may delete both *that* and the relative pronoun under certain conditions. It is plausible that a person will learn a grammar generating restrictive and nonrestrictive relatives differently if these idiosyncracies are exemplified in his basic data; but how he could learn which meaning is associated with each variety is not so clear. The major semantic difference between the two types seems to be that the proposition expressed by the relative clause is presupposed in the restrictive case and asserted in the nonrestrictive case. Virtually all of the distributional characteristics distinguishing between the two types seem irrelevant to this semantic difference. The only distributional reflection I know about of the semantic affinity between sentences containing nonrestrictive relative clauses and conjoint assertions of sentences is the behavior, pointed out by Thorne (1971), of adverbs like *incidentally* and *frankly*. Consider the following pattern of grammatical and ungrammatical sentences.

(3) *The girl that frankly he liked left the room blushing.
(4) *The girl frankly he liked left the room blushing.
(5) The girl, who frankly he liked, left the room blushing.
(6) The girl left the room blushing, and, frankly, he liked her.
(7) Anne, who frankly he liked, left the room blushing.

Frankly occurs as a so-called sentence adverb only in the main clause of an asserted sentence and of a nonrestrictive relative clause. It occurs in restrictive relative clauses only as a manner adverb, in which role it also occurs in nonrestrictive relatives and main clauses:

(8) The girl (that) he had frankly praised left the room blushing.
(9) {The girl/Anne} , who he had frankly praised, left the room blushing.
(10) {The girl/Anne} left the room blushing, and he had frankly praised her.

These parallels are the most cogent distributional justification for generating nonrestrictive relative clauses from conjoined assertions, but I find it quite implausible that such recondite examples could be the basis for a child's learning that nonrestrictive relatives are asserted. Apparently, some information about meaning is crucial here, but again the truth value of certain sentences in various situations may be sufficient to decide those options that linguistic universals leave open about the meaning of relative clauses.

The difference in meaning between questions (11) and (12) is reflected in the different answers appropriate to each [(11) is pronounced with final rising intonation and (12) with final falling intonation, as indicated by "?R" and "?F"]:

> (11) Did you hear a shriek or a moan?R
> (12) Did you hear a shriek or a moan?F

Yes and *no* are inappropriate answers to (12) under all circumstances, whereas in certain situations *yes*, and in every other situation *no*, is appropriate to (11). The semantic difference between yes-no and alternative questions correlates with the difference in intonation and two other restrictions I know of. There are no syntactically negative alternative questions, in contrast to so-called negative questions:

> (13) Didn't you hear a shriek or a moan?R
> (14) *Didn't you hear a shriek or a moan?F

Alternative questions permit only *some* where yes-no questions permit *some* or *any*:[11]

> (15) (a) Do you want some beer or some whiskey?R
>   (b) Do you want any beer or any whiskey?R
> (16) (a) Do you want some beer or some whiskey?F
>   (b) *Do you want any beer or any whiskey?F

It is not at all clear how the existence of these restrictions could determine that a yes-no question based on a proposition A v B requests the truth value of A v B, while an alternative question based on the same proposition requests the truth value of A and of B. On the other hand, once a child notices that adults answer alternative questions differently than yes-no questions (casual observation suggests this occurs quite a while after he learns to interpret yes-no questions), he possesses a vital clue to the difference in meaning. One could suppose that these observations plus linguistic universals necessitate that alternative questions be interpreted in a unique way, thus providing some semantic information needed for language learning.

From these inconclusive remarks on the nature of basic data let us turn to some ways of selecting a grammar once the data are given. If we could formulate an effective procedure for calculating the projection function π—i.e., a finite recipe for mechanically passing in a finite number of steps from any set of basic data to the correct grammar(s)—we would have invented a discovery procedure for grammars. Unfortunately, the over-whelming majority of effective procedures are enormously time-consuming to carry through, but if our procedure could be carried out practically – say, by a fast computer – it would be of the greatest interest. The interest would decrease to the extent that it was less than practical. Of course, no one has actually specified a discovery procedure, even an impractical one; but structural linguists appear to have tried to do so. Chomsky argued against this effort (1957, pp. 52-57) as being both unlikely to succeed and needlessly overambitious. His doubts about its success had two roots. Structuralists were attempting to develop discovery procedures that utilized segmentation and classification as the basic computational devices, and the kind of grammar to which such techniques must lead is inadequate to describe certain known complexities of English. Furthermore, of the grammar classes then known, every one either demonstrably excluded a descriptively adequate grammar for some language or else contained too many grammars compatible with any reasonable set of data for the correct one(s) to be efficiently selected. Of Chomsky's two objections, the first is obviously specific to the kind of calculating procedure embodied in structuralist methodology and does not preclude the invention of a different sort of practical discovery procedure. The second, on the other hand, might turn out to apply with equal force to other approaches to the projection problem.

Instead of a discovery procedure, Chomsky advocated developing an *evaluation procedure* which might not permit us automatically to construct a correct grammar when presented with a set of basic data. Such a procedure would, however, effectively indicate for any two grammars G_i and G_j and any basic data D_k whether it "prefers" G_i to G_j as a description of D_k. Its preferences automatically define the function which maps any set D_k of basic data to the set of maximally preferred grammars. If this function is identical to the projection mapping π, then the evaluation procedure in question is a solution to the projection problem. Different evaluation procedures thus express different hypotheses about the projection function. An evaluation procedure which correctly solves the projection problem would not fabricate for us the correct grammar of a given language, but it would at least tell us when our own constructions are advancing toward that goal and when they are retreating. Chomsky further suggested defining preferability in terms of two other concepts: compatibility of a grammar with a set of data, and value of a grammar as specified by an *evaluation measure*. A grammar G_i is defined to be preferable to G_j for basic data D_k if G_i is compatible with D_k, and furthermore, should G_j be compatible with D_k, then the value of G_i is greater than that of G_j. Little light has been shed on the required definition of compatibility (see Chomsky 1962, p. 535; 1965, p. 32). Explicating this notion depends on knowing how a language learner extracts his basic data from his experience, and consequently little can be said at present. Obviously a grammar should be compatible with a set of data only if it generates all sentences reliably specified in the data as grammatical, none specified as ungrammatical, etc.

By contrast, certain aspects of the contemplated evaluation measure have received considerable study. Much work has gone into developing a notational system for phonology with the idea that the value of a grammar's phonological component be inversely proportional to the number of specified features in the particular notation representing that component (e.g., Halle 1962; Chomsky and Halle 1968, chaps. 3, 8; Bach 1968). Evaluation measures for other aspects of a grammar, however, have not been investigated with anything like the same thoroughness, and no one to my knowledge has even proposed an evaluation measure for complete grammars. Thus we are very far from solving the projection problem in the manner Chomsky recommended. Just how far can be seen by asking what success has been achieved even in the single area of phonology. Harms (1966) and Chomsky and Halle (1968, pp. 345-49) have proposed quite different phonological components for a grammar of Southern Paiute. The two phonologies dovetail with precisely the same syntactic (and semantic) components for a Southern Paiute grammar, and furthermore are both compatible with the data recorded by Sapir (1930). Which one is preferable, then, ought to be decided by the phonological evaluation measure that has been so laboriously developed. No one, however, would seriously suggest counting the number of specified features required for each analysis and declaring one a winner on that basis; the measure is simply not that reliable. A decision between these analyses must presently be made by considering such questions as whether other languages contrast vowels but not consonants for the feature of voicing. We would choose the analysis which, conjointly with grammars of other languages, maximizes the universal properties of language, not necessarily the more highly valued one. We just do not have an evaluation procedure which can be counted on in cases of much complexity to prefer an analysis that is also preferable on other grounds. The Paiute example is anything but isolated. Chomsky and Halle (1968, chaps. 3, 4) and Ross (Forthcoming) have proposed different phonological components for English, Halle (1959) and Lightner (1965, Forthcoming) for Russian, and the same considerations hold. In neither case can one expect with much confidence that the analysis which requires fewer specified features to express in the appropriate notational system will turn out to be better motivated on other grounds. Though existing evaluation measures make demonstrably correct predictions in certain cases, new situations are constantly turning up where they are inadequate and must be revised.

One reason for this is the tremendous latitude in present theories of generative grammar, which permits a number of analyses to be given for any single set of data, analyses that differ widely and in some unforeseeable ways from one another. Thus when we engineer an evaluation measure in a given case to prefer what we know to be the better of two analyses, there is often a third (fourth, fifth, ...) analysis which our theory of grammar permits, unbeknownst to us, and which is inferior to the two analyses we had in mind and at the same time preferred to both by our evaluation measure. We would naturally expect to be burned by this problem when we first start trying to develop an evaluation procedure, but after years of effort it is still a common occurrence. Thus the existence of a great variety of theoretically permitted grammars, which creates such obstacles to a discovery procedure, is hardly less of a stumbling block to the development of an evaluation measure. Worse yet, the same superfluity of grammars would continue to be a problem even if we succeeded in developing an apparently successful evaluation procedure.

To see why, recall that any proposed evaluation procedure is an empirical hypothesis about how humans project from basic data to matured linguistic competence and therefore must itself be justified empirically. Let us consider, then, how one could test the correctness of any proposed solution to the projection problem. In principle, there is a simple test: one could (*a*) determine the basic data from which someone learned his native language, (*b*) ascertain which grammar(s) the proposed solution selects for those data, and (*c*) check that the predictions made by (at least one of) the grammar(s) agree with the native speaker's linguistic intuition. Of course, in practice it may be quite difficult to determine just which data a person used in acquiring his native language as well as to ascertain precisely what his linguistic intuition about various sentences is. Furthermore, even perfect accord between his linguistic intuition and a grammar's prediction is not sufficient to establish that he has internalized that grammar. [12] Still, it is useful to think of this test as establishing a standard of correctness for proposed solutions to the projection problem.

One aspect of a speaker's linguistic intuition is the knowledge of what each sequence of sounds means. We assume that there is a universal system of phonetic representation and a universal system of semantic representation and represent this knowledge as a set of ordered pairs, each having as its first member a phonetic representation, which stands for a sound sequence, and as its second member a semantic representation, which stands for an associated meaning. Linguistic intuition includes judgments of other kinds too, e. g., of grammaticality, ambiguity, segmentation into constituents, conformity, and potential for coreference. If two grammars make identical predictions with respect to properties that linguistic intuition ascribes to sentences, we shall say that they are *strongly equivalent* because they are indistinguishable by this empirical criterion no matter how different they may be in certain formal respects. Strong equivalence means just that grammars generate the same phonetic representations, the same pairing of phonetic and semantic representations, and so forth; it does not require that they generate these things by means of the same set, or even remotely similar sets, of rules.

Suppose now that for some theory of grammar, for example

Chomsky's (1965) theory of transformational grammar, there were an algorithm, an effective procedure, which mapped any grammar countenanced by the theory into a different yet strongly equivalent grammar. Such an algorithm would permit us automatically to convert any successful evaluation procedure into a different evaluation procedure, also successful. To say an evaluation procedure E_1 is successful is to say that the hypothesis π_1 it expresses about the projection function satisfies the following condition: $\pi_1(k)$ is not empty; furthermore, j is in $\pi_1(k)$ only if on the basis of data D_k a human could learn a language such that G_j is in complete agreement with his linguistic intuition, for all j and k. Suppose that E_1 is, in fact, successful in this sense and that ψ is a bijective recursive function such that $G_{\psi(i)}$ is strongly equivalent to G_i for all i.[13] We define a new evaluation procedure E_2 by stipulating that E_2 prefers $G_{\psi(i)}$ to $G_{\psi(j)}$ for D_k if and only if E_1 prefers G_i to G_j for D_k. For any basic data D_k, E_2 projects to $G_{\psi(i)}$ just in case E_1 projects to the strongly equivalent grammar G_i, because E_2 mirrors the preferences of E_1 exactly but under the influence of the function ψ. Hence, since E_1 is successful, it follows that $\pi_2(k)$ is not empty and, furthermore, that $j \in \pi_2(k)$ only if on the basis of D_k a human could learn a language in complete agreement with G_j; i.e., E_2 is also successful. For this reason, any claim that π_1 is really the projection mapping, rather than the very different function π_2, has no justification on fundamental empirical grounds, namely, agreement with native speakers' linguistic intuition. Correspondingly, we have no justification for supposing that E_1 is the empirically correct evaluation procedure and not E_2.

This unhappy state of affairs would result from the existence of an algorithm ψ preserving strong equivalence of grammars. I suspect it can be shown that such an algorithm does exist for current theories of transformational grammar, though the argument is beyond the scope of this paper. Its existence is a consequence of the excessive latitude current versions of transformational theory permit for describing a given speaker's linguistic intuition. Because existing theories are not restrictive enough, the principal available type of empirical data cannot play the decisive role one might expect it to in selecting either particular grammars or the theory of grammars. Often important decisions about linguistic theory rest on linguists' intuitions of "revealingness" or "naturalness" of particular analyses, an undesirable situation since perceptions about such matters sometimes differ from person to person. Scientists' intuitions of this sort are valuable guides to research, but are surely not convincing evidence for acceptance or rejection of an empirical hypothesis.

Why is transformational theory in this condition? In the 1950's, during the first few years of effort to construct a grammatical theory that overcame the limitations of immediate constituent analysis, relatively few examples of grammatical transformations had been discovered. To suppose that the general properties of such rules were adequately exemplified by so limited a sample would have been unwise. It made no sense to theorize that transformations could only transpose subject and object noun phrases (like the passive rule) or prepose parts of the verbal auxiliary (like the question transformation), because one knew that the immediate future held a new grammatical transformation with a somewhat different function. On the other hand, a substantive theory of transformational grammar had to define "grammatical transformation." The solution to this problem was to characterize transformations in terms of certain very general formal properties that were shared by all the instances known at that time. This saved the theory from vacuity, and left a great deal of freedom for new discoveries because the defining properties were *very* general. In the intervening years, some hundreds of purported examples of grammatical transformations have appeared, and they have turned out to fit a surprisingly limited number of patterns. The vast majority of the rules countenanced by formal definitions of transformations, for instance rule (17) and an infinity of possible variations on it, depart radically from these patterns:

$$(17) \quad NP - V - NP - [_S NP{-}V{-}NP]_S$$

$$
\begin{array}{ccccccc}
1 & 2 & 3 & & 4 & 5 & 6 \implies \\
3 & 2 & 1 & & 6 & 5 & 4
\end{array}
$$

Condition: $2 = 5$

Nonetheless, refined and improved versions of these definitions continue in the same mold, quite general and purely formal, as the original, taking little advantage of the restricted range of observed variation in transformations. What was necessary in the mid-fifties is no longer appropriate. Effort should now be given to defining "transformational grammar," and, accordingly, "grammatical transformation," in a highly restrictive fashion.

Bach has done some exploratory work that points in a direction well worth following. He has shown (1965) that certain transformations not only appear in a variety of distantly related or unrelated languages in precisely the same form or very similar forms, but also have the same function in each of them. English and Japanese each have relative-clause-forming transformations and the similarities are manifold. Some other languages have relative clauses formed by different transformations, but in all these cases the transformations share a very significant common denominator. Similarly, questions are formed by a very limited range of different transformations (Bach 1971). Not only that, but in these instances a rule's form corresponds in a suggestive way to its function in these languages. This indicates that much more work ought to be done on the possibility that strong substantive constraints exist, relating the form of a transformation to the semantic role it plays in a language, and that furthermore there is a finite number of transformations from which grammars may draw. One might speculate that a grammar may either contain a transformation for forming, say, comparatives, or not; that if it does, then that transformation must be chosen chosen from a finite list of options, all sharing properties that are traceable to the semantic nature of comparison. Among all languages the number of "constructions" such as comparative may be limited, and for each possible construction there may be just a finite number of transformational realizations. This possibility is worth pursuing because it is plausible in light of the past decade's revelations about transformations and because, if true, it permits a tremendous strengthening of transformational theory. If we formulate a theory of transformational grammar along these lines and find no falsifying evidence from the realm of native speakers' linguistic intuition, we should possess a theory that really permits empirical justification of grammars. Since there would be only a finite number of different transformational components permitted and since each grammar would generate an infinite number of predictions about linguistic intuition, there should exist divergent predictions from any two grammars about some specific intuition; so we could check which, if either, is correct. In fact, given a representative sample of basic data from a language, a discovery procedure could project it to the correct grammar simply by testing each of the *finite* number of grammars permitted by the theory for compatibility with the data; if the data are representative, only one grammar should fit. Quite likely, one could even develop a *practical* discovery procedure, by taking account of certain earmarks that would be associated with each of the finite number of permitted transformations.

    If one desires to solve the projection problem, this seems to me the most promising direction for future research. If it leads where I have speculated, one outcome would be a discovery procedure that could conceivably open up significant new avenues for research in language acquisition. Eliminating the existing obstacles to an evaluation procedure will have opened the way to a discovery procedure.

NOTES

This work was supported in part by NSF Grant GS 2468 and in part by a grant from the University Research Institute, University of Texas at Austin.

[1] I have borrowed this term from *Syntactic Structures* (Chomsky 1957, p. 15). The apparent discrepancy between Chomsky's use of the term and mine results from the fact that he was employing it prior to drawing the distinction between a grammar (which, of course, generates every sentence in any sample of its language) and an explanatory theory of language (which selects a grammar on the basis of a sample of its language).

[2] I suspect that Chomsky intends this term to cover all the demands we would make of an explanatory linguistic theory, even though he consistently uses it to refer only to the criterion of solving what I am here calling the "projection problem" (see Chomsky 1964b, pp. 28-29; 1965, pp. 25-26; Chomsky and Halle 1965, pp. 99-100).

[3] There is another lowering of goals here as well, in that the projection problem allows data other than simply examples of observed utterance tokens—i.e., a corpus—to serve as "input" to the grammar selection scheme.

[4] Since there is no reason to rule out *a priori* the possibility that there might be even infinitely many grammars that could be acquired given certain sets of basic data and since in such cases we wish to have a tractable finite specification of the set of grammars acquired, we need to assume given some Gödel numbering of the set $\varphi_1, \varphi_2, \varphi_3, \ldots$ of all recursive functions. We can then define the projection function π to be the function such that for all i, the recursive function $\varphi\pi(i)$ has as its range (set of values or "outputs" arising from any "input") the set of all numbers j such that grammar G_j can be acquired on the basis of data D_i.

[5] See Peters and Ritchie (1971) for an argument that apparently can be extended to establish this statement.

[6] Of course, there is in addition a problem in determining what constitutes the set of basic data from which a person learned his language. The solution to this problem, too, is supposed to go hand in hand with a solution to the projection problem since, it has been thought, only one choice of a set of grammars for each set of data would allow development of a general scheme for projecting from a reasonable (small enough, yet sufficiently varied) set of data to grammars consistent with the linguistic intuition of a speaker who learned his language on the basis of that set of data (Chomsky 1957, pp. 14, 49-50). This view, that pursuit of explanatory adequacy is essential to attainment of descriptive adequacy, has been advanced repeatedly (Chomsky 1962, pp. 532-33; 1964a, pp. 224, 241; 1964b, pp. 52-53; 1965, p. 26).

[7] Chomsky and Halle naturally expect their proposed solution of the projection problem to disclose certain facts regarding the descriptively adequate grammar [i.e., the "correct account of the linguistic intuition of the native speaker" (Chomsky 1964b, pp. 28-29)] acquired by a speaker on the basis of any set of data he considers. They assert (Chomsky and Halle 1968, pp. 331-32), however, that the strongest claim that can be supported on the basis of their proposed solution is that "if it were the case that language acquisition were instantaneous, then [the underlying phonological forms of the grammar their solution selects for English] would be psychologically real"—i.e., their grammar would be descriptively adequate in this respect. Their reason for qualifying the claim to descriptive adequacy is that "the order of presentation of linguistic data is, for the moment, an extrinsic factor that has no place in [their] theory."

There is, however, no need for the qualifying condition which Chomsky and Halle seem to feel must be appended to every claim of descriptive adequacy. A correct solution to the projection problem is perfectly reliable as an indicator of the descriptively adequate (i.e., psychologically real) grammar whether or not it is a point-by-point model of the acquisition process. In fact, what they really seem to be concerned with in this case is a situation in which some speakers may not have certain linguistic experiences early enough for the speakers' fully matured linguistic competence to be affected by them; that is, the speakers may not be exposed to certain facts before they cease learning their native language and thus these facts may not form part of their basic data at all.

[8] See, for example, Chomsky (1962, p. 530), Chomsky and Halle (1968, pp. 331-32), McCawley (1968, p. 560). To my knowledge, however, no one has yet demonstrated that order of presentation was a determining factor in any particular case—that is, no one has gone beyond speculation on this matter.

[9] This position seems to be held by McCawley (1968, p. 560) and Chomsky and Halle (1968, pp. 331-32).

[10] Apparently Chomsky and Halle share this opinion. They say (1968, p. 331), "To us it appears that this more realistic study is much too complex to be undertaken in any meaningful way today and that it will be far more fruitful to investigate in detail, as a first approximation, the idealized model outlined earlier . . . . " The "more realistic study" referred to pertains to the sequence of stages a child goes through in language acquisition – on the odd choice of adjective, I will comment shortly. The "idealized model outlined earlier" is the familiar Chomsky-Halle approach to solving the projection problem, which I will discuss later.

[11] I am indebted to LeRoy Baker for pointing this out to me.

[12] Every speaker has internalized a set of generalizations (which a grammar is supposed to model) about his language, and these generalizations assign specific properties to individual sentences. A speaker has linguistic intuition about certain properties of individual sentences or pairs of sentences: for example, that *What we danced on was the bandstand* is grammatical while *What we danced at was midnight* is not, and that *That is a talkative family of midgets* is synonymous with *That is a family of talkative midgets* but that *That is a large family of midgets* is not synonymous with *That is a family of large midgets*. No speaker, however, has linguistic intuition about the generalizations that make these particular judgments possible; as a native speaker of English, for example, no one can intuit the generalization that covers passive constructions.

I want to emphasize that linguistic intuition is only about particular instances and not about the generalizations that cover these instances. There is no harm in assuming that for each possible phonetic sequence a speaker has linguistic intuition about grammaticality, ambiguity, meaning, etc., and that for each possible pair of phonetic sequences he has linguistic intuition about synonymy, conformity, etc. There is, however, a great deal of potential harm in assessing the correctness of a grammar by reference to any intuition a speaker might claim to have about which generalizations he has internalized. Such intuition is characteristically unreliable and is not a suitable foundation for a scientific theory of which generalizations a speaker has in fact internalized. Linguists too sometimes develop intuition about which generalizations are linguistically significant. Obviously, though, these intuitions are not data but at best useful guidance in how to use data to justify claims about which generalizations have been internalized.

Note, therefore, that a speaker's linguistic intuition does not uniquely determine a grammar. Since speakers have no reliable intuitions about which generalizations they have internalized, our evidence about these generalizations is necessarily indirect. But the particular judgments of grammaticality, synonymy, etc. which a speaker makes are characterized by infinitely many different sets of generalizations, any one of which he might have internalized. So any grammar which models one of these sets will be in complete agreement with the speaker's linguistic intuition.

[13] The assumption that ψ is bijective is made for expository ease only and can be eliminated along the following lines. Let ψ be a recursive function such that $G_{\psi(i)}$ is strongly equivalent to G_i for all i. Define a recursive function ψ' on the range of ψ by the condition that $\psi'(j)$ is equal to the least i such that $j = \psi(i)$. Since each grammar G_i is strongly equivalent to $G_{\psi(i)}$, we can restrict our attention to the set of grammars $G_{i'}$ with i' in the range of ψ without diminishing descriptive adequacy. Consider, now, a theory which specifies the various $G_{i'}$ as admissible grammars and which contain an evaluation procedure E_2 that prefers $G_{i'}$ to $G_{j'}$ for D_k if and only if E_1 prefers $G_{\psi'(i')}$ to $G_{\psi'(j')}$ for D_k. Then from any set of D_k of basic data, the new theory projects to those grammars $G_{j'}$ such that E_2 does not prefer any $G_{i'}$ to $G_{j'}$ for D_k; in other words, to those grammars $G_{\psi(j)}$ such that E_2 does not prefer any $G\psi_{(i)}$ to $G\psi_{(j)}$ for D_k, since i' and j' are in the range of ψ. But these are just the grammars $G_{\psi(j)}$ such that E_1 does not prefer any $G_{\psi'(\psi(i))}$ to $G_{\psi'(\psi(j))}$ for D_k, because of the relationship between E_2 and E_1. To complete the proof, note that $\psi'(\psi(i)) = i$ and $\psi'(\psi(j)) = j$ for all i and j in the range of ψ'.

REFERENCES

Bach, E. 1965. On some recurrent types of transformations. In *Georgetown University Monograph Series on Languages and Linguistics*, vol. 18, ed. C. W. Kreidler, pp. 3-18. Washington, D.C.

_____. 1968. Two proposals concerning the simplicity metric in phonology. *Glossa* 2: 128-49.

_____. 1971. Questions. *Linguistic Inquiry* 2:153-66.

Chomsky, C. 1968. The acquisition of syntax in children from 5 to 10. Research Monograph No. 57. Cambridge: M.I.T. Press.

Chomsky, N. 1955. *Logical structure of linguistic theory*. Microfilm. Cambridge: M.I.T. Library.

_____. 1957. *Syntactic structures*. The Hague: Mouton.

_____. 1962. Explanatory models in linguistics. In *Logic, methodology and philosophy of science: proceedings of the 1960 International Congress*, ed. E. Nagel, P. Suppes, and A. Tarski, pp. 528-50. Stanford, Calif.: Stanford University Press.

_____. 1964a. A transformational approach to syntax. In *The structure of language: readings in the philosophy of language*, ed. J. A. Fodor and J. J. Katz, pp. 211-45. Englewood Cliffs, N.J.: Prentice-Hall.

_____. 1964b. *Current issues in linguistic theory*. The Hague: Mouton.

_____. 1965. *Aspects of the theory of syntax.* Cambridge: M.I.T. Press.

_____, and Halle, M. 1965. Some controversial questions in phonological theory. *Journal of Linguistics* 1: 97-214.

_____, and Halle, M. 1968. *The sound pattern of English*. New York: Harper & Row.

Halle, M. 1959. *The sound pattern of Russian*. The Hague: Mouton.

_____. 1962. Phonology in generative grammar. *Word* 18: 54-72.

Harms, R. 1966. Stress, voice and length in Southern Paiute. *International Journal of American Linguistics* 2: 228-35.

Lenneberg, E. H. 1962. Understanding language without ability to speak. *Journal of Abnormal Social Psychology* 65: 419-25.

_____. 1967. *Biological foundations of language*. New York: John Wiley.

Lightner, T. M. 1965. Segmental phonology of modern standard Russian. Ph.D. dissertation. Cambridge: M.I.T.

_____. Forthcoming. *Russian phonology*. Edmonton: Linguistic Research, Inc.

McCawley, J. D. 1968. Review of T. A. Sebeok (ed.), *Current trends in linguistics, vol. 3: theoretical foundations*. 44: 556-93.

Peters, P. S., Jr., and Ritchie, R. W. 1971. On restricting the base component of transformational grammars. *Information and Control* 18: 483-501.

_____. Forthcoming. On the generative power of transformational grammars. *Informative sciences*.

Ross, J. R. Forthcoming. Reanalysis of English word stress.

Sapir, E. 1930. Southern Paiute, a Shoshonean language. *Proceedings of the American Academy of Arts and Sciences* 65, nos. 1-3.

Thorne, J. P. 1971. On non-restrictive relative clauses. Unpublished paper.

Chapter 6

EXPLANATION IN PHONOLOGY

Paul Kiparsky

1. FORMAL AND FUNCTIONAL EXPLANATION

The study of the formal properties of phonological systems has progressed to a point where it may be possible to return, with much greater precision and generality than could be achieved before, to traditional functionalist questions: how phonological structure is grounded in the requirements of speech performance, in the broad sense of perception, production, and acquisition. The interest and importance of these questions is obvious. However, the research paradigms of generative phonology have in several respects not been particularly conducive to their investigation.[1] Insufficient attention has been paid even to posing the relevant questions sufficiently clearly to allow empirical studies to get under way. Perhaps one reason for this is the sharp distinction which has developed in practice between work on linguistic competence and work on speech performance. More serious is the fact that many functional regularities differ in a basic way from the sorts of phenomena that have been primarily investigated in generative grammar, and cannot be "captured" by notational conventions and an evaluation measure based on simplicity. For example, we shall see

189

below that recent attempts to reduce certain types of functional regularities to grammatical simplicity by means of derivational constraints fail for intrinsic reasons to provide an explanatory account of these regularities.

The questions which will be raised in this paper will be about the explanation rather than the description of phonological and morphological facts. The paper deals with the form and substance which functional explanations may have in these areas of linguistic structure. In spite of the fact that it continues a very traditional line of investigation, it is in many ways preliminary and speculative. The data used to illustrate and motivate the proposed generalizations come from well-documented languages and should not be controversial, though its interpretation in a few cases may be.

Let me begin by reviewing briefly the nature of explanation in phonology as it emerges from Chomsky and Halle (1968). The notational devices and the evaluation measure jointly characterize the notion "linguistically significant generalization," in a way which is empirically testable through the investigation of linguistic universals, language acquisition, and linguistic change. As this explanatory paradigm is well known, I will simply give a short illustration of its functioning, and then proceed to point out some respects in which the paradigm breaks down. This will then lead into the general topic of functional conditions as a basis of explanation in phonology and morphology.

The examples which I will analyze come from a discussion of movable accent of the phonologically predictable type in Itkonen (1966). Itkonen cites the accentual systems of two Finno-Ugric languages, Eastern Cheremis and Komi. In certain dialects of Eastern Cheremis, and in Proto-Cheremis, vowels are divided into two groups: full and reduced vowels (what the feature correlates of this distinction are need not be settled here). On the basis of this distinction in the vowels, the accentuation of a word is predictable as follows:

> 1. "[a] ... the accent falls on the syllable containing the last full vowel of the word. [b] If the word has only reduced vowels, the accent is usually on the first syllable" (Itkonen 1966, p. 156).

In the Eastern Permyak dialect of Komi (which Itkonen assumes represents Proto-Permic in this respect) vowels are divided into heavy and light. The accentuation of a word is determined by the following rule, which is exactly the mirror image of the Cheremis rule:

> 2. "[a] The accent normally falls on the syllable containing the first heavy vowel of the word. [b] If the word has only light vowels, the accent is on the last syllable" (Itkonen 1966, p. 156).

For both Cheremis and Komi, a verbally formulated stress rule contains two separate statements: one for words which contain full (or heavy) vowels, and another for words which do not. No *instrinsic* connection between the [a] and [b] cases is shown. There is no reason, apparently, why 1[b] should read "first syllable" and 2[b] "last syllable," rather than vice versa.

Things are different if we work within a formal theory. Suppose that we write formally the Cheremis rule for words containing full vowels (case 1[a]). The simplest rule which puts the accent on the last full vowel is this:

$$V \rightarrow [+\text{acc}] \ / \ \underline{\quad} \ [C_0 \ \breve{V} C_0]_0 \ \#$$

where V indicates any vowel, $\breve{V}$ a reduced vowel, and C a consonant. The rule discounts any syllables with reduced vowels at the end of the word and stresses the last vowel of the remaining portion.[2] This rule generalizes to the special case of words with only reduced vowels. By the normal conventions of disjunctive ordering, it stresses the *first* syllable of such a word. That is the correct result.

The inverse case of Komi naturally works just as well. The simplest rule for accenting the first "heavy" vowel of a word (case 2[a]) is the following:

$$V \rightarrow [+\text{acc}] \ / \ \# \ [C_0 \ \breve{V} C_0]_0 \ \underline{\quad}$$

where $\breve{V}$ indicates a "light" vowel. This rule gives the correct accentuation, on the final syllable, of words with only light vowels (2[b]).

What phonological theory says, then, is that the accentuation of words containing only reduced (or light) vowels does not have to be specifically learned, but can be inferred from the accentuation of words containing both types of vowels. The notational conventions of generative phonology, in our case the use of subscripts and the principle of disjunctive ordering, together with the evaluation measure, which selects the simplest formulation of the rule, jointly make a correct prediction about the accentuation of one type of word on the basis of the accentuation of the other. The value of an abstract formulation of the theory and of grammatical descriptions is shown by examples of this type, where the formalism leads to a conclusion which would not necessarily be anticipated on the basis of a merely verbal statement of the facts. It is in this sense that generative phonology goes beyond simply making traditional process phonology more precise, and yields a deeper understanding of the structure of phonological systems than previously was possible.

The bases of explanation in current generative phonology are the formal constraints given jointly by the notational conventions and the evaluation measure. These formal constraints may be *absolute* or *relative*. Absolute constraints are given by the form of the notation itself, which limits the class of possible grammars. For example, a rule could simply not be written within the current framework which would drop the middle segment in words of a certain class (in words with an even number of segments, say, the two middle segments). The theory correctly makes this linguistically impossible rule unstatable in an absolute sense. Relative constraints are given by the interplay of the notational devices and the evaluation measure. The explanation in the examples I have cited is based on such relative constraints. The theory does not claim that Cheremis words containing only reduced vowels *must* have initial stress. Rules for stressing such words elsewhere than on the initial syllable could be formulated; they would merely be more complex than the actual rule. The claim is rather that a certain natural projection will be made from the general case [a] to the special case [b], which will be abandoned only if contrary evidence is encountered.

What basis does this claim have in actual linguistic fact? Before answering this question, let us review in a general way the sorts of specific factual consequences which *could* be derived from it.

The claim relates most directly to language acquisition. It says that the child projects correctly according to certain abstract formal principles from one set of data, which he may reasonably be expected to encounter first, to the full system that includes special cases whose relation to the normal cases may superficially appear quite irregular. For example, if in some language with an accent system like that described by rules 1 or 2 the child has not encountered words stressed by 1[b] or 2[b], but forms such words on the basis of morphological rules he has learned, he should be able to stress them correctly. Such predictions are in principle quite testable, for example, by study of the "mistakes" made by children, which permit conclusions to be drawn about the system of rules the child has formed, and experimentally by asking the child to make up new words, asking him to repeat words given to him with neutral stress. The formal principles in question are so general that many languages will provide significant empirical tests for them.

Implicit in these consequences for first language acquisition is another set of predicted consequences for language change, which provide a second major source of empirical evidence for linguistic theory. For example, the generally well-supported assumption that "sound change" is the addition of phonological rules to grammar entails that historical stress shifts of the [a] type will normally involve, as a special case, stress shifts of the [b] type—in general, that "sound change," far from being a purely physiological process, is subject to the same abstract formal constraints as the synchronic phonological rules of a grammar. Likewise, the assumption that "analogical change" is the simplification of grammars (in the linguistic sense of simplicity, intended to be specified by the notational conventions of generative grammar) entails that stress systems having subrule [a] will, if they do not have subrule [b], tend to acquire it. In more general terms, it is claimed that the notational conventions, to the extent that they correctly characterize the linguistic notion of "simplicity," provide a characterization of the form and direction of generalization in linguistic change. And finally, we should expect the formal groupings of rules to result in entities whose unity is reflected in common changes—e.g., that [a] and [b] should be reordered or generalized in the same way (see Kiparsky 1968 for discussion).

A third reflection of these formal conditions has to do with linguistic universals, including implicational ones, and with facts about the relative "naturalness" of various properties of rules and grammars. On the basis of the investigation of large numbers of languages one might be able to verify the claims which the formalism implicitly makes about what sort of rules should tend to co-occur. The fact that rule pairs such as the [a] and [b] cases of the stress rules mentioned above are expressible as subcases of a general process of stress assignment means that such rule pairs should be characteristic of languages in general. The more specific the formal relationship expressed by the formalism, the clearer the exclusion of an accidental relationship. Because of its greater accessibility, synchronic evidence predominates quantitatively in discussions of universal grammar, although it can be difficult to interpret when detailed questions are at issue.

The role of what I refer to as relative constraints is usually said to be that of selecting the right grammar from among the alternative grammars for a set of data. In terms of a less overschematized model of language acquisition, in which the process is not viewed as instantaneous, we can replace this interpretation by viewing the relative constraints as a ranking of grammars which determines the order in which the grammatical system of the child unfolds. That order has little to do with the order in which it encounters the "primary linguistic data," but rather depends on the relative linguistic complexity of the grammatical structure underlying this data. This is shown, in phonology, by such observations as Jakobson's (1942) that the elements of phonological systems are acquired roughly in the order of increasing markedness. Especially striking is Jakobson's point that unmarked segments often occur early in language acquisition even when no models for them exist in the adult system. For example, stop systems of the English type, with, e.g., [p^h] : [b], but not [p], appear in many children to develop out of initial stop systems with the maximally unmarked series (e.g., [p]), an analog in child language to the fact that languages with a single stop series (such as Finnish, Menomini, or Polynesian languages) in general have that maximally unmarked series.

This paradigm of formal explanation in generative grammar has certain limitations. In theory, the evaluation measure is supposed to operate *globally* on the whole phonology and lexicon (indeed, the whole grammar). If so, cases should arise where overall decisions of a sort that frequently arise in phonology—for example, between adding a segment to the inventory of phonemes and adding a phonological rule to the grammar—are made on the basis of simplicity. Decisions of this nature have in fact sometimes been made on formal simplicity considerations. However, it is important to note that in no case has the resulting analysis been shown to be correct on independent grounds. The cases in which the formal paradigm has been confirmed empirically (by either synchronic or diachronic evidence) are all instances of *local* decisions. Examples are cases of disjunctive ordering of the type illustrated above (Chomsky and Halle 1968), and the collapsing of rule pairs by the notational convention of braces (Kiparsky 1968). The only interesting global consequence of the paradigm of formal explanation in generative grammar that has ever been proposed was the analysis of "accidental gaps" in the lexicon. Halle (1962) suggested that the distinction between accidental gaps such as *blik* and systematic gaps such as *bnik* is automatically drawn by the notational devices in conjunction with the simplicity metric. Accidental gaps, according to this proposal, are those gaps whose exclusion by morpheme structure rules does not pay off because the needed rules cost more (in terms of numbers of feature specifications) than they save in the lexicon. However, this treatment of accidental gaps has been withdrawn by Chomsky and Halle (1968) in favor of one which, while more adequate in a descriptive sense, does not provide an explanatory account, and so provides no confirmation of the notational devices and the simplicity metric. The explanatory function of these, therefore, remains relatively small at present.

This circumstance is reflected in the nature of the issues in phonological theory debated in recent years. On the one hand, proposals concerning the notational conventions are characteristically introduced on the basis of arguments based on descriptive rather than explanatory adequacy. For example, in Anderson's work on rule ordering (1969) it is shown that certain facts in Icelandic and other languages cannot be stated unless the hitherto accepted constraints on ordering are relaxed in certain ways. On the other hand, proposals based on considerations of explanatory adequacy have been made, but these have generally taken the form of substantive rather than formal conditions on grammars, such as various constraints on abstractness of underlying representations, or on the naturalness of phonological rules (e.g., Stampe 1969).

In some respects, furthermore, the paradigm of formal explanation breaks down altogether even with respect to what appear to be purely formal generalizations. A case in point are the ordering asymmetries proposed in Kiparsky (1968). The concepts of "feeding" and "bleeding" order were there defined in purely formal terms as relations between pairs of rules with respect to the derivations of the grammar. But the greater "simplicity" of the unmarked order types cannot be reduced to brevity by means of any reasonable "notational conventions." Yet the evidence for these ordering relations, especially in the case of feeding order, is of the same nature and quality as that for the relative constraints which the formalism does capture. Stampe (1969) has shown that children can initially apply rules in their unmarked order contrary to what the adult grammar requires, whereas cases of children's deviation in favor of marked ordering are not on record. Given that children initially select the optimal hypothesis, this is what we would expect on the basis of the assumption of ordering asymmetry. For historical evidence, see Kiparsky (1968) and King (1969). The point could also be established on synchronic grounds if, for example, Anderson (1969) is correct in claiming that unmarked ordering predominates in the phonological rules of languages, or in proposing that local ordering is to be constrained in terms of unmarked ordering. It is suggestive that such diverse representatives of "traditional grammar" as Boas and Pāṇini seem to have viewed unmarked ordering (certainly the feeding subcase) as the norm from which deviations had to be indicated by special proviso.

The limitations of formal explanation are much more serious than even these facts indicate. In this paper I propose to review various types of regularities in phonology and morphology which are based on general conditions of a *functional* nature. To account for them we have to add to the theory substantive conditions which pertain not to the form of grammars (i.e., to the system of rules that generates a language) but to their output. These conditions, which are relative rather than absolute, appear to be of two general types, which we can term "syntagmatic" and "paradigmatic." At the level which we are dealing, these amount to phonological and morphological conditions, respectively.

Syntagmatic or phonological conditions put certain relative constraints on the phonotactic structure of the output. I will argue that the theory of derivational constraints and "conspiracies" fails to provide an adequate explanatory account of these constraints on phonotactic structure, and that a notion of "negative target" is needed for this purpose.

The paradigmatic or morphological conditions which I will propose are closely related to traditional ideas about analogy and sound change, some of which were unjustly rejected by Bloomfieldian structuralism (Bloomfield 1933). We have, on the one hand, *distinctness conditions*, which, as an initial approximation, state that there is a tendency for semantically relevant information to be retained in surface structure. Secondly, there are *leveling conditions*, which state that allomorphy in paradigms tends to get eliminated.

All these conditions are functional. Syntagmatic, phonotactic conditions can be related to the requirements of speech production. Retention of functional information in surface structure would appear to be motivated by the requirements of speech perception, and elimination of allomorphy in paradigms by language acquisition.

Let us make it clearer and more precise what is meant by a "tendency" here, and how the existence of such tendencies is to be empirically justified.

One of the reasons why functionalism has generally failed to get off the ground is that it has been content with making vague statements to the effect that there exist certain "tendencies." It is necessary to give a precise interpretation to this claim before anything can be done with it. I would like to propose that a tendency for some condition A to be implemented is for a language meeting condition A to be more highly valued, other things being equal, than a language not meeting condition A.

From this interpretation it follows that functional conditions, if correct, can be justified in the same way as other aspects of linguistic theory, namely by showing that they explain facts about language acquisition, linguistic change, or linguistic universals. At the risk of repetition, I will mention some of the ways in which this in principle can be done. With reference to language acquisition, it means showing that functional conditions account for facts about child language not predicted by the present theory, i.e., that children's "mistakes," and the grammatical systems which are revealed by these mistakes to have been acquired, have functionally characterizable properties which are not explained by the principles of projection embodied in the notational devices of standard generative grammar. The historical arguments will involve showing, for example, that functional conditions define the targets for those "analogical changes" which cannot at present be characterized as grammatical simplifications. In that case, functional conditions will be justified by enabling a satisfactory theory of analogy to be formulated. Finally, it should be shown that there are "linguistically significant generalizations" which cannot be expressed in an otherwise adequate formal framework, but which have a ready functional interpretation.

The beginnings of such a demonstration are found below. Only in one case will reference be made to language acquisition. The major part of the evidence comes from linguistic change and synchronic structure. I will try to show that an understanding of both sound change and analogy depends in essential ways on functional conditions. I hope to establish also that a great part of the phonological and morphological phenomena that constitute counterexamples to the claims of current phonological theory are explicable on a functional basis. Besides "conspiracies" these include various types of ordering paradoxes that require derivational or transderivational constraints, and the systematically variable application of optional rules uncovered by Labov (1968, 1969).

2. CONSERVATION OF FUNCTIONAL DISTINCTIONS

In this section and in the following one I will argue that the morphology of a language is subject to overall paradigmatic conditions of a functional nature, which are reflected both in its synchronic structure and in the phonological and morphological changes it undergoes. This section deals with the realization of morphological categories in surface structure.

It has been clearly established by now that phonological processes, including even quite "low-level" rules, and specifically also sound changes, can be subject to conditioning according to morphological categories. But such morphological conditioning seems to be limited in an interesting way by functional conditions. It characteristically originates as a blocking of rules in environments in which their free application would wipe out morphological distinctions on the surface. The same functional conditions seem to underlie certain cases of "analogical change" which have as their target the retention of a morphological distinction. Especially notable is the fact that some specific kinds of morphological categories are, in many languages and at many points of time, consistently stabler than others, in that they both put up a stronger "resistance" to phonological rules which eliminate their distinctive surface characteristic, and are more frequently restored by morphological change.

The strongest of the cases which will be discussed here constitute counterexamples to the present theory of generative phonology. On the synchronic level, they involve formally unnatural or even unstatable regularities, such as ordering paradoxes, "conspiracy" phenomena, and optional rules with consistently variable frequencies of application. Diachronically, many of them originate as analogical changes which cannot be represented as simplifications. If we can show that these regularities can be stated and explained in functional rather than in formal terms, we shall have shown that functional constraints have to be included in linguistic theory.

A simple illustration of the sort of phenomenon that I will be concerned with here is found in those varieties of American English which have the rule that drops word-final -*t*, usually optionally. Where this -*t* is the past tense ending, some speakers drop it only when the present and past tense forms of the verb show a different stem vowel (Twaddell 1935, p. 79).[3] These speakers have *keep - kep', creep - crep', sweep - swep'* etc., but retain -*t* obligatorily in cases like *steep - steeped, heap - heaped* on the one hand, and *step - stepped* on the other.

Labov et al. (1968, p. 130) showed a similar distinction between *t*-deletion in these types of past tense forms in the speech of Black teenagers in New York City. Here the rule is generalized so as to apply even when no vowel change takes place. However, -*t* was deleted more frequently in the type *kept* than in the type *passed*. The percentages of deleted -*t* in cases like *kept* were 50 percent before consonants and 31 percent before vowels; the corresponding figures for *passed* were 38 percent and 14 percent.

The vowel of the stem cannot in the present theory of generative phonology serve to determine whether or not -*t* may be dropped. If -*t* is dropped before the vowel shortening rule applies, then *keep* and *steep* cannot be distinguished from each other; and if -*t* is dropped after the shortening rule applies, then *keep* and *step* cannot be distinguished. There is no single point in the derivation at which the crucial information, whether a vowel *change* has taken place, is available. There is another way to formulate the condition on the deletion of -*t*, however. The vowel change in past tense forms is due to the phonological rule which shortens vowels before two consonants, e.g., /kēp+t/ → *kept*. According to a plausible analysis of

Chomsky and Halle (1968), the shortening fails to apply in past tense forms like /stēp#t/ (*steeped*) because the ending is here separated from the stem by an internal word boundary, as is normal for inflectional and more productive derivational suffixes in English. In *kept*, they suggest, this internal word boundary is reduced to a simple morpheme boundary (+) by a readjustment rule. Therefore, it is possible to formulate *t*-deletion, in these dialects, as being dependent on this same distinction between the # and + boundaries. When a # boundary precedes, the rule is either completely blocked, or less frequently applied than when a + boundary precedes.

This description of the application of *t*-deletion in terms of different boundaries does not yet constitute an explanation. I contend, furthermore, that it does not even constitute the basis of the true explanation. The facts fit into a general, cross-linguistic pattern of phenomena only if we view *t*-deletion as being dependent on whether or not there is a vowel difference between the present and past forms of the verb. The rule is blocked (or, in some dialects, applied less frequently) when its application makes the past and present forms indistinguishable (*pass:passed*), but applies freely where this distinction is retained because of the vowel difference (*keep:kep'*).

Consider the rule of German which drops *e* in unstressed syllables. In nouns, the plural ending -*e* is not subject to deletion (*die Tore*), whereas the phonologically identical dative singular ending -*e* is optionally dropped (*dem Tor[e]*). In the standard language, plural -*e* does not drop even when the stem undergoes umlaut (*die Bäume*) and no homonymy between singular and plural would result. In some dialects, however, *e*-deletion is extended to plurals as well. In Mecklenburg (Nerger 1869, pp. 173-77) *e*-deletion applies in plurals only where its operation does not result in singular-plural identity: namely, when *neither* umlaut *nor* lenition of the stem-final consonant (which in this dialect must precede *e*-deletion) is applicable to the plural form; e.g., *spēr:spēre* 'javelin(s)', but *gast:gest* 'guest(s)' (with umlaut), *brêf:brêv* 'letter(s)' (with lenition). It should be noted that this is not an absolute rule—Nerger notes exceptions in both directions—but a fairly clear general tendency. The complementarity between stem change and *e*-deletion is important in standard German as well, though it plays no role in the plural (Venneman 1968, Kiparsky 1971).

The mere existence of such morphological conditioning in rules is not of course in itself enough to prove that functional factors are at work. The first step toward the required proof is showing that substantive aspects of the morphological conditioning are constant from language to language. There could not be a functional explanation of the greater stability of plural -*e* compared to dative singular -*e* in German if it turned out that in the next language a plural ending was less stable than a phonologically identical dative ending. But on the other hand, it is difficult to see what other explanations there could be than functional ones if plural endings proved to be stabler in *every* language in which an asymmetry of this sort exists. I would like to propose, as a subhypothesis, that plural endings are in fact, other things being equal, universally stronger than case endings. This is not to say that these grammatical categories condition every rule, but rather that *if* a rule is conditioned by them, the relative strength of the conditioning categories is predictable.

If this is correct, it may be that we shall be able not only to distinguish generally between "strong" categories, such as tense and number, and "weak" categories, such as case, but to set up a hierarchy of categories according to their relative strength. We shall see that things are actually even more complicated, and that the strength of a category in a language may depend on other aspects of its grammar, though in a way which strongly confirms the functional interpretation here proposed. I now turn to various sorts of phonological phenomena which provide evidence for such a general hierarchy.

Labov's investigations of synchronically variable rules have yielded clear indications of morphological conditioning which, on a statistical plane, parallels the substance of that which we find in obligatory rules. For deletion of -*s* in the speech of Black adolescents in New York City, Labov et al. (1968, 158ff.) found plural *s*-deletion to be much less frequent than deletion of the verb ending -*s* or genitive -*s*. The percentage of plural deletion always stayed below 30 percent, whereas that of the third singular always was over 50 percent, sometimes reaching close to 100 percent, with the genitive showing similar behavior.

Sound change gives converging evidence. Historical grammars generally state sound changes in terms of their beginning and end points. Any such macroscopic statement—e.g., "final -*e* is dropped"—represents in several respects a considerable smoothing of the actual event it refers to. Statistics based on spellings in texts written at the time of a sound change show that changes can occur in some morphological categories before others. Furthermore, they show that as the frequency with which the new rule applies grows larger with time, the *relative* frequencies for the categories tend to remain stable. And, significantly, the relative differentiation of categories is comparable to what we find in synchronic rules, whether variable or obligatory.

Consider the statistics compiled by Moore (1927) for the loss of Middle English -*n*. The findings, for the fifteen separate texts which Moore examined, are summarized in table 1. reproduced from Moore, where the frequencies indicate the proportion of *n*-deletion according to grammatical categories.

As Moore points out, there is a constant differentiation between the first three lines and the last two. In the former, -*n* is a case suffix, and is relatively often lost; in the latter, -*n* is a plural suffix, and is less often lost. The differentiation among the subcases of these two major groups shows no comparable systematicity. It is particularly striking that *every* text shows this same distinction, though some show it more strongly than others. (A reflex of the distinction is -*n* retained in *oxen, children.*)

Table 1

Function of -n	Grammatical Category	1	2	3	4	5	6	7	8	9	10	11	12	13	14	15	Total
									Texts								
Case marker	Wk. noun, s	.05	.20	.21	.25	.61	.49	.47	.28	.37	.38	.63	.84	.68	.84	.72	.38
	Wk. adj	.36	.26	.14	.14	.50	.51	.28	.48	.50	.53	.67	.63	.63	.83	.86	.50
	St. adj. d. s. pl.	.20	.18	.36	.49	.24	.19	.29	.69	.64	.79	.59	.72	.92	1.00	.88	.43
Plural marker	Wk. noun, pl	.01	.06	.14	.21	.07	.04	.26	.00	.07	.00	.00	.00	.25	.08	.28	.11
	St. noun, d. pl.	.04	.13	.18	.14	.02	.14	.24	.14	.14	.02	.14	.05	.71	.07	.36	.15

Frequency of deletion of final -*n* in 15 Middle English texts.

A study by Lindgren (1953) on the loss of -*e* in Middle High German, carried out with similar statistical techniques, but on a much larger scale, gives similar results. Lindgren examined texts from many different dialects covering a period of several hundreds of years. The loss of -*e* turned out to be morphologically differentiated. This morphological differentiation is parallel to the Middle English case in that plural -*e* was dropped relatively rarely compared to phonologically identical instances of -*e* representing case.

All these examples involve quite low-level phonological processes. Indeed, in the case of variable rules the question arises whether the different frequencies with which the rules are applied in different cases are to be given in the grammar at all, or whether they are consequences of some general constraints on speech performance. I return to this question below. However, it is important to note that functional differentiation is not *only* found in low-level rules such as *e*-deletion. The relative strength of plurals, for example, plays an important role in purely morphological processes, and especially in so-called analogical change.

A general conclusion to be drawn from the historical morphology of many Indo-European languages is that, other things being equal, lost plural distinctions are more likely to be analogically restored than lost case distinctions. Consider the extension of the English -*s* plural (and, earlier, of -*n* plurals) and the spread of -*er*, -*en*, -*s* and umlaut as new plural markers in German, which are scarcely paralleled by similar large-scale reinstatement of case endings, under ostensibly similar circumstances, with equally good "proportional models" available. See Pandit (1961) for a Gujerati example; also see Jespersen (1949).

A reflection of this can be seen in a general property of Indo-European paradigms. Syncretism (i.e., homonymy) of case forms is very common between, e.g., dative and ablative, or ablative and genitive. But syncretism of number, tense, or mood is rare. There are few cases of a case form serving equally for singular and plural. Greek -*phi*, or the Finnish comitative, are exceptional examples of this.[4]

The effect of such categorial polarization on morphological rules and analogical processes can be seen even more clearly in languages with complicated inflectional and derivational systems. I will cite a few cases in Sanskrit in which formally quite peculiar and unnatural conditions on rules are explicable as consequences of the functional factors here proposed.

The gerund of prefixed verbs in Sanskrit ends in -*ya*, cf., *vi#bhaj+a+ti* 'hands out', *vi#bhaj+ya* 'having handed out'. When this form is derived from causative stems, the causative suffix -*ay*- in which these stems end is dropped in some verbs, e.g., *vi#bhāj+ay+a+ti* 'causes to hand out', *vi#bhāj+ya* 'having caused to hand out'. In others it is retained, e.g., *vi#kram+ay+a+ti* 'causes to step out', *vi#kram+ay+ya* 'having caused to step out'. Whether or not the causative suffix is retained is determined by the way in which the causative stem if formed from the simple stem. Most verbs lengthen the root vowel in causatives (*bhajati* → *bhājayati*), whereas others, a synchronically unpredictable class, retain it short (*kramati* → *kramayati*). Some verbs—mainly those ending in -*a*—add *p* before the causative suffix -*ay*- (*gāyati* 'sings' → *gāpayati* 'causes to sing'). The conditions under which -*ay*- is retained are, in Whitney's formulation (1889, p. 385), the following: "[causative] stems showing in the root-syllable no difference from the root retain *ay* of the causative-sign in the gerund, to distinguish it from that belonging to the primary conjugation." This rule is illustrated in the examples of simple and causative forms in table 2.

			Gerund	Causative	Caus. Ger.
(1)	vibhajati	'hands out'	vibhajya	vibhājayati	vibhājya
	avatarati	'comes down'	avatīrya	avatārayati	avatārya
	utpadyate	'arises'	utpadya	utpādayati	utpādya
	upavasati	'fasts'	upoṣya	upavāsayati	upavāsya
	ānayati	'brings'	ānīya	ānāyayati	ānāyya
	anujānāti	'excuses'	anujñāya	anujñāpayati	anujñāpya
	uttisthati	'gets up'	utthāya	utthāpayati	utthāpya
	abhijigharti	'sprinkles'	abhighṛtya	abhighārayati	abhighārya
(2)	vikramati	'steps out'	vikramya	vikramayati	vikramayya
	avagacchati	'understands'	avagamya	avagamayati	avagamayya
	unnamate	'rises'	unnamya	unnamayati	unnamayya
	ujjvalati	'flares up'	ujjvalya	ujjvalayati	ujjvalayya
(3)	prāpnoti	'reaches'	prāpya	prāpayati	prāpayya[5]
	(root *āp*)				

The deletion of the causative suffix *ay* in gerunds depends on the *relation* between the simple root and the causative form of the root: it takes place if they are phonologically distinct and fails if they are phonologically identical. In other words, the deletion is blocked where its application would eliminate the distinction between simple and causative forms.

Wackernagel and Debrunner (1954, 110) point out that many morphological rules in Sanskrit that introduce the common secondary derivational suffix -*a* in various meanings are restricted to words whose initial syllable does not have /*āu*/ as its nucleus. They ascribe this curious restriction to the fact that vṛddhi of the first syllable (essentially, insertion of long *ā*), which is the main morphological mark of this formation, would be vacuous in words of exactly this structure. For example, to denote authorship (Pāṇini 1962, 4.3.101 *tena proktam*) the suffix -*a* with vṛddhi is normally added, but names with *ā, ai, an* in the first syllable take -*īya* instead (Pāṇini 1962, 4.2.144 *vṛddhācchaḥ*). In designations of grammars and works on linguistic theory: *pātañjalam mahābhāṣyam* 'Patañjali's Big Commentary', but *pāṇinīyam vyākaraṇam* 'Pāṇini's grammar'. Likewise *candra* → *cāndra*, *jinendra* → *jainendra*, *apiśali* → *āpiśala*, but *vyādi* → *vyādīya*. Similarly in patronymic names (*bida* → *baida*, but *vāmadeva* → *vāmadevya*, with suffix -*ya*) and in metronymic names (*śikṣitā* → *śaikṣita*, but *vāsavadattā* → *vasavadatteya*).

The distribution of -*a* is tied to potential ambiguity only in a general

way. The suffix is avoided in stems with *ā, ai, au* not just when they end in
-a, where truncation of the stem produces real homonymy between base
form and derivative (and even here older Sanskrit often shows an accent
difference which prevents homonymy), but also in the less frequent case
when they end in *-i*, where no homonymy can arise. Furthermore, there are a
few exceptional words which have *ā, ai, au* in the first syllable, end in *-a*, and
still take the secondary suffix *-a* (Wackernagel and Debrunner 1954, 110–to
their examples add *kāśakṛtsna* → *kāśakṛtsna* 'written by [the linguist]
kāśakṛtsna'). These facts make it difficult to exploit the overall regularity in
the distribution of suffixes by a derivational constraint in the grammar.

The development of the aorist tense inflection in Sanskrit offers a
striking illustration of the global effect which functional conditions can have
on a paradigm. The active aorist endings were

	Singular	Dual	Plural
1.	-am	-va	-ma
2.	-s	-tam	-ta
3.	-t	-tām	-ṣ (-an)

In the second and third person singular, the ending consists of a single
obstruent. Since Sanskrit has a rule dropping word-final obstruents when
preceded by a consonant, the 2.3.p.sg. endings were subject to loss by this
rule whenever they were preceded by a consonant. This situation existed in
two large groups of forms. It existed in verbs which took the suffix *-s-* after
the root in the aorist. For example, the singular paradigm of *prā* 'fill' goes

1. /a+prā+s+am/ → *aprāsam (cf. ayāsam)
2. /a+prā+s+s/ → aprās
3. /a+prā+s+t/ → aprās

The situation also existed in verbs which did not take the aorist suffix *-s-*, if
these verbs had roots ending in consonants. For example, the singular
paradigm of *kṛ* 'do' in the *Rigveda* was:

1. /a+kar+am/ → akaram
2. /a+kar+s/ → akar
3. /a+kar+t/ → akar

When the root both ended in a consonant and took the aorist suffix *-s-*, both
suffixes were deleted; e.g., the Rigvedic singular paradigm of *yaj* 'sacrifice'
(with *a* → *ā* due to the suffix *-s-*):

1. /a+yāj+s+am/ → ayākṣam
2. /a+yāj+s+s/ → ayāj [ayāṭ]
3. /a+yāj+s+t/ → ayāj [ayāṭ]

Metrical considerations indicate that the loss of final obstruents by the rule in question took place during, or not long before, the composition of the *Rigveda*.[6] In later Vedic, and in classical Sanskrit, a series of morphological changes took place whose effect was to eliminate, in different ways, the ambiguity between the second and third persons singular introduced into the paradigms by the final obstruent deletion rule.

What appears to have been historically the first development (Narten 1964, p. 19) resulted in a rule deleting the *inner* (instead of the outer) obstruent(s) in a terminal cluster. This rule was almost completely[7] restricted to verb inflection, i.e., precisely to those cases in which it was functionally motivated. The new version of the obstruent deletion rule resulted in derivations such as

> 2p. /a+yāj+s+s/ → RV ayās (replacing ayāṭ)
> 3p. /a+prā+s+t/ → AV aprāt (replacing aprās)

This system did not stay long in the language either. Already in the Vedic period it too began to be replaced by what became the classical form of aorist inflection. This developed through two main innovations. The first of these was that *-i-* became inserted after the aorist suffix when a single obstruent followed, i.e., in exactly those cases where the terminal cluster rule was potentially applicable to delete the ending. This inserted vowel broke up the cluster and caused the personal endings to be retained. The new paradigm of *yaj* was

> 1. /a+yāj+s+am/ → ayākṣam
> 2. /a+yāj+s+s/ → ayākṣīs (replacing ayāṭ, ayās)
> 3. /a+yāj+s+t/ → ayākṣīt (replacing ayāṭ, *ayāt)

The *-i-* insertion rule was not applicable in the second large group of verbs in which the personal endings were originally subject to deletion by the terminal cluster rule, namely in those verbs which formed their aorists without the suffix *-s-*, but whose roots ended in consonants, e.g., *akar* 'you, he made'. What happened here was that for exactly these verbs, the aorist ceased to be formed without *-s-*. This resulted in the new paradigms:

> 1. /a+kār+s+am/ → akārṣam
> 2. /a+kār+s+s/ → akārṣis (replacing akar)
> 3. /a+kār+s+t/ → akārṣīt (replacing akar)

where *-i-* is inserted by the rule just mentioned. The s-less aorist was retained *only* in verbs with roots ending in a vowel, i.e., exactly where the terminal cluster simplification rule was not applicable to the personal endings, e.g., in *dā* 'give':

1. /a+dā+am/ → adām
2. /a+dā+s/ → adās
3. /a+dā+t/ → adāt

Deletion of the 2.sg. and 3.sg. endings also arose in the imperfect of the small and unproductive class of athematic verbs (which added their personal endings directly to the root) when the root ended in a consonant:

1. /a+han+am/ → ahanam
2. /a+han+s/ → ahan
3. /a+han+t/ → ahan

These imperfects are rare compared to the aorists discussed above. Changes paralleling those that took place in the aorist were not carried through consistently in the imperfect. However, there are examples showing both inner obstruent deletion in terminal clusters (/a+śās+t/ → aśāt 'he ordered') and insertion of vowels breaking up the cluster. In the verb as 'be' the 3.sg. imperfect is, in Vedic,

/a+as+t/ → ās

and, by -ī- insertion,

/a+as+t/ → āsīt

which becomes the standard classical form. The verb ad 'eat' inserts -a- in precisely the 2.3.sg. imperfect forms, and conjugates without a vowel everywhere else:

/a+ad+s/ → ādas
/a+ad+t/ → ādat

This complex of morphological changes is a historical "conspiracy" whose target is the retention of distinct person inflection in the second and third singular of the past tense paradigms.

At this point the reader may sense a contradiction. Remember that Labov's findings show the third singular -s to be a *weak* category, subject to much more frequent deletion than plural -s. How does this fit in with the above Sanskrit facts, which would seem to indicate that person is a strong category? I think the answer lies in a distinction which has to be drawn between languages like English, which must retain unstressed subject pronouns, and languages like Sanskrit, which can delete them. The hypothesis which I would like to advance is that person inflection on the verb is a strong category *only* in languages which delete unstressed subject pronouns. What little evidence I have on the question confirms this hypothesis. In Estonian, a language in which unstressed subject pronouns can be deleted, -n has been lost *except as a first person singular ending;* e.g., /kanta+n/ 'of the base' (Finnish *kannan*) → Est. *kanna*, but /kanta+n/ 'I carry' (Finnish *kannan*) → Est. *kannan*. Kettunen (1962 , p. 106) points out that *n*-deletion was a variable rule in some early seventeenth-century texts, where its application in part depended on phonological conditions (less deletion before a following vowel). The present situation is the result of a morphological polarization of this variable rule. On the other hand, languages in which unstressed subject pronouns are retained seem to show no comparable resistance to the leveling of the person endings in the verb paradigm (see Pandit 1961, for Gujerati).

Very tentatively, then, we can sum up the division of categories as follows:

Weak	*Strong*
case	number
verb agreement (in lan-	tense
guages with no pronoun	gender
deletion)	verb agreement (in languages
	with pronoun deletion

Evidently the weak categories are those which register information that is relatively redundant. Cases (at least grammatical cases, which our data consists of) are specified by transformations on the basis of the tree configuration at a late stage in the derivation of a sentence. Verb agreement is predictable in a similar way, and loses its redundancy only when the subject with which agreement takes place is deleted. On the other hand, number and tense are specified in the deep structure and are associated with largely fixed meanings of their own. Their status as strong categories is therefore not surprising. This is not true of gender, unfortunately. I have placed it on the strong side because of the German data, which indicate that feminine -e is highly resistant to loss. I am totally unable to suggest a reason for this behavior. To that extent the functional basis of morphological conditioning of phonological processes remains unsubstantiated.

3. PARADIGMATIC COHERENCE

One of the stock examples of analogical change is the generalization of *r* throughout the inflectional paradigm of a class of Latin *s*-stems, e.g., *honōs* → *honor.* The oblique case forms of these nouns were subject to rhotacism, yielding an *s ⁓ r* alternation which was eliminated in the new paradigm:

N.	honōs	honor
G.	honōris	honōris
A.	honōrem	honōrem

.   .

.   .

.   .

Old Paradigm   *New Paradigm*

It looks like the base forms are changing here.[8] In the older system, the base forms were /hon+ōs/, /arb+ōs/, etc., and the *r* in the case forms apart from the nom.sg. were derived by the rhotacism rule

$$s \rightarrow r \;/\; V \underline{\quad} V$$

In the newer system, the paradigm can be derived by starting from underlying /hon+ōr/. No stem change now takes place in the oblique cases. The shortening of *ō* to *o* in the nom.sg. *honor* is by a regular shortening of vowels before a certain class of consonants in word-final position.

But it is not quite so simple as that. Suppose that the change is correctly describable as a replacement of the old underlying form /honōs/ by a new underlying form /honōr/. Within the framework of the present theory, there is no reason to expect this replacement of underlying forms to take place at all. Adoption of the new base form /honōr/ in no way simplifies the grammar. The rhotacism rule, while inapplicable to /honōr/, must still be retained in the grammar, because it is needed for numerous other nouns which did not generalize the *r*, such as *genus ~ generis, ōs ~ ōris,* as well as for other *s ~ r* alternations, e.g., *es-t* 'is' *er-at* 'was'.

In fact, the situation is even worse for the present theory: the change actually *complicates* the grammar. A number of words which changed their nominative singular from *-ōs* to *-or* continued to show *s* before derivational suffixes beginning with consonants. The most notable group of such derivatives are the adjectives in *-tus: honestus* 'honest' (from *honor*), *arbustus* 'wooded' (from *arbor* 'tree'), *angustus* 'tight' (from *angor* 'constriction'), *rōbustus* 'robust' (from *rōbur* 'oak'), *augustus* 'august' (from *augur* 'augur'). This suffix is not very productive, and there are some problems with the vowel of the stem (why *-e-* in *honestus*?). Nevertheless, it seems likely that the adjectives were felt to be synchronically related to the corresponding nouns. If that is the case, then we must draw one of two conclusions from them. The first possibility is that the underlying forms did not change after all, but retained their old form with *s*. The *-s-* in the adjectives then causes no difficulty, but to get *honor* and the other nominative singulars in *-or* we need an extra rule which changes *s* to *r* in these nouns (but not in *ōs, cinis* and many others). This might be done by

extending rhotacism for certain nouns to the environment V _____ # or to
the environment _____ + Case (which would include the nominative). In
either case the grammar would become more complicated through this
development. The second possibility is that the underlying form did indeed
change from /honōs/ to /honōr/. Now the noun inflection is derived without
a hitch, but we need some rule, otherwise unnecessary, which turns *r* to *s*
before certain consonantal suffixes, so that derivatives like *honestus* will be
correctly formed. This alternative also represents a complication of the
grammar.

Present phonological theory therefore not only fails to characterize
the change from *-ōs* to *-or* as a simplification of the grammar, but actually
characterizes it as a complication. However, given the two paradigms, a
practising historical linguist would correctly conclude that *honōs* is older
than *honor*, even if he had no textual evidence for this fact. *Honōs* > *honor*
is a possible change (given the rest of the data), but *honor* > *honos* is an
impossible or at least unlikely change. The reason for this asymmetry, given
our assumption that analogical change results in a more highly valued
grammar, must be that the grammar with *honor* is more highly valued than
the grammar with *honōs*, in spite of the fact that current theory, in which
simplicity is the only criterion for evaluating alternative grammars, leads us
to the reverse conclusion.

The fact that analogical leveling sometimes takes place only within
certain paradigms, and not in all allomorphs of a morpheme or class of
morphemes, is commonplace in historical linguistics. See, for example, the
discussion in Paul (1920, pp. 206-7), where cases are given from German
which are formally parallel to the Latin case just discussed. Thus, the
German alternation between [x] before consonants and word boundary, and
[h] before vowels (which drops intervocalically) has been retained in
derivation (*sehen* ‑ *Sicht, fliehen* ‑ *Flucht*) but almost completely eliminated
in inflection (*sieht, sah, flieht, floh*). This again represents the typical
distribution of leveling in inflection versus retention in derivation.

But the consequences of this fact for phonological theory have not
been seen. The notion of an inflectional paradigm plays no role in current
generative phonology. Note especially that the postulation of special
boundaries before inflectional endings is *not* an adequate descriptive solution
to the problem which these examples raise, quite apart from its failure on
the explanatory level. In the German example, inflection and derivation
differ even where there are no endings (and therefore no different
boundaries) involved at all: compare *schmähen* 'despise' ‑ *Schmach*
(derivation) with *sehen* ‑ *sah* (inflection). Facts of this sort evidently require
some sort of revision in the theory of generative phonology.

I suggest that we have here evidence for a second functional factor in
phonology and morphology, which we may call *paradigm coherence*. This
says that *allomorphy within a paradigm tends to be minimized*. We have seen
a case in which this principle is implemented *at the cost of complicating the*

system of rules. The result of the change in Latin was to generalize the *-r* form in the declension while breaking the phonological regularity in the distribution of *r* and *s*.

The effect of paradigm leveling is also produced by simplification of the structural analysis and by that type of reordering which eliminates a bleeding order (Kiparsky 1968). What examples like the one given above indicate is that paradigm coherence is an independent factor, and not wholly reducible to formal properties of rules and relations between rules.

As a further argument in favor of the principle of paradigm coherence I should like to adduce a type of reordering which has the one-way character of the cases investigated in Kiparsky (1968), but which escapes the generalizations there proposed. The usual conditions of maximizing feeding order and minimizing bleeding order are irrelevant here. What rather seems to determine the directionality of the reordering is paradigm coherence.

The clearest case I know involves two well-known rules in German phonology: the rule which devoices obstruents word-finally and before suffixes beginning in a consonant:

$$\text{A.} \quad [\text{+obstr}] \rightarrow [\text{-voiced}] \ / \ \underline{\hspace{1cm}} \ \left\{ \begin{matrix} \text{+C} \\ \# \end{matrix} \right.$$

(e.g., Tag [tāk] - Tage [tagə])

and the rule which deletes [g] after a nasal (which can only be [ŋ]):

$$\text{B.} \quad g \rightarrow \emptyset \ / \ [\text{+ nasal}] \ \underline{\hspace{1cm}}$$

German dialects differ in their treatment of words like *lang*. The pronunciation is [laŋk] in some dialects, and [laŋ] in others. This difference corresponds to a difference in the order of the devoicing and *g*-deletion rules, as can be seen in the following derivations:

Dialect Group I

	/laŋg/	/laŋg+e/
A. Devoicing	laŋk	—
B. g-deletion	—	laŋe

Dialect Group II

	/laŋg/	/laŋg+e/
B. g-deletion	laŋ	laŋe
A. Devoicing	—	—

It is fairly certain on historical grounds that dialect group I has the original ordering of rules, and that dialect group II has innovated by reordering the rules. The Middle High German spelling *lanc* indicates that the system of dialect group I prevailed at this time; see Vennemann (1969) for discussion of these rules.

The relationship between devoicing and *g*-deletion is the unusual one of *mutual bleeding*. Only one of the two rules can apply to an input representation. If *g*-deletion applies first to /laŋg/, it deprives devoicing of a chance to operate. If devoicing applies first, it in turn deprives *g*-deletion of a chance to operate. Whichever of the two rules is ordered first bleeds the other and is the only one that can apply in forms that meet the structural analysis of both rules. Under the usual ordering conditions, then, both orders, being bleeding orders, are equally marked and no directionality of reordering is provided for.

Perhaps it is possible to construct some more elaborate theory of ordering, which imposes an asymmetry of the right kind in cases of mutual bleeding, too. It would have to state that the unmarked order here is that order in which a whole paradigm is subject to the *same* rule (*g*-deletion in our example) rather than some forms being subject to one rule and others to a different rule. The surface consequence of making whole paradigms subject to the same rule or rules is of course normally going to be precisely the effect we have been talking about: minimization of allomorphy.

Nevertheless, formal conditions on ordering are not, I believe, the correct solution to the problem. The reason is that even if they could be formulated in such a way as to always specify that order which gives paradigm coherence (which they at present do not), they still would fail to relate the cases of leveling in which rule order is not involved at all. Again, a unified functional goal, namely paradigm coherence, is implemented in formally diverse ways.

Paradigm leveling is also the only explanation I can see for some of the facts that have been reported in the literature on child language. Kazazis (1969) describes a case in the Greek speech of his daughter Marina. In Greek, velars are palatalized to palatals before front vowels, yielding such paradigms as that of *exo* 'have':

Sg. 1. [éxo]
     2. [éxʼis]
     3. [éxʼi]
Pl. 1. [éxume]
     2. [éxʼete]
     3. [éxune]

During a short period in her linguistic development, Marina failed to apply the palatalization rule *in the verb paradigm*. Instead of [exʼete], she pronounced [exete] with a velar. Does this mean that she had not yet acquired the palatalization rule at this point? The answer is no: "Marina was at that time perfectly capable of pronouncing palatal spirants, and she did so in environments where there was no obvious velar - palatal alternation, such as within a stem" (p. 385). The rule was suspended *only in paradigms.*

This is a clear case where the principles of projection which the present theory of generative phonology attributes to the child are making the wrong prediction. They let us expect either that the rule should be dropped (i.e., not learned) everywhere, with resulting elimination of the alternation between [x'] and [x] and that between the other palatalized - nonpalatalized consonant pairs, or else that it should be acquired and applied in its most general form. The child is rather applying the rule except where its application would produce paradigmatic alternations of velars and palatals. This is in good agreement with what we know to be the typical historical development of palatalized-nonpalatalized consonant alternations in Indo-European verb paradigms: they have been leveled out in Sanskrit, and in varying degrees in some Slavic languages. The general point that analogical change is optimalization of the grammar due to retention into adult speech of features of child language is not vitiated but rather strengthened by this example. What is wrong is simply the assumption that optimality is a function of length under the notational conventions of generative grammar. These have to be augmented, as such examples show, by an independent principle of paradigm regularity.

The elimination of distinctions associated with functionally important categories tends to be retarded in places where it results in merger (as in the dialects which allow *t*-deletion in *kept* but not in *heaped* because *t*-deletion in the latter results in ambiguity of tense—see section 2). If paradigm coherence is a target of linguistic change, we would expect conversely that the elimination of arbitrary distinctions should tend to be *accelerated* in places where it results in merger. There are some cases where this in fact happens. A good example is the elimination of the Verner's law alternation in the Germanic languages.

The loss of free accent had turned the interchange between the reflexes of the Germanic voiced and voiceless continuants into a process governed by an arbitrary morphological categorization. The alternation was eliminated in all the Germanic languages, aside from a few residual cases. The interesting point about this process of elimination in verbs is that (at least in West Germanic) it depends on the type of ablaut to which the verb is subject. Generally the alternation is first eliminated where there is no associated vowel difference. In the past tense Old English retain it in snāð - snidon 'cut' (I class), cēas - curon 'chose' (II class), cwæð - cwǣdon 'spoke' (V), but not in slōʒ -slōʒon 'hit' (VI class). Similarly in Old High German (see Paul 1920, p. 203). Note that while rule simplification would account for the overall loss of the residue of Verner's law, it would *not* account for the differences between the strong verb conjugations in this respect.

Recently James Harris (1970) has made a strong case for paradigmatic uniformity as a principle in the evaluation measure. The main part of his argumentation is based on historical facts. Accepting the

assumption that a certain type of linguistic change results in more highly
valued grammars, Harris goes on to show that several Spanish changes which
we would regard as belonging to this type are not characterized as
simplifications by the present theory of generative phonology. The common
feature of these cases is that they establish paradigm uniformity. He
concludes that "paradigmatic relationships, or analogy if you like, play a role
in the organization of grammars, both synchronically and diachronically, and
therefore must be incorporated into linguistic theory."

Two other recent articles provide more ammunition to support this
position. Kisseberth (1970*d*) shows that in Klamath (Oregon) an *a* is inserted
in the context C_CC just in case there was a vowel in this position at an
earlier point in the derivation: "A sequence $C_aC_bC_c$ takes an *a* between its
first two consonants just in case that sequence derives from V* (C_o)
$C_aVC_bC_c$. Insertion of *a* must not take place if a $C_aC_bC_c$ sequence is
underlying or derived from V* (C_o)$C_aC_bC_c$". Kisseberth is able to show
clearly that the vowel must be deleted and missing from the representation
at a certain stage in the derivation prior to the insertion rule. I return to this
example later, noting here only that preservation of stem shape here leads to
an ordering paradox, which leads Kisseberth to propose a derivational
constraint.

The example is reminiscent of the well-known problem of zero grade
in roots of the *CreC* and *CerC* type in Greek. The basic facts are as follows.
In certain morphological environments, a zero-grade rule operates to delete *e*
in verb roots, e.g., *léipō* 'leave' - aorist middle *elipómēn*. In the same
environments, roots of the form *CreC* and *CerC* are reduced, not to **CrC*,
but to *CraC* and *CarC*, e.g., *térpō* 'amuse' - *etarpómēn*, *trépō* 'turn' -
etrapómēn. As a rule, the *a* goes on the same side of the *r* as the original *e*.
The exceptions to this rule are almost all old Homeric forms, and are cases of
CerC - *CraC*, such as *dérkomai* 'see' aor. *édrakon* (almost never *CreC* - *CarC*).
This, together with the fact that in nouns, *CraC* is the rule (*pater+si* → *patrsi*
→ *patrasi*), suggests an older system with the following derivations:

	leip	derk	trep
zero grade	lip	drk	trp
ϕ → a / Cr_C		drak	trap

The new system, where the type *derk* - *drak* disappears, and *terp* - *tarp* takes
over, represents a formal complication of the rules in terms of the usual
theory of generative phonology. We can either say that a new branch of the
zero-grade rule was added, which changed *e* → *a* in the neighborhood of *r*, or
retain a general zero-grade rule but have two branches of *a*-insertion, with
verbs marked for which one they undergo. In the former case we lose the
generality of the ablaut system; in the latter case the rules fail to reflect the
fact that it is predictable where *a* gets inserted. Again, a paradigmatic leveling
takes place at the price of a systemic complication.

Carstairs (1970) has shown paradigmatic regularities in the noun declension of ancient Greek which cannot be represented within the standard theory of generative phonology, and which again indicate the need for incorporating paradigmatic leveling into linguistic theory as a principle of the evaluation measure.

The common feature of these examples is the conflict between a paradigmatic condition and the simplicity of the phonological rules. The conflict was here resolved in favor of the paradigmatic condition. But this is clearly not always the case. In simplification of the structural analysis of a rule, and in reordering into a feeding order, the simplicity of the system of rules is often established at the expense of paradigmatic uniformity. The investigation of what determines the trading relation between the two sometimes conflicting principles is an enormously difficult task, but one which is necessary if the notion of paradigmatic conditions is to yield precise predictions about the direction of possible analogical change. It requires investigation into the structure of paradigms at a level which generative grammar at present may not be ready for.

4. CONSPIRACIES AND DERIVATIONAL CONSTRAINTS

There have been some attempts to account for facts of this sort within the formal paradigm of explanation. To my knowledge the earliest discussion is by Venneman (1968), who on the basis of the complementarity of *e*-deletion and vowel change in dental stems in the German conjugation suggested that phonological rules may need to be given access to paradigmatic information. What he proposed has recently come to be termed a *derivational constraint*. The topic has been raised again independently in a series of articles on phonological problems in American Indian languages by Kisseberth (1970*a, b, c, d*).

Kisseberth has argued that some of the kinds of phenomena discussed above require us to abandon certain formal constraints on phonological rules which have so far been assumed to be valid. Practically all versions of generative phonology say that the applicability of a rule to an item is determined just by whether that item has, through the ordered application of the earlier rules to the underlying form, acquired a representation which fits the structural analysis of the rule. Kisseberth proposes to relax this constraint in at least two respects.

(1) Phonological rules are to have access to the derivational history of their input, i.e., to be able to make crucial reference to earlier representations which a form has had in its derivation, for example, to the underlying representation. A case in point is Klamath, where a vowel must be reinserted in the place from which it has been deleted earlier in the derivation. Kisseberth (1970*d*) argues that the theory has to be changed (he leaves it open exactly how this is to be done) so as to enable the vowel

insertion rule to "look back" at an earlier stage in the derivation to determine where the vowel is to be placed.

(2) A phonological rule can also be constrained by global phonotactic conditions of the language, which block the application of the rule in cases where its output would violate the phonotactic condition. On the basis of a reanalysis of Newman's and Kuroda's work on Yawelmani Yokuts, Kisseberth (1970a) describes that part of Yokuts phonology which has to do with consonant clustering. He shows that these rules form a "conspiracy" to avoid clusters of three consonants (as well as #CC and CC# clusters). Some rules eliminate such clusters when they arise in morpheme combinations (there are no CCC clusters inside morphemes, this itself being part of the conspiracy), and others are prevented from applying in exactly the cases in which they would introduce CCC clusters if they did apply. For example, three-consonant clusters are broken up by an epenthesis rule:

$$\phi \rightarrow V \ / \ C\_\_\_C \ \begin{cases} \# \\ C \end{cases}$$

where V is i, in some cases a. An example of the latter type—avoidance of introducing three-consonant clusters—is the rule

$$\breve{V} \rightarrow \phi \ /VC\_\_\_CV$$

which deletes short vowels between consonants *wherever a CCC cluster does not result.* Kisseberth's suggestion is that the grammar has a derivational constraint which blocks rules from creating CCC clusters. The vowel deletion rule can then be written in the somewhat simpler form

$$\breve{V} \rightarrow \phi \ / \ C\_\_\_C$$

where the rest of the environment is predictable from the general derivational constraint. In this way the generality of the phonotactic constraint is reflected in the greater simplicity of some of the phonological rules in the language.

In traditional descriptive grammar, as exemplified in Whitney's *Sanskrit Grammar* (1889), or in the three volumes of Boas' *Handbook of American Indian Languages* (1911, 1925, 19), the use of equivalent "derivational constraints" of both types is common. For example, in his Takelma grammar Sapir (1925) distinguishes between "organic" (= underlying) diphthongs and "inorganic" (= derived) diphthongs. The former receive a rising accent under certain conditions, whereas the latter, like short vowels, can never receive a rising accent even when the conditions are otherwise met. For example, *bilàuk'* 'he jumped' has an inorganic a, as shown by *bilwá?s* 'jumper', whereas *gayaũ* 'he ate it' has an organic diphthong (and hence a rising accent)—cf. *gayawâ?n* 'I ate it'. The accent rule, as stated by Sapir, in effect "looks back" at the underlying form of a *but can be solved by rule ordering.*

diphthong to determine how it is accented. The "inorganic *a*" is inserted by a rule whose formulation in Sapir's grammar (p. 28) illustrates his use of the second type of derivational constraint, where rules "look forward" at their output. Sapir says that consonant combinations "which are either quite impossible in Takelma phonetics, or at any rate are limited in their occurrence to certain grammatical forms" are "limbered up" by the introduction of an "inorganic" *a*. Elsewhere (pp. 36-41) he then lists the possible consonant clusters of Takelma. In order to apply the *a*-insertion rule correctly, we must refer to the list, and insert *a* into any clusters in the input form which are not contained in the list.

There is an important difference, however, between this type of example and those on which Kisseberth has based his arguments. Sapir's rules can be restated, without loss of generality, in the standard theory of generative phonology, or in any framework where phonetic forms are derived from underlying forms by a set of ordered rules, which cannot refer back to earlier stages of the derivation, or to global conditions on the output. The need for making reference to earlier stages in the derivation here, as often, disappears as soon as the rules are placed in the right order. Had Sapir in his earlier work operated with ordered rules (as in Sapir 1930), he would have been able to simply state the rules in the following order:

1. Place rising pitch on long vowels and diphthongs.
2. Insert inorganic *a*.

Given this order of application, we derive

	/bilwkʻ/	/gayau/
1. rising pitch	—	gayaũ
2. inorganic *a*	bilauk	—

with the correct accentuation. And on the other hand, Sapir's statement of *a*-insertion in terms of blocking impossible clusters has an element of circularity. Since impossible clusters appear to be just those into which *a* is inserted, the statement that *a* is inserted to break up impossible clusters has no explanatory value. The cases which Kisseberth has brought out are not so simple. In them, the current theory of generative phonology fails to bring out important regularities. It is to enable these regularities to be expressed that Kisseberth has proposed the introduction of new formal devices into the theory.

Do derivational constraints represent an adequate solution to the problems raised by these examples, and do they extend to the other types of phenomena mentioned in sections 1-3 above? In proceeding to seek an answer to these questions, let us keep in mind that the function of the notational conventions, insofar as they place relative rather than absolute constraints on grammars, is strictly explanatory. Their role in the paradigm of formal explanation is to enable "linguistically significant generalizations" to be expressed, and, just as importantly, to prevent "spurious generalizations" from being expressed.

A review of the conspiracies which have been described yields the interesting result that their target configurations are chosen from a rather small set. The targets are generally negative. Phonotactic conspiracies function to avoid certain complex syllable types or complex prosodic configurations. Conspiracies against consonant clusters seem to be common: see Kisseberth (1970*a*–Yokuts), Kisseberth (1970*c*–Tonkawa), Kiparsky (1971–Finnish, Sanskrit). Another type is the conspiracy against vowel sequences, a case of which has been noticed by Ross (Forthcoming) in English. A strong form of both operates in Japanese to give a *CVCV* syllable structure (Nishihara 1970). Miller (1970) has analyzed the diverse processes whereby V̆CC sequences are eliminated in Middle Indic (to either V̆C or V̄CC). In prosody, a common type is the elimination of adjacent stresses in favor of an alternating stress pattern, as in Tunica (Kisseberth 1970*b*), and even in English and German (see above). A partial conspiracy involving liquid dissimilation has been pointed out in English by Ross (personal communication). It is manifested in the following ways: (1) In the morpheme structure constraint that allows morphemes like *flicker, trickle,* but prohibits **fricker, *flickle* (in view of *brother,* etc. this constraint may be restricted to "descriptive verbs," as proposed by Bloomfield). (2) In the dissimilation rule that turns the adjective-forming suffix *-al* (as in *autumnal*) into *-ar* after stems with *l* (e.g., *cellular, circular*). (3) In a constraint on the derivational morphology that prevents the nominalizing suffix *-al* from being added to verbs containing *l* (e.g., *betrayal, rehearsal, acquittal, dismissal, burial,* but never **applial, *displayal, *allowal, *dispellal, *recoilal, *collectal,* etc.) Liquid dissimilation seems to be a fairly common rule, although I do not know another case in which it figures as the target of a conspiracy.

The very interesting cases in Korean discussed by Kim (1969) do not really represent a conspiracy in the same sense, but rather a deeper phonetic parallelism between apparently diverse phonological processes in the language, which phonetic theory as yet cannot satisfactorily express. I will also set aside cases in which some phonological rule mirrors a morpheme structure condition in its content. The most common type of case here is that of a sound change which both remains as a productive rule in the phonology and causes a corresponding change in the morpheme structure conditions. What synchronically is overlap between a phonological rule and a morpheme structure condition is historically a single phonological process which is reflected, though restructuring, in several places in the grammar. The existence of such cases is simply a consequence of how languages change, and does not pose a problem for linguistic theory. More interesting is the possibility that the phonological structure of the lexicon might itself delimit the sound changes a language undergoes. For some discussion of the relation between morpheme structure conditions and phonological rules, see Kiparsky (1971).

Apart from these special cases, to which the term "conspiracy" is not applicable in the same sense as to the others, and for which a different explanation must be given, it seems to be true that phonological conspiracies always function to avert configurations which must be characterized as complex or highly marked, in terms of universal grammar. We have already noted two points in support of this conclusion: (1) Only a restricted set of conspiracy targets is encountered; and (2) If some language has a conspiracy avoiding strings of the form A, then rules eliminating A will be frequent also in other languages, even outside of any conspiracies. In general, relative linguistic complexity can be established in the ways discussed in section 1, by utilizing the evidence of child language, linguistic change, and linguistic universals. For example, if it is universally true that a language that has CCC clusters necessarily also has CC clusters, but not vice versa, or that children learn CC clusters before they learn CCC clusters, then we can say that CCC clusters are linguistically more complex than CC clusters. In this way the hierarchical complexity relations established in a theory of natural phonology may provide an essential basis for an explanation of the phenomenon of conspiracies.

The second major type of target of conspiracies appears to be the sorts of paradigm conditions we already encountered in sections 2 and 3. This is true at least for category distinctness. An example is the conspiracy relating to the past tense verb endings in Sanskrit (section 2). One of the other examples discussed there—the overall incompatibility of -a with vacuous stem vṛddhi in secondary derivation—we now see to be, in effect, a conspiracy, since the incompatibility is a global characteristic not reflected in any single rule. Another English example is the systematic stress relation between English nouns and verbs, which is not the result of any one stress rule, but of features of several rules which conspire to make any stress difference show up as a stress farther to the left on the noun than in the verb (Ross Forthcoming). As in the Sanskrit case, the effect is to decrease cases of derivation which are phonetically null.

It will not be essential for the remainder of my argument that the targets I have proposed should prove to be correct in detail. The essential point is that the configurations that phonological conspiracies conspire against are limited by substantive constraints to configurations of the sort we would on general grounds hold to be linguistically complex, and that the few morphological conspiracies which have been so far proposed seem to implement general paradigmatic conditions of the sort which on other linguistic grounds must be incorporated into linguistic theory.

Can this be reflected in a theory of derivational constraints? The explanatory role of the formalism of derivational constraints in phonology is to simplify the formulation of particular rules by eliminating from them whatever elements are predictable by an overall constraint. In line with the

Are deriv'l constraints adequate to reflect the nature of "conspiracies"

paradigm of formal explanation, this converts "linguistically significant generalizations" into simplifications of the grammar. However, a formal notation cannot claim to provide an explanation until it not only is rich enough to express the generalizations, but its expressive power is also limited in such a way that the notation cannot be used to express generalizations that could not hold in real languages. In what follows I want to show that derivational constraints of the sort that have been proposed, or could be reasonably devised, have some intrinsic inadequacies in both respects. I will first consider the ways in which derivational constraints are an excessively strong device.

How can we limit the formalism to allow conspiracies against three-consonant clusters, but not, for example, conspiracies against CVCV ... syllable structure, or against words beginning with single consonants, or against medial clusters of the form "sonorant + obstruent stop" (e.g., *rt, mp, nt*)? Evidently the difference between the kinds of conspiracies that occur and the kinds of conspiracies that do not occur is not of form but one of content. There is no way to place purely formal restrictions on derivational constraints so as to limit its expressive power to those conspiracies which are "natural." Accordingly, it becomes necessary to impose limitations of substance, rather than of form, on this type of derivational constraint. We may have to say that conspiracies can only function to reduce, not to increase the linguistic complexity of the output. This may ultimately prove to be somewhat too strong. It is evident, however, that *some* such naturalness constraints must be placed on the formalism.

In itself, the need for these substantive constraints still does not invalidate the concept of derivational constraints in any way. There is no reason why the use of a formal notation in grammars should not be subject to substantive constraints. On the contrary, this is exactly what we would expect. For example, it is clear that variables over feature specifications are necessary for assimilatory phenomena such as that expressed by the common rule

$$[+\text{obstr}] \rightarrow [\alpha\text{voiced}] \ / \ \_\_ \begin{bmatrix} +\text{obstr} \\ \alpha\text{voiced} \end{bmatrix}$$

but that the use of variables has to be limited by substantive constraints, to prevent the statement of absurd rules such as

$$[+\text{voiced}] \rightarrow [\alpha\text{obstr}] \ / \ \_\_ \begin{bmatrix} +\text{back} \\ \alpha\text{nasal} \end{bmatrix}$$

In the case of "conspiracies," however, the question arises whether the facts which the formalism is supposed to explain cannot be in their entirety explained by the substantive constraints, which must in any case be part of any theory of phonology. The alternative approach which I have in mind is quite simply this: three-consonant clusters, adjacent stresses, and so on, are linguistically complex configurations, and rules eliminating or avoiding them are accordingly highly natural and occur frequently in the languages of the world. It is therefore only to be expected that there should be some languages in which several rules should eliminate or avoid these configurations, and that there should be languages in which no instances of these configurations appear on the surface. This is no more surprising than it is, in view of the fact that extraposition of sentences and heavy noun phrases is a common kind of transformational rule in languages of the world, that some languages (English may be one) have several such rules of extraposition, and that some languages have no surface structures with sentences flanked by constituents of a higher sentence.

What I am questioning, then, is whether there is any fundamental sort of difference between the cases in which just one or two rules reflect general phonological conditions of this type, and the cases in which several rules are involved, which would be termed a "conspiracy." I have so far challenged the explanatory value of introducing derivational constraints to incorporate conspiracies into the derivations in the phonological component, and advocated doing away with derivational constraints for this purpose by an Occam's Razor type of argument. Concrete empirical differences are clearly also involved: for example, is there any evidence for a true "functional unity" of the rules in a conspiracy which would not simply be characterizable by their sharing a common target? Are there cases in which they are subject to parallel historical changes at some point in the development of a language? Are there cases in which apparently diverse changes in the rules of a language at some point of time can be shown to be consequences of the imposition of a single derivational constraint? Are there cases where the rules in a conspiracy have the same set of lexical exceptions? This would be strong evidence in favor of derivational constraints. However, I have not found any such cases.

From another direction, the proposal to solve the problem of conspiracies by means of derivational constraints is weakened by some formal difficulties.

Derivational constraints simplify only rules that *fail* to apply wherever their output would violate the phonotactic constraint. For instance, some of the environment of the vowel deletion rule in the Yawelmani Yokuts example (see above) can be eliminated. How is one to express as a simplification of the grammar the conspiratorial status of rules that actively eliminate strings which violate the phonotactic constraint? For example, no part of the vowel epenthesis rule which breaks up three-consonant clusters in Yawelmani Yokuts is redundant even given the general derivational constraint. But rules of the latter type are surely just as frequent participants in conspiracies as rules of the former type, which derivational constraints can at least begin to accommodate in a direct way. Kisseberth (1970b) has proposed a principle to meet this difficulty: "A derivational constraint does not add to the complexity of a grammar as a whole if the sequence which it prevents rules from creating is *identical to* the

sequence to which some phonological rule applies." For example, the
derivational constraint which says that no rule can introduce CCC clusters is
free in Yawelmani Yokuts because there exists the epenthesis rule which
destroys CCC clusters. To account for the observation that morpheme
structure conditions often conform to a conspiracy, Kisseberth (1970c)
likewise suggests that "constraints on sequences of segments in morphemes
automatically constitute derivational constraints." Suppose we take this to
mean that derivational constraints that reflect morpheme structure
constraints are also "free." Then the question still remains what happens in
case a language has both a morpheme structure constraint which conforms to
a conspiracy, and a rule which eliminates sequences which the conspiracy
excludes? How would it be formally characterized as more highly valued
than a language in which only one of these belonged to the conspiracy? And
what about a case like Yawelmani Yokuts, where there is not only such a
morpheme structure condition, but *several* rules which eliminate the CCC
clusters which the conspiracy excludes, viz., consonant deletion rules in
addition to the vowel epenthesis rule mentioned above. The approach of
building conspiracies into the derivational process would have to find some
way of formally reflecting as a grammatical simplification the fact that each
of these rules belongs to the conspiracy.

Similar formal problems arise because of the fact that not only
phonological rules, but also morphological rules can participate in a
conspiracy, as in Ross's case of liquid dissimilation in English, where a
constraint on derivational morphology interacts with a phonological rule and
a morphological constraint. We might perhaps say, again, that a
morphological rule is highly valued or "free" if its output meets the
condition of the conspiracy.

Worse yet, we have seen cases where a rule participates in a
conspiracy not directly, but by feeding or bleeding appropriately another
rule. For example, the insertion of -*i*- between the aorist -*s*- and the 2.3.sg.
personal endings -*s*, -*t* in Sanskrit contributes to the retention of the person
endings only indirectly, by blocking the application of the terminal cluster
simplification rules. We would therefore have to say something like this: a
rule is highly valued (or "free") if its application creates representations to
which other rules are applicable in such a way as to implement the
conspiracy.

Note also that to incorporate morphological (paradigmatic)
conspiracies in the derivations of a grammar, derivational constraints are not
always sufficient. And some still more powerful device—viz.,
"transderivational" constraints—would be needed. The target of category
distinctness is not a property of the output of the derivation, but a property
of the relation between this output and other surface forms. A formal
account would have to say that the application of rules can depend on
whether or not the ultimate result of applying them, taking into account the

effect of subsequent rules, bears a given relation to certain other surface forms. It would also have to provide a mechanism for formally simplifying a rule subject to such a constraint relative to one not subject to it. For example, in Sanskrit the limitation of the *s*-less aorist to roots ending in vowels should on this approach not have to be stated in the grammar, but would follow from a general derivational constraint. Likewise, the *s*-insertion rule would have to be stated as context-free. A formalism strong enough to accomplish this (none has ever been proposed) will not be easy to stop from running amok.

All this brings us to a conclusion which lies at the heart of the second major objection to derivational constraints as a solution to the problem of conspiracies in phonology: the formal devices by which a constraint on the output can be effected are highly heterogeneous. Therefore, factoring out those parts of the structural analyses of rules which are in the conspiracy is technically feasible only in a small part of the relevant rules. Adding a list of auxiliary principles to the evaluation measure to take care of the kinds of rules which escape this formal simplification misses the general point that *any* rule or condition in the grammar is a potential participant in a conspiracy. What is significant and narrowly constrained about conspiracies, in short, is their content and not the means by which they are brought about.

Nevertheless, this does not exclude the possibility that some form of derivational or even transderivational constraints may after all be needed in grammar. I am rather criticizing their adequacy as explanatory theories. It may well be the case that derivational constraints have to be introduced into the theory for descriptive adequacy. Facts such as King's (1970) observations on the elision of the copula in English, or the sort of ordering paradoxes illustrated in Kenstowicz and Kisseberth (1970) may well motivate some form of derivational constraints on purely descriptive grounds. It remains to be seen whether King's facts can be dealt with in a more interesting way as our understanding of the interaction of syntax with stress assignment and related phenomena grows (cf. Bresnan 1971), and it also remains to be seen how many ordering paradoxes have, like the Klamath case, a functional under-pinning which explains them on principles independent of the formalism.

5. THE ROLE OF FUNCTIONAL CONDITIONS IN LINGUISTIC THEORY

We have looked at some types of phonological phenomena which have recently been adduced as counterexamples to the formalism of generative phonology: variable rules, conspiracies, and certain ordering paradoxes. Our conclusion was that most instances of these phenomena have a functional basis. We have distinguished three sorts of general conditions to which they can be reduced: distinctness of categories, paradigm coherence, and optimalization of phonotactic structure. From a formal point of view, these targets are reached in several ways:

(1) Conditions are placed on the structural analysis or on the ordering of a rule, which block the rule in just those cases in which its application would go counter to the target (e.g. English *t*-deletion), or triggering it in just those cases in which its application would secure its realization (e.g., Sanskrit *t*-insertion).

(2) Other phonological or morphological rules are introduced in a "conspiracy" to implement the target.

(3) The actual frequencies with which optional rules are applied are such as to favor surface structures conforming to the targets.

The targets are evidently rooted in the requirements placed on language by speech "performance." More specifically, it seems plausible to assume that category distinctness derives from perceptual requirements, and optimalizes language for the hearer by providing more clues to meaning in surface structure. Phonotactic conditions presumably optimalize language for the speaker by keeping down the need for executing complex articulatory movements. The status of paradigm coherence is less clear. Presumably it can be related to language acquisition, though the other aspects of speech performance may also play a role.

These performance-based targets are put into effect by mechanisms which are, in general, unquestionably part of grammar,[1] i e., linguistic competence. We could not exclude them from grammar in the way that certain functionally motivated but formally unstatable constraints in syntax, such as restrictions on self-embedding, or on scrambling up to ambiguity, can be taken out of grammar and accounted for within a theory of performance. This is so because the phonological rules in question are, for example, ordered with respect to other rules, can have lexical exceptions, and are subject to change in time. Though grounded in performance, they are not themselves performance conditions, but are language-specific and must therefore be learned as part of the grammar of the language.

There is, however, one case in which it is not so clear what to make of the facts. This is the case of optional rules applying with systematically variable frequencies depending on phonotactic and paradigmatic conditions. For example, one might ask whether the relative frequencies indicated in table 3 (after Labov et al. 1968, p. 130) were specified by the grammar of those whose speech they characterize.

Table 3

		___##C	___##V
C ___	(fist)	90	50
C+___	(kept)	50	31
C#___	(passed)	38	14
V ___	(red)	22	04
V+___	(said)	29	12
V#___	(stayed)	22	04

Per cent of *t*-deletion in certain environments.

Note carefully what the issue is here. In asking whether variable rule application falls outside of grammar I am *not* asking whether it should be shoved under some rug where linguists put things that do not interest them. On the contrary, it would be a gain for linguistics if the variable frequencies, or some aspect of them, could be predicted by a theory of speech performance, for then we would have been able to substitute a general explanation for a description of language particular facts. My question is rather whether the variable frequencies are part of the statement of the grammatical rules, or whether they might be predictable, wholly or in part, by universal conditions. That is, the question is whether the child has to *learn* to drop -*t* according to such a table, or whether he does so for reasons which have nothing to do with the specifics of English phonology. Labov (1969) has claimed that these frequencies are part of linguistic competence, and has developed a formalism for expressing them in grammatical rules. The alternative hypothesis would be that they are the result of general functional conditions impinging on speech performance. In this example, the conditions would relate to phonotactics and distinctness. Both preceding and following consonants increase the frequency of deletion (avoidance of consonant clusters). On the other hand, deletion is less frequent where it would make the past and present tenses identical.

This possibility is at the moment remote, however. We are far from being able to propose functional explanations for all of the frequency relations that have been found in optional rules. Even in the above table, it remains unclear why there is more deletion in C___ than in C+___, but less deletion in V___ than in V+___. And this is not a unique query.

The sort of evidence from which we would conclude that variable frequencies of rule application are not specified in the grammar would be that the frequency relations vary systematically with the speech situation according to the change in functional factors involved. For example, the relative importance of the distinctness factor should rise with increasing difficulty of communication, as on a telephone, and rapid speech should lead to a greater importance of phonotactic factors. Some facts pointing in this direction are mentioned by Labov et al. (1968, p. 137).

Functional conditions, then, enter the linguistic system in a grammaticalized form. At that point they begin to interact and conflict not only with each other, but with formal generality in the usual generative phonological sense. We have seen examples of this interaction and conflict above. At present I do not see how to predict which condition wins in a conflict of this kind. Note that this still does not reduce the theory to anywhere near vacuity. A unique claim is still being made in cases where only one condition is applicable.

The great difficulty with functional explanations in linguistics (and partly in other fields as well) has always been finding the general theories without which functional explanations of specific phenomena can have no empirical substance. It is easy to point at a specific historical event or synchronic fact and suggest an *ad hoc* "reason" for it. But however plausible such explanations may seem, they carry no force until backed up by general claims, which go beyond the case at hand, and which for that reason can be put to a test.

This difficulty was not always recognized explicitly by traditional proponents of functional explanations. Hence Bloomfield's scathing attacks on Horn and Havers were in a way perfectly justified:

> A teleologic "explanation" can be given without difficulty for any and every happening. If we create a vacuum over one end of a *U*-shaped tube containing water (the principle of the pump), the water will rise at this end: Nature abhors a vacuum. But the water rises only to a height of 33 feet above the level of the water outside: well, Nature's horror of a vacuum goes only so far and, after that, is offset by the weight of the water. Teleology cuts off investigation by providing a ready-made answer to any question we may ask. (Bloomfield 1934).

Proposing an empirically testable version of functionalism involves giving a general, cross-linguistic characterization of what the functional factors are, and how they impinge on linguistic structure. I have tried to begin this here. I have suggested a way in which the concept of a "tendency," which lends functionalist discussions their characteristic unsatisfactory fuzziness, can be made more precise in terms of hierarchies of optimality, which predict specific consequences for linguistic change, language acquisition, and universal grammar. Enormous areas of vagueness obviously remain. But there is enough to show that the project is a worthwhile one.

NOTES

This work was supported in part by the National Institutes of Mental Health (Grant No. MH-13390-04).

[1] In syntax, the problems have been raised by Bever (1970) and Bever and Langendoen (1971).

[2] The subscript notation is normally used on single segments only. However, there is no reason to restrict it so. If subscripts are not used, we have to use the star notation, and, since application for the star is defined as conjunctive, an extra rule is then needed to wipe out all except the rightmost or leftmost of the stresses which are assigned by the main rule. But this would not affect the point of the example, since the generalization from one word type to the other is still correctly made by the formalism.

[3] Twaddell mentions a functionalist explanation of this rule, but rejects it as "psychologistic" and "mentalistic."

[4] See Bolling's postscript to Moore (1927).

[5] However, Pāṇini 1962, 6.4.57 allows optionally also *prāpya*.

[6] See Wackernagel (1896, 304-5).

[7] The only exceptions may be a couple of nouns like *puroḍās* 'sacrificial cake', from *puroḍās+s*.

[8] This is what I proposed in my dissertation. James Harris several years ago called my attention to the difficulties which words like *honestus* pose for this solution.

REFERENCES

Anderson, S. 1969. West Scandinavian vowel systems and the ordering of phonological rules. Ph.D. Dissertation, M.I.T.

Bever, T. G. 1970. The cognitive basis for linguistic structures. In *Cognition and language learning*, ed. J. R. Hayes. New York: Wiley.

Bever, T. G., and Langendoen, D. T. 1971. The interaction of speech perception and grammar in linguistic evolution. In *Historical linguistics in the light of generative grammar*, ed. R. Stockwell. Bloomington: Indiana University Press.

Bloomfield, L. 1933. *Language*. New York: Holt.

_____. 1934. Review of Havers's *Handbuch der erklärenden Syntax*. *Language* 10: 32-39.

Boas, F. 1911, 1925, 1938. *Handbook of American Indian languages*, vols. I, II, III. Washington: Government Printing Office.

Bresnan, J. 1971. On sentence stress and syntactic transformations. *Language* 47: 257-81.

Carstairs, A. 1970. A transderivational constraint in Greek phonology. Dittoed.

Chomsky, N., and Halle, M. 1968. *Sound pattern of English*. New York: Harper and Row.

Halle, M. 1962. Phonology in generative grammar. *Word* 18: 54-72. Reprinted in *The structure of language*, ed. J. Fodor and J. Katz, Englewood Cliffs, N. J.: Prentice-Hall, 1964.

Harris, J. 1970. Paradigmatic regularity and naturalness of grammars. Paper read at the December 1970 meeting of the Linguistic Society of America.

Itkonen, E. 1966. *Kieli ja sen tutkimus*. Helsinki: Werner Söderström.

Jakobson, R. 1968. *Child language, aphasia, and phonological universals*. English translation by A. Keiler. The Hague: Mouton.

Jespersen, O. 1949. *Efficiency in linguistic change*. Historisk-filologiske Meddelelser 27.4. Reprinted in *Selected writings* Tokyo: Senjo, n.d.

Kazazis, K. 1969. Possible evidence for (near-) underlying forms in the speech of a child. In *Papers from the fifth regional meeting of the Chicago Linguistic Society,* ed. R. Binnick et al. Chicago: University of Chicago Linguistics Department.

Kenstowicz, M., and Kisseberth, C. 1970. Rule ordering and the assymmetry hypothesis. In *Papers from the sixth regional meeting of the Chicago Linguistic Society*. Chicago: University of Chicago Linguistics Department.

Kettunen, L. 1962. *Eestin kielen äännehistoria*[3]. Helsinki: Suomalaisen Kirjallisunden Seura.

Kim, C. -W. 1969. Two phonological notes. Dittoed.

King, H. 1970. On blocking the rules for contraction in English. *Linguistic Inquiry* 1: 134-36.

King, R. 1967. Functional load and sound change. *Language* 43: 831-52.

_____. 1969. *Historical linguistics and generative grammar*. Englewood Cliffs, N. J.: Prentice-Hall.

Kiparsky, P. 1968. Linguistic universals and linguistic change. In *Universals in linguistic theory*, ed. E. Bach and R. Harms. New York: Holt, Rinehart.

_____. 1971. Lectures on phonology. In *Proceedings of the International Seminar on Linguistic Theory*, Tokyo.

Kisseberth, C. 1970*a*. On the functional unity of phonological rules. *Linguistic inquiry* 1: 291-306.

_____. 1970*b*. The Tunica stress conspiracy. Mimeographed, to appear in *Linguistic inquiry*.

_____. 1970*c*. Vowel elision in Tonkawa and derivational constraints. Mimeographed.

_____. 1970*d*. A global rule in Klamath phonology. Mimeographed.

Labov, W., Lohen, P., Robins, C., and Lewis, J. 1968. A study of the non-standard English of Negro and Puerto Rican speakers in New York City. Cooperative Research Report no. 3288, vol. I. New York: Columbia University.

Labov, W. 1969. Contraction, deletion, and inherent variability of the English copula. *Language* 45: 715-62.

Lindgren, K. 1953. *Die Apokope des mhd. -e in seinen verschiedenen Funktionen*. Ann. Ac. Sc. Fenn. B78, 2. Helsinki.

Miller, G. 1970. The Pāli two-mora conspiracy. Dittoed.

Moore, S. 1927. Loss of final *-n* in inflectional syllables of Middle English. *Language* 3: 232-59.

Narten, J. 1964. *Die sigmatischen Aoriste im Veda*. Wiesbaden: Harrassowitz.

Nerger, K. 1869. *Grammatik des meklenburgischen Dialektes*. Leipzig: Brockhaus.

Nishihara, S. 1970. *Phonological change and verb morphology of Japanese*. Ph.D. dissertation, University of Michigan.

Pandit, P. B. 1961. Historical phonology of Gujarati vowels. *Language* 37: 54-66.

Pāṇini. 1962. *The Ashṭādhyāyī of Pāṇini*, vols. I, II. English translation by Ś. Vasu. Delhi: Motilal Banarsidass.

Paul, H. 1920. *Prinzipien der Sprachgeschichte*[6].

Ross, J. R. Forthcoming. The English stress conspiracy.

Sapir, E. 1925. *The Takelma language of southwestern Oregon*. In Boas (1925).

_____. 1930. Southern Paiute, a Shoshonean language. *Proceedings of the American Academy of Arts and Sciences*, 65, nos. 1-3.

Stampe, D. 1969. The acquisition of phonetic representation. In *Papers from the fifth regional meeting of the Chicago Linguistic Society*, ed. R. Binnick et al. Chicago: University of Chicago Linguistics Department.

Twaddell, W. F. 1935. *On defining the phoneme*. *Language* monograph no. 16. Page references are to the reprint in *Readings in linguistics*, ed. M. Joos. New York, 1958.

Venneman, T. 1968. On the use of paradigmatic information in a competence rule of modern German phonology. Paper read at the summer meeting of the Linguistic Society of America, Ann Arbor, Mich.

_____. 1969. German : a case for abstract phonology. Forthcoming.

Wackernagel, J. 1896. *Altindische Grammatik I*. Göttingen: Vandenhoeck and Ruprecht.

Wackernagel, J., and Debrunner, A. 1954. *Altindische Grammatik II. 2*. Göttingen: Vandenhoeck and Ruprecht.

Whitney, W. P. 1889. *Sanskrit grammar*[2]. Cambridge: Harvard University Press. Reprinted 1961.

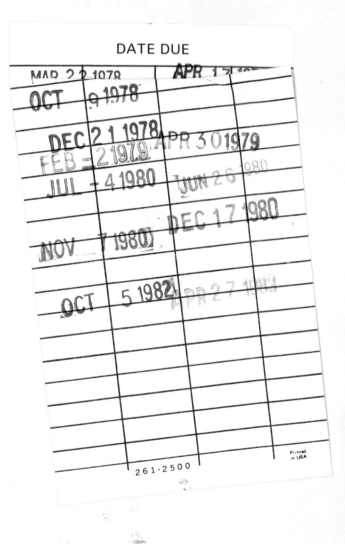

DATE DUE

MAR 2 2 1978	APR 1 7 1978	
OCT 9 1978		
DEC 2 1 1978	APR 3 0 1979	
FEB - 2 1979		
JUL - 4 1980	JUN 2 6 1980	
NOV 7 1980	DEC 1 7 1980	
OCT 5 1982	APR 2 7 1983	

261-2500